T5-BCA-313

Criminal Justice

Recent Scholarship

Edited by
Marilyn McShane and Frank P. Williams III

A Series from LFB Scholarly

Mental Illness and Violence
The Importance of Neighborhood Context

Eric Silver

LFB Scholarly Publishing LLC
New York 2001

Library of Congress Cataloging-in-Publication Data

Silver, Eric, 1965-
Mental illness and violence : the importance of neighborhood context / Eric Silver.
p. cm. -- (Criminal justice)
Includes bibliographical references and index.
ISBN 1-931202-06-0 (alk. paper)
1. Violence--Social aspects. 2. Violence--Psychological aspects. 3. Mentally ill offenders. I. Title. II. Criminal justice (LFB Scholarly Publishing LLC)
HM1116 .S55 2001
616.85'82071--dc21

00-013135

ISBN 1-931202-06-0

Printed on acid-free 250-year-life paper.

Manufactured in the United States of America.

CONTENTS

ACKNOWLEDGMENTS

This book has benefitted greatly from thoughtful comments provided by Steven Messner, Henry J. Steadman, Scott J. South, and Edward P. Mulvey. Their guidance and suggestions greatly enhanced the overall quality and relevance of the work. Special thanks also go to John Monahan, Director of the MacArthur Foundation's Research Network on Mental and the Law, for providing me with the data upon which this study was based, and to the National Consortium on Violence Research for providing funding for this work.

This book marks the completion of a goal that would never have been attained were it not for support and guidance provided by my wife, Laura. There were many times when I questioned my ability to see this goal through. During my moments of doubt, it was Laura who kept me directed by believing in me and by her willingness to do more than her fair share in keeping our home-life happy and stable. Were it not for her support this goal would have been abandoned long ago. I would also like to thank my parents, Iris and David Silver and Tom and Kathy Piraino for their constant support, and my two beautiful children, Jasmine and Benjamin, for keeping me ever-mindful of the fact that there is more to life than work.

This document also marks the culmination of a great deal of learning and professional development for which I am deeply thankful to the following people. First, is Steven Messner. I took my first course with Steve in Research Methods in 1990. From that time forward I have sought Steve out for guidance in all aspects of my academic career. Steve chaired my Master's Thesis Committee, my Deviance Comprehensive Exam Committee, and my Dissertation Committee, from which this book emerged. Steve has taught me - through advice and example - about the profound interconnectedness between theoretical thinking and sound empirical research.

Next, I thank Henry J. Steadman, President of Policy Research Associates, for inspiring my substantive interest in violence and mental illness and for providing me with countless opportunities to grow professionally - from a research assistant face-editing data forms in 1988 to a senior data analyst and published author in 1999. From Hank I have learned that when it comes to communicating research findings, simpler is better and less is more. These lessons grow out of Hank's unyielding emphasis on the notion that social science research ought always to be conducted with an eye toward practical and policy implications - a perspective that has had a profound impact on my view of what constitutes a worthwhile research project.

Next, I would like to thank Steven Banks. Although Steve was not an official member of my dissertation committee, I have worked alongside him on many research projects over the years and, in the process, have learned a great deal from him about how to think about data analysis. Steve's approach to data analysis and, in particular, his ability to communicate a profound - almost philosophical - understanding of the meaning of statistical concepts and techniques - has greatly affected how I view the data analytic process. Steve has taught me to view each analytic problem from multiple perspectives before arriving at a solution (by periodically asking me questions like "would you use a screwdriver to hammer a nail?"), and that no analytic technique - no matter how sophisticated - can overcome the limitations of a poorly defined question. I have almost never left an encounter with Steve Banks during which I did not learn something new.

Finally, I would like to thank Edward P. Mulvey for taking an interest in my professional development. Over the past several years, Ed has given of his time providing me with invaluable professional and substantive advice in his dual roles as NCOVR Mentor and guardian angel. It was Ed who first suggested that I apply for the NCOVR fellowship that wound up supporting this research. Ed's own career, which combines a strong substantive/policy focus with a broad methodological sophistication continues to be an inspiration to me.

CHAPTER 1

Overview of the Research

Over the course of the twentieth century, a great deal of scholarly attention has been devoted to studying the social ecology of crime and violence (Shaw and McKay, 1942; Lander, 1954; Bordua, 1958; Chilton, 1964; Byrne and Sampson, 1986; Reiss and Tonry, 1986; Sampson and Groves, 1989; Sampson, Raudenbush and Earls, 1997; for a comprehensive review, see Sampson and Lauritsen, 1994; LaFree, 1999). This research has consistently shown that rates of violence vary across nations and, within a single nation, across different communities and neighborhoods. Yet, we know relatively little about how the ecological characteristics of communities influence the violent behavior of particular individuals. Indeed, we know less about the relationship between neighborhood characteristics and the violent behavior of persons with mental illnesses.

In this book, I draw upon the social disorganization perspective to examine the contribution of individual- and neighborhood-level risk factors for violence among a sample of individuals recently discharged from a psychiatric hospital after an acute inpatient stay. Not since Faris and Dunham's (1939) pioneering study of the spatial and social distribution of mental illnesses in the city of Chicago has the social disorganization perspective been systematically applied to a mentally ill sample. However, Faris and Dunham (1939) did not attempt to describe or explain the *violent behavior* of mentally ill persons. Their main interest was in relating various types of mental disorders (e.g., schizophrenia, alcohol and substance abuse, and affective disorder) to social conditions in Chicago neighborhoods.

This book expands upon Faris and Dunham's (1939) original work by focusing on the relationship between neighborhood conditions and violence among mentally ill persons. Specifically, the book brings to bear recent reformulations and extensions of Shaw and McKay's (1942) social disorganization model of crime and delinquency (Kasarda and Janowitz, 1974; Kornhauser, 1978; Bursik, 1988; Sampson, 1988, Sampson and Groves, 1989; Cullen, 1994) to derive testable hypotheses regarding the violent behavior of persons with mental disorders. The basic premise of this book is that the social and organizational characteristics of neighborhoods explain and/or condition variations in the violent behavior of discharged psychiatric patients that can not be attributed to their individual characteristics.

The analyses contained in this book combine individual-level data from the MacArthur Foundation's Violence Risk Assessment Study - the largest study of risk factors for violence among discharged psychiatric patients ever conducted (Monahan and Steadman, 1994; Steadman, Mulvey, Monahan, Robbins, Appelbaum, Grisso, Roth, and Silver, 1998; Silver, Mulvey, and Monahan, 1999) - with objective data on the characteristics of the neighborhoods in which patients resided after discharge - gathered from 1990 U.S. Census Summary Tape Files. The kinds of violence to be assessed by this project include battery resulting in injury, sexual assaults, assaultive acts that involved the use of a weapon, or threats made with a weapon in hand. These are serious acts of violence.

The vast majority of research on community violence by discharged psychiatric patients has focused on individual characteristics. In a recent, comprehensive review of the literature on patient violence, Webster, Douglas, Eaves, and Hart (1997) identified 20 individual-level predictors of violent behavior that they organized into three substantive domains: (1) historical; (2) clinical; and (3) risk management. Importantly, none of the risk factors they highlighted took account of the neighborhood contexts within which discharged psychiatric patients live.

Yet, without taking into account the neighborhood contexts in which discharge patients live, interpreting individual-level relationships is tricky. With rare exceptions (Silver, Mulvey, and Monahan, 1999), the question of whether the variations in violent behavior attributed to the individual characteristics of discharged psychiatric patients also reflect differences in the types of neighborhood settings in which patients reside, has not been raised. Little is known about whether, and if so, how neighborhood-level variables contribute to the risk for violence posed by discharged psychiatric patients. Even less is known about whether neighborhood-level and individual-level characteristics interact to increase or decrease the potential for violent behavior.

In general, studies of individual behavior that do not consider the effects of neighborhood conditions may lead to a mis-estimation of the importance of particular individual-level factors (Farrington, 1992; Sampson and Lauritsen, 1994; Duncan, Connell, and Klebanov, 1997; Sampson and Morenoff, 1997; Ellen and Turner, 1997). Further, without measuring neighborhood characteristics, it is impossible to determine the extent to which the associations between individual characteristics and violent behavior vary across neighborhood settings. The current study takes the position that a full understanding of the behavior of individuals requires data on individual- and community-level characteristics.

Although rarely featured in inquiries into the relationship between mental illness and violence, sensitivity to multi-level issues has become an important focus of recent sociological and criminological inquiries (Sampson, 1985; Miethe and McDowall, 1993; Sampson and Lauritsen, 1994; South and Crowder, 1997; Elliot, Wilson, Huizinga, Sampson, Elliot, and Rankin, 1996). In a recent study of victimization risk, Miethe and McDowall (1993) demonstrated that individual characteristics that protect one against victimization risk in one type of neighborhood are not necessarily protective of risk in other types of neighborhoods. Their study used Seattle survey data collected on 5,098 adults in combination with neighborhood-level measures reflecting key explanatory variables drawn from routine activities and social disorganization theory. They found that regardless of individuals' life-style and routine activities, people who lived in areas with high levels of socioeconomic deterioration had greater risks of both violent and property victimization than did residents of more affluent areas. In addition, they found different effects for individual-level predictors across different types of neighborhoods. Specifically, measures of guardianship and target attractiveness influenced risk of burglary only for residents of middle- and upper-class areas. In lower-class areas, these individual-level risk factors had little effect on burglary risks. Miethe and McDowall's (1993) study demonstrates how incorporating individual and neighborhood measures into studies of crime and violence can reveal new information about the causes and correlates of individual behavior and risks.

The approach taken in this book is similar to that taken by Miethe and McDowall (1993) except that, rather than focus on victimization risk for the general population, I focus on the violent behavior of persons recently discharged from psychiatric hospitals after treatment for an acute mental illness. This approach has important implications for informing legal and social policy related to patient violence. If, for example, individual-level factors are found to be more important than contextual conditions, then the risk of violence posed by discharged psychiatric patients may be more effectively reduced through individual treatment interventions, regardless of neighborhood setting. If, however, contextual factors are also responsible for variations in psychiatric patient violence, then risk reduction strategies must also be designed to take into account the contexts into which patients are discharged. Finally, by disentangling individual-level and community-level effects and by examining the interactions between them, this book provides much-needed data on whether and how community-level risk factors condition individual risk for violence among discharged psychiatric patients. Such data can be used to determine whether context-specific risk management intervention strategies are needed.

The MacArthur Violence Risk Assessment Study

This study uses data from the MacArthur Violence Risk Assessment Study, a three-site, longitudinal study of discharged psychiatric patients (n=1,136) conducted between 1992 and 1995 (Steadman et al., 1998). An extensive battery of research instruments was administered to subjects during their psychiatric hospital stays and then up to five times during the first year following their discharge from the hospital. Data on the personal, historical, clinical, and interpersonal characteristics of individual patients were collected, along with in-depth information on violent acts they were committed in the community following hospital discharge. The purpose of the MacArthur Violence Risk Assessment Study was to evaluate individual-level characteristics (e.g., personal, historical, and clinical factors) and situational characteristics (e.g., access to lethal weapons, social supports, etc.) in order to identify risk factors that could be used by clinicians in psychiatric hospitals, managed care, and community mental health settings to assess and manage risk for violence (Monahan and Steadman, 1994).

A unique aspect of this book is that it contains analyses that link individual-level data from one of the three sites of the MacArthur Violence Risk Assessment Study - the Pittsburgh site - to information on the characteristics of the *communities* in which patients resided after discharge from the hospital. This data linkage was made possible by converting post-discharge addresses that had been obtained for subjects at the Pittsburgh site into census tract identifiers. Census tract identifiers were determined by the University of Pittsburgh's Center for Social and Urban Research using mapping procedures to geo-code subjects addresses.

Using census tract identifiers, a multi-level data set was created by linking patient records to tract-level data from the 1990 U.S. Census. This augmented data set enables hypotheses to be tested regarding the joint influences of neighborhood-level and individual-level risk factors on the violent behavior of discharged psychiatric patients. Specifically, tract-level measures will be used to characterize the Pittsburgh neighborhoods in which the discharged patients lived. These characteristics will be derived from factor analyses of selected 1990 U.S. Census Summary Tape File (STF) variables (see Sampson, Raudenbush, and Earls, 1997 for a recent example of this approach). Thus, a contextual analysis will be conducted that draws on social disorganization theory in order to understand the causes and correlates of violence among discharged psychiatric patients.

Overview of Chapters

Chapter two reviews the literature on mental disorder and violence. In the chapter, I provide a brief description of the policy context within violence and mental illnesses typically are discussed. I also provide an overview of recent research on the relationship between mental disorder and violence. I end chapter two by highlighting the lack of attention that has been paid to neighborhood-level factors in this literature. In chapter three, I provide an overview of the research literature on social disorganization, I identify the neighborhood conditions that are relevant for understanding the behavior of persons with mental illnesses, and I discuss the importance of multi-level models for understanding the role of contextual factors. Chapter four presents the research hypotheses that will be tested in subsequent chapters. Chapter five describes the data collection procedures, the operationalization of measures, and the statistical procedures that are used. Chapter six presents descriptive and bivariate results of the study. Chapter seven presents multivariate results. Finally, chapter eight discusses the implications of these results for social disorganization theory. I conclude the final chapter with a discussion of the implications of the study for risk assessment and risk management policy.

Summary

This study is the first to apply social disorganization theory to the violent behavior of discharged psychiatric patients. This study also is the first to attempt to disentangle the extent to which patient differences in violent behavior reflect individual-level processes (e.g., symptomatology, diagnosis, personality disorder, psychopathy, etc.), or whether (and to what extent) such differences are due to neighborhood-level processes, such as are featured in the literature on social disorganization. An understanding of how neighborhood contexts structure the behaviors of discharged psychiatric patients holds great potential for both extending the scope of sociological theory and informing mental health policies related to the prediction and management of patient violence. In short, this study seeks to broaden the focus of future research and policy in the area of mental disorder and violence.

CHAPTER 2

Research and Policy Issues in the Study of Mental Illness and Violence

The perception that mental illness leads to violence is not limited to the general public; it occupies a central position in American mental health policy, supporting legal practices such as involuntary civil commitment and involuntary outpatient treatment. This chapter provides an overview of research and policy bearing on the relationship between mental illness and violence.

Perceptions of an Association

The belief that there is an association between mental disorder and violence has deep roots in Western culture. As Monahan (1992a) points out, references in Greek and Roman literature to the aggressiveness of the mentally ill appear as early as the fifth century B.C.. Monahan notes that Plato, in *Alcibiades II*, describes a dialogue between Socrates and

Alcibiades in which Alcibiades makes the claim that many citizens of Athens are "mad." Socrates refutes this claim by arguing that the rate of mental disorder could not be very high since the prevalence of violence in Athens was very low. The assumption that high violence rates imply high rates of mental illness was not debated.

Much more recently, in Colonial America, Benjamin Franklin invoked the notion of an association between mental disorder and violence to convince the Pennsylvania Assembly to include a ward for the mentally ill in the first general hospital built in the New World, by arguing that:

> "the number of persons distempered in mind and deprived of their rational Faculties has increased greatly in this province. Some of them going at large are a Terror to their Neighbors, who are daily apprehensive of the Violences they may commit" (Monahan, 1992a).

Later, in England in 1843, on the day after Daniel McNaughten's acquittal by reason of insanity of murdering the secretary of the Prime Minister, the *London Times* published the following excerpt on its editorial page: "Ye people of England exult and be glad, For ye're now at the mercy of the merciless mad."

The perception of an association between mental disorder and violence persists today. This perception has led researchers to focus on the various ways in which persons with mental illnesses are stereotyped by the general public and the media (Szasz, 1974; Scheff, 1984; Link, Cullen, Frank, and Wozniak, 1987; Link and Cullen, 1990). Persons with mental illnesses are frequently portrayed in the media and other forms of public discourse as threats to community and individual safety (Silver, Cirincione, and Steadman, 1994; Monahan, 1992a; Steadman and Cocozza, 1978; Steadman, 1981). A content analysis conducted for the National

Institute of Mental Health (Gerbner, Gross, Morgan, and Signorielli, 1981) found that 17 percent of all prime time American television dramas depicted a character as mentally ill, and 73 percent of these mentally ill characters were portrayed as violent (compared with 40 percent of the nonmentally ill characters). In addition, 23 percent of mentally ill characters were portrayed as homicidal, compared with 10 percent of nonmentally ill characters. Such images are not limited to television. A content analysis of stories from the United Press International database (Shain and Phillips, 1991) found that 86 percent of all print stories dealing with former mental patients also featured a violent crime.

A recent study conducted by Pescosolido, Monahan, Link, Steuve, and Kikusawa (1999) using data from 1,444 respondents to the "Problems in Modern Living" module of the 1996 General Social Survey (GSS), illustrates the extent of public concern regarding the potential for violence posed by persons with mental illness. Respondents were shown a vignette describing an individual meeting the Diagnostic and Statistical Manual (DSM)-IV criteria for schizophrenia, major depression, alcohol dependence, drug abuse, or a control case (a person with mental health problems meeting no DSM-IV criteria). Race/ethnicity, sex and education levels were varied in the vignettes. To measure dangerousness to others, respondents were asked: "In your opinion, how likely is it that [NAME] would do something violent toward other people?. Is it: very likely, somewhat likely, not very likely, or not likely at all?" Pescosolido and colleagues found that a substantial proportion of the public held an exaggerated view of the level of violence risk posed by persons with mental illnesses: 33.3% of the public believed that people with major depression (and no substance abuse problems) were "somewhat" or "very" likely to engage in violent behavior toward others and 60.9% of GSS respondents believed that individuals with schizophrenia (and no substance abuse) were "somewhat" or "very" likely to engage in violence. With regard to the effects of drug and alcohol abuse, 82.1% of GSS respondents viewed persons with alcohol dependence to be either "somewhat" or "very" likely to engage in violence toward others, and 92.2% of respondents viewed persons with drug abuse problems as either "somewhat" or "very" likely to be violent to others.

Further, a study conducted by Link et al. (1987) demonstrates how the belief that mentally ill people are dangerous leads to their stigmatization. These researchers investigated the extent to which a person's status as a "former mental patient" fostered social distance on the part of others, measured by questions tapping the willingness of respondents to have as co-workers or neighbors persons described in vignettes as having once been in a mental hospital. Consistent with other research (Gove, 1980), Link and colleagues found no main effect of the former patient label. But when they disaggregated their subjects - adults drawn from the general population - by means of a perceived dangerousness scale into those who believed that mental disorder was linked to violence and those who did not, strong labeling effects emerged. Subjects who believed that there was no connection between mental disorder and violence exhibited what might be called an "affirmative action" position (Monahan, 1992b): they responded as if they were more willing to have as co-workers or neighbors someone who had been in a mental hospital. People who believed that persons with mental disorders were prone to violence, however, strongly rejected the former patients. The public's perception that mentally ill people are dangerous thus contributes to the stigma they experience.

The notion that mental illness and violence are related

is not only found among the general public; it occupies a central position in American mental health law and policy. In particular, the dangerousness standard - which allows for the involuntary treatment of persons believed to be at risk of harming others - is widely used by courts to support legal practices such as involuntary civil and outpatient commitment. The following section reviews the legal and policy contexts in which the belief that mental disorder predisposes one to violence has become institutionalized.

Violence, Mental Disorder, and Mental Health Law and Policy in the United States

Several shifts in the socio-historical climate have converged to keep the topic of violence and mental disorder prominent in the area of mental health law policy (Mulvey and Lidz, 1995; Borum, 1996; Appelbaum, 1997). Based on a comprehensive review of civil commitment procedures around the world, Appelbaum (1997) reports that from the formulation of the first statutes governing civil commitment to the asylums of the early 19th century to roughly the mid-1960's, the focus of civil commitment law remained unchanged: persons who were mentally ill and *in need of treatment* could be involuntarily committed to treatment settings for mental health care. By the mid-1960's, however, the appropriateness of this paternalistic approach to treatment was called into question. First, critics asked whether mental illness really existed, or whether it was a myth (Szasz, 1974; Laing, 1967). The notion that mental disorder was simply a construct that allowed society to exercise social control over unusual but harmless deviant behavior attracted a good deal of support (Scheff, 1984).

Second, exposés revealed abysmal conditions in many

state hospitals - where the majority of chronically ill patients were living. Researchers began to suggest that long-term hospitalization itself might be the cause of many of the symptoms associated with chronic mental illness, representing a syndrome called "institutionalism" (Goffman, 1961; Wing, 1962). The argument was simultaneously made that patients could be better taken care of in their own communities (Ewalt and Ewalt, 1969). Third, the civil rights movements of the 1950's and 1960's in conjunction with the activist stance of the courts during that period, brought renewed interest to theories of law that emphasized the rights of disenfranchised groups against the power of the government, including persons with mental illness. Fourth, with budgets of departments of mental health accounting for the largest share of expenditures in many states, legislatures were eager to embrace any option that would reduce hospitalization and thereby lower the costs of caring for persons with mental disorders (Johnson, 1990; Isaac and Armat, 1990). Finally, as public and private mental health systems became subsumed by various forms of managed care, the risk for committing violence posed by psychiatric patients has increasingly been factored into cost-containment calculations (Borum, 1996). Specifically, the fact that patients who become violent tend to utilize higher-cost services such as inpatient hospitalization has been suggested as justification for their exclusion from benefit plans.

In the wake of these trends, the concept of risk of harm to others has come to occupy a pivotal role in both civil and criminal aspects of mental health law (Monahan and Steadman, 1994; Mulvey, 1994, Appelbaum, 1997). Risk of harm now enters into criminal justice decision making as courts must decide whether an individual acquitted by reason of insanity "poses a substantial risk of serious bodily harm to others" in order to justify involuntary commitment to a mental hospital (American Bar Association, 1989). On the civil side, the dangerousness criterion has become a primary justification for the use of involuntary hospitalization. As Appelbaum (1997) points out, with the advent of the dangerousness standard, the law allowing hospitalization of persons solely because they were 'in need of treatment' - the historic standard of commitment in this country - was abandoned (p.137). Mulvey and Lidz (1995) summarize this situation as follows: "...whereas 15 years ago the use of dangerousness as a criterion for committing psychiatric patients was an issue of contention, currently almost every state legislature has mandated the use of such a standard" (p.130).

These changes are reflected in the American Psychiatric Association's model state law on civil commitment (American Psychiatric Association, 1983) which explicitly allows for the involuntary commitment of mentally disordered individuals who are "likely to cause harm to others." Going further, the guidelines for involuntary civil commitment of the National Center for State Courts recommend that clinical predictions of dangerousness be used to justify involuntary civil commitment (National Center for State Courts, 1986). Finally, the landmark decision by the California Supreme Court in *Tarasoff v. Regents of the University of California* (1976), which held that psychotherapists who know or should know of their patient's likelihood of inflicting injury on identifiable third parties have an obligation to take reasonable steps to protect the potential victim(s), further established risk of harm as a central component of psychiatric practice (Monahan, 1993; Borum, 1996).

The judicial and legislative emphasis on dangerousness as a key standard in decisions involving involuntary hospitalization has placed enormous pressure on mental health clinicians to make assessments of the potential for future violence posed by individuals with mental disorders. This has led to numerous studies beginning in the 1970's aimed at evaluating the accuracy of clinical predictions of dangerousness (Steadman and Cocozza, 1974; Thornberry and Jacoby, 1979; Steadman and Morrissey, 1982). This research has had to overcome serious methodological and ethical difficulties inherent in studying the accuracy of clinical predictions because under usual circumstances, clinical opinions regarding dangerousness *determine who becomes at risk for committing a violent act.* A properly controlled study requires that all patients, both those considered dangerous and those considered not dangerous, be released into the community so that they are all given the opportunity to commit a violent act. Under such conditions, such patients could be followed to determine their actual rates of violent conduct (see Webster, Harris, Rice, Cormier, and Quinsey, 1994 for a review of this issue).

A 1966 decision of the U.S. Supreme Court provided Steadman and Cocozza (1974) with the rare opportunity for such a study. The case involved Johnny Baxstrom, who served out his sentence in a hospital prison as a mentally ill inmate and, as was common practice, was civilly committed upon the expiration of his sentence based on a psychiatric assessment that he was dangerous - without the right of a jury trial on the issues of mental illness and dangerousness. In *Baxstrom v. Herold*, the Supreme Court ruled this procedure unconstitutional and, as a result, nearly 1,000 inmates of hospitals for the criminally insane were transferred to civil hospitals. Eventually, about half of these former inmates were released to the community, creating a natural experiment that Steadman and Cocozza capitalized on to test the positive predictions of dangerousness that had resulted in the inmates' initial hospitalizations. Steadman and Cocozza found that, of a sample of 98 patients released from civil hospitals, 20 were arrested during the four and a half year follow-up period, and of these 20 arrests, 13 were for nonviolent offenses. An additional seven subjects were rehospitalized. Thus, of the 98 pre-Baxstrom predictions of dangerousness, only 27 could be classified as correct, leading Steadman and Cocozza (1974) to question the ability of hospital clinicians to accurately predict dangerousness.

Similarly, in *Dixon v. Attorney General of the Commonwealth of Pennsylvania* (1969), Section 404 of the Pennsylvania Mental Health and Mental Retardation Act was ruled unconstitutional, resulting in the transfer of 586 male patients of Farview Hospital for the criminally insane to civil hospitals. Many patients were eventually discharged to the community, enabling Thornberry and Jacoby (1979) to replicate the Baxstrom study design. A total of 414 subjects had a chance to offend during the three-year follow-up period. Of this group, 98 (24%) were arrested at least once. This finding corresponded to the Baxstrom rate of 28.6%, leading the authors to conclude that the "predictions made by the Fairview staff that the Dixon patients were as a group dominated by likely recidivists are not confirmed" (p. 179).

Despite their far-reaching implications, both the Steadman and Cocozza (1974) and Thornberry and Jacoby (1979) studies have been criticized on methodological grounds. Most important, they relied upon retrospective analyses involving indirect and potentially inaccurate measures of both clinicians' predictions and community violence (Lidz, Mulvey and Gardner, 1993). In particular, the fact that patients had been involuntarily hospitalized prior to the court decisions more likely reflected the institutional inertia of mental hospitals in continuing to house those persons over whom they had custody, rather than reflect a definitive prediction of dangerousness (Mulvey, personal communication). This operationalization of the 'clinical prediction' may have resulted in an underestimation of predictive accuracy. In addition, these studies measured violent behavior using police arrests, commitment hearing reports, or clinical records, all of which may underestimate the true rates of community violence (Lidz, Mulvey, and Gardner, 1993; Monahan and Steadman, 1994).

A more recent study conducted by Lidz, Mulvey and Gardner (1993) using a different study design, found better accuracy rates than those previously reported. Rather than rely on legal criteria (e.g., dangerousness) to indicate a prediction of future violence, these researchers examined two samples of psychiatric patients, matched on age, race, sex, and admission status (i.e., voluntary vs. involuntary). One group included individuals assessed by psychiatric emergency department clinicians as likely to be violent to another person during the follow-up period; the other group served as a comparison. Subjects were followed in the community for up to 6 months. Patients provided self-reports of violent incidents, and a "collateral" (i.e., an individual with detailed knowledge of the patient's life) provided this same information. In addition, official arrest records were reviewed. Lidz, Mulvey and Gardner (1993) found that clinicians were not only able to identify a more violent group of patients, but that the types of violence of the predicted-violent group were more serious than the comparison group. However, the overall accuracy of the clinicians was still quite modest and, for female patients, was not statistically significant.

Despite a general consensus that clinicians are at best unimpressive predictors of dangerousness, the "problem of dangerousness has stayed in the mainstream of research and debate" (Mulvey and Lidz, 1995: p.130). By the early 1980's, researchers began to focus on providing statistical information that could be used to improve the accuracy of clinical predictions (Webster et al., 1994). This "second generation"of risk research (Monahan, 1988) has focused less on evaluating the accuracy of clinical predictions of violence than on (1) empirically assessing the relationship between mental disorder and violence; and (2) identifying specific risk factors that clinicians could use to support predictions of future violence. The results of these studies have led to dramatic improvements in our understanding of the relationship between mental disorders and violence.

The Relationship Between Mental Disorder and Violence

Due primarily to the policy context described above, the strength of mental disorder as a risk factor for violence has received a good deal of research attention (Monahan and Steadman, 1994; Mulvey, 1994, Monahan, 1992b). Questions such as 'Are persons with mental disorders more dangerous than persons without mental disorders ?" and "What risk factors are associated with the dangerous behavior of persons with mental disorders?" are central to informing legal and social policies aimed at treating persons with mental disorders.

Research on the relationship between mental disorder and violence has generally followed one of two approaches (Monahan, 1997a, 1992b). The first approach seeks to estimate the relationship between mental disorder and violence by studying people *unselected* for mental health treatment. The second approach seeks to estimate the relationship between mental disorder and violence by studying people who have been *treated* for mental disorders (in hospitals or other treatment settings).[1] Substantively, these sampling strategies raise important questions concerning the types of conclusions that can be drawn from research. Studies of untreated populations are well-suited to examining the *fundamental relationship* between mental disorder and violence because the samples studied are, in principle, free of selection biases that may distort the association. Such studies enable direct comparisons between the violence rates of persons with and without mental disorders.

In contrast, studies of *treated* populations are, by definition, influenced by selection factors and therefore raise difficulties in drawing conclusions about the fundamental relationship between mental disorder and violence. Monahan (1992b) cautions that several sources of systematic bias render studies of treated populations inappropriate for drawing such conclusions. First, since these studies measure the violent behavior of subjects who have been hospitalized for mental health treatment, none of them can estimate the extent of violence that is due to the systematic selection of a disproportionately violent subset of persons into psychiatric hospitals. Second, studies of violence after hospitalization (i.e., following discharge) suffer from the additional selection bias that only those patients clinically predicted to be non-violent generally get released. Finally, to use the prevalence of violence before hospitalization as an index of the fundamental relationship between mental disorder and violence necessarily confounds rates of violence with the legal criteria for hospitalization. Specifically, the

---

[1]Note that studies of the prevalence of mental disorders among samples incarcerated in prisons and jails have also been conducted. For a review, see Monahan (1997a).

"dangerousness standard" for civil commitment (described above) systematically increases the likelihood that violence will precipitate hospitalization thereby inflating the observed pre-hospitalization prevalence rate of violence among patients.

Although inappropriate for making inferences regarding the fundamental relationship between mental disorder and violence, studies of treated populations are extremely important for answering *policy relevant questions* regarding the handling of persons treated by the mental health system in psychiatric hospitals, community-based treatment, and managed care settings. How much violence is expected to be committed by *psychiatric patients* after they are discharged from psychiatric hospitals? What risk factors can help to predict violence by discharged patients? Do rates of violence remain constant after discharge or do they change over time?; and Who are the victims of patient violence? Answers to such questions are crucial for the formulation of policies aimed at managing the risk of violent behavior among discharged patients.

The next two sections of this chapter review the research literature on the relationship between mental disorder and violence. The first section examines studies comparing the rates of violence by persons with mental disorder (both treated and untreated) with those of the general population. The second section reviews studies of the correlates of violence among persons who have been hospitalized for mental health treatment.

Comparisons with Non-Disordered Samples

At least two types of research designs have been used to evaluate the association between mental illness and violence.

The first relies on arrests or convictions to measure violence; the second design incorporates other data on violent acts regardless of whether they result in arrest or conviction. Although no single design is sufficient for determining whether and how mental illness is related to violence, these two approaches complement one another, enabling general conclusions to be drawn.

Arrest-Rate Studies of Discharged Psychiatric Patients. Studies conducted between the 1960's and 1980's typically have relied on individual arrest and conviction records in order to estimate and compare the underlying rates of violent behavior exhibited by psychiatric patients and nonpatients. While arrest-rate studies have been criticized for relying on official reports of arrests (see below), two strengths of this approach should be highlighted. First, because the outcome measure is based on official data, it is not subject to the kinds of reporting biases (e.g., social desirability bias) typically found in studies that rely on individuals' self-reports of violence. Second, arrest-rate studies have generally been prospective in the sense that patients were followed after being discharged from treatment. Thus, the chronology of events is known. In her review of arrest-rate studies, Rabkin (1979) observed that, whereas investigations conducted prior to 1965 showed no elevated rate of arrests for former patients, studies conducted after 1965 consistently showed the opposite result. In addition, as noted by Link, Andrews, and Cullen (1992), arrest-rate studies conducted after Rabkin's review consistently find an increased risk of arrest associated with patient status.

However, arrest-rate studies have been criticized on several grounds (Link and Stueve, 1995; Link, Andrews, and Cullen, 1992). First, differences between the arrest rates of patients and the general population may indicate less about the association between mental illness and criminal behavior than about the association between mental illness and the arrest process. This criticism has been referred to as the "criminalization of mental illness" thesis (Bonovitz and Bonovitz, 1981; Teplin, 1983; Abrahamsen, 1952). For example, based on observations of police-citizen encounters (involving over 2,200 hours of ride-alongs with police over a 14-month period), Teplin (1984) found that mentally disordered persons were more likely to be arrested than nonmentally disordered persons (47% versus 28%), controlling type of offense. Thus, higher arrest rates among discharged patients may, in part, be the result of differential police treatment, and not to differences in underlying rates of dangerous behavior.

Second, higher arrest rates among former patients may not only result from the systematic selection of a disproportionately violent subset of persons into psychiatric hospitals due to the reliance on dangerousness standards (see above), but may also be due to a process of selection that has been referred to as both the "medicalization of deviance" and the "psychiatrization of criminal behavior" (Monahan, 1973; Steadman, Cocozza, and Melick, 1978). The medicalization/psychiatrization of deviance argument is as follows: Because the scope of medical intervention has expanded over time to include more types of deviant behaviors (including violent behavior), persons who formerly had been channeled to the criminal justice system for punishment are now referred to psychiatrists and other mental health professionals for treatment. Thus, patient populations may now contain more persons with violent tendencies than used to be the case (Steadman, 1981), not because there is a strong connection between mental illness and violence but because the medicalization/psychiatrization process has systematically augmented the number of psychiatric patients with violence-related problems. In support of this thesis,

Steadman, Cocozza and Melick (1978) found that successive cohorts of New York State Psychiatric Hospital patients contained increasingly higher proportions of people who had been arrested before their most recent hospitalization.

A third limitation of the use of arrest-rates as indicators of psychiatric patient violence stems from the fact that the patients included in these studies were typically drawn from public mental hospitals or clinics that tend to serve populations from low-income areas where rates of violence are high, even for people who are not mentally ill. In addition, these facilities tend to serve the chronically mentally ill which further limits their generalizability (Cohen and Cohen, 1984). Thus, the higher arrest rates of former psychiatric patients (compared to the general population) found in these studies may generalize only to people with chronic disorders and may in fact have less to do with mental illness than with the social environments from which public hospital and clinic populations tend to be drawn.

Studies Incorporating Self-Reports of Violent Behavior. Consistent with recent studies based on arrest data, studies using other data sources to measure violence have found an association with mental disorder that cannot be explained away by selection factors, inadequate sampling or measurement, or with demographic and ecological controls (Swanson and colleagues, 1990, 1993, 1994; Link, Andrews, and Cullen, 1992; Link and Stueve, 1994; Steadman and Felson, 1983). The first such investigation, reported by Swanson, et al. (1990), was based on data from three of the five communities surveyed in the National Institute of Mental Health's Epidemiological Catchment Area (ECA) surveys (Robins and Regier, 1991) - the largest community study of mental disorders ever conducted in the United States. Representative, weighted samples of adult household residents of Baltimore, Raleigh-Durham, and Los Angeles were administered structured diagnostic interviews between 1980 and 1983. Data from these interviews were pooled to form a database of 10,059 respondents.

The Diagnostic Interview Schedule (DIS), a structured interview designed for use by trained lay persons, was used to measure mental disorders according to DSM-III criteria. Five items on the DIS - four embedded among the criteria for antisocial personality disorder and one that formed part of the alcohol abuse/dependence diagnosis - were used to indicate violent behavior. The ECA items pertaining to violent behavior were (1) Did you ever hit or throw things at your wife/husband/partner? [If so] Were you ever the one who threw things first, regardless of who started the argument? Did you hit or throw things first on more than one occasion? (2) Have you ever spanked or hit a child, (yours or anyone else's) hard enough so that he or she had bruises or had to stay in bed or see a doctor? (3) Since age 18, have you been in more than one fight that came to swapping blows, other than fights with your husband/wife partner? (4) Have you ever used a weapon like a stick, knife, or gun in a fight since you were 18?; and (5) Have you ever gotten into physical fights while drinking?

A respondent was counted as violent if he or she endorsed at least one of these items and reported that the violent act occurred during the year preceding the interview. This index of violence, as Swanson, et al. (1990) note, must be, for a number of reasons, considered a "blunt measure." First, it was based on self-report data without corroboration from either collateral informants or official records. Second, the questions overlapped considerably in terms of the types of behaviors measured. Third, the questions did not allow differentiation in terms of the frequency or the severity of violence. Thus, a respondent who reported multiple acts of felonious assault (even homicide) could not be distinguished from someone with only a single, less serious episode to report. These limitations prevented Swanson, et al. (1990) from inferring the *actual degree of dangerousness* exhibited by persons with specific mental disorders.

Nonetheless, the results reported by Swanson, et al. (1990) represented a dramatic leap forward in providing empirical evidence on the relationship between mental disorder and violence among persons *not selected for treatment* in the mental health system. Specifically, Swanson and colleagues found that: (1) the prevalence of violence was more than five times higher among mentally disordered persons compared to nondisordered persons; (2) the prevalence of violence was remarkably similar among persons who met the criteria for major mental disorders, such as schizophrenia, major depression, or mania/bipolar disorder; (3) the prevalence of violence among persons who met the criteria for a diagnosis of alcoholism was 12 times that of persons with no mental disorder diagnoses; and (4) the prevalence of violence for persons who met the criteria for drug abuse was 16 times that of persons with no disorders. When both demographic and clinical variables were combined in a logistic regression equation to predict the occurrence of violence, the following variables were found to contribute significantly: age, socioeconomic status, presence of diagnosed substance abuse disorder, and presence of diagnosed major mental disorder. The significant association between race and violence disappeared when SES was controlled.

In a follow-up study of these data, Swanson (1993) tested the hypothesis that the observed relationship between violence and dual diagnosis (e.g., possessing both a major mental disorder and an alcohol or substance abuse diagnosis) is spurious because violence and dual diagnosis have common sociodemographic correlates (e.g., both tend to cluster among young males of low SES). If this hypothesis was true, then when sociodemographic variables, such as age, gender, and SES were controlled, the association between violence and dual diagnosis would be greatly diminished. However, Swanson (1993) found that the effects of dual diagnosis were highly significant and stronger than the effects of sociodemographic characteristics.

In another study using the Epidemiological Catchment Area data, this time exploring the effects of psychotic symptomatology, Swanson, et al. (1996) attempted to replicate a finding initially reported by Link and Stueve (1994) that psychotic symptoms which produce feelings of personal threat or involve the intrusion of thoughts that can override self-control - a symptom cluster labeled by Link and Stueve (1994) as "threat/control-override" - were significantly related to violent behavior. Swanson et al. (1996) found that ECA respondents who reported threat/control-override symptoms were about twice as likely as those with other psychotic symptoms to engage in assaultive behavior, and about five times more likely to engage in violence than those and no mental disorder. The interaction between substance abuse disorders with threat/control-override symptoms added significantly to the risk of violent behavior.

In considering the results from the ECA studies, it is important to note that only 3% of all violent incidents reported in the ECA data were committed by mentally ill persons (Wessely, 1993). Thus, although mental disorders were found to be associated with violence, the actual amount of violence committed by persons with mental disorders was relatively small. In addition, as will be discussed in more detail below, it is important to highlight that no neighborhood-level data were included in the ECA studies. It is therefore impossible to determine whether the associations with violence reported by Swanson et al. (1990) were the same across neighborhood settings, or to determine how these associations might change if neighborhood characteristics were controlled.

Furthermore, it is possible that the spuriousness of the relationship between dual diagnosis and violence studied by Swanson (1993) is rooted less in the sociodemographic characteristics of individuals than in the characteristics of the neighborhoods in which mentally disordered persons with substance abuse problems reside. To the extent that substance abuse disorders are found to be more prevalent among persons in disadvantaged neighborhoods (i.e., neighborhoods in which all persons - regardless of mental illness - are at greater risk of engaging in violence), omitting neighborhood characteristics from the analysis may lead to erroneous conclusions about the association between mental illness and violence. Finally, it is plausible to hypothesize that psychiatric symptom such as threat/control-override which consist of "feelings of personal threat" are, to some extent, dependent upon the threatening nature of certain neighborhood settings (Aneshensel and Sucoff,1996). Without measuring neighborhood characteristics, there is no way to assess whether the association between threat/control-override symptoms and violence has been overstated.

In a study conducted in the Washington Heights Area of New York City, Link, Andrews and Cullen (1992) found significantly higher rates of reported violence among current and former psychiatric patients than among a random sample of subjects drawn from the general population. This result maintained after controlling for age, sex, education, race, and the homicide rates of the census tracts in which subjects resided. Violence was operationalized using two data sources: official arrest records and subject self-reports. In addition, Link and colleagues tested the hypothesis that the increased rate of violence in their patient group might be attributable to psychotic symptomatology. Indeed, their analyses revealed that psychotic symptoms mediated the differential rates of violence of the patient and nonpatient groups leading them to conclude that "much of the difference between mental patient groups and the never-treated group in the rates of violent/illegal behavior can be explained by the level of psychotic symptomatology" (p. 288). Although not the primary focus of their analyses, the results presented by Link, Andrews and Cullen revealed that over and above the significant effect of patient status and other individual characteristics, individuals from more violent neighborhoods were more likely than those from less violent neighborhoods to report having been arrested, having been involved in physical fights, and having used a weapon in a fight.

In seeking further specification of the symptom patterns associated with violence among persons with mental disorders, Link and Stueve (1994) reanalyzed their data this time focusing specifically on delusions involving "threat/control-override" symptoms. As described earlier, these symptoms include: feeling "that there were people that wished to do you harm," "that your mind was dominated by forces beyond your control," and "that thoughts were being put into your head that were not your own." Link and Stueve found that threat/control-override symptoms were significantly related to violent behavior, while other psychotic symptoms were not. Link and Stueve concluded that the apparent relationship between violence and psychotic symptoms is spurious, due almost entirely to a prior correlation with threat/control-override symptoms. No attempt was made by Link and Stueve to relate threat/control-override symptoms to neighborhood violence rates despite the possibility that one of the main symptom components (e.g., the belief that "people wished to do you harm") may vary by neighborhood context (Aneshensel and Sucoff, 1996).

In summarizing their work, Link and colleagues caution (1994) that the fact that psychotic symptoms explained differences between the rates of violence of mental patients and never-treated residents does not mean that psychotic symptoms are a potent source of violent behavior. They state: "Such symptoms are relatively rare and are in no way as important as the influx of drugs, the breakdown of communities, and other similar factors as causes of violent/illegal behavior" (p.290). Link and colleagues' research demonstrated that compared to the risk associated with demographic characteristics, the risk associated with mental patient status is relatively small. They argue that if higher rates of violent/illegal behavior are a "rational" justification for the differential treatment of mental patients, one might just as well advocate such differential treatment for men and high school graduates as opposed to women and college graduates.

A more recent study conducted by Steadman et al. (1998) compared the rates of violence among a sample of 336 psychiatric patients released into the Pittsburgh area to a sample of nonpatients matched on sex, age and ethnicity and drawn from the same neighborhoods into which the patients were discharged. (The Steadman et al. study used the same data upon which this book is based). In this study, violence was measured using a combination of data sources including subject self-report, collateral informant report, and official arrest and rehospitalization data. Steadman and colleagues found no significant difference between the rates of violence of discharged psychiatric patients who did not have a co-occurring substance abuse diagnosis and the rates of violence of others living in the same neighborhoods. However, the rate of violence of discharged psychiatric patients *with* a co-occurring substance abuse diagnosis was found to be two times higher than nonpatients living in the same neighborhoods during the first 10 weeks after hospital discharge. Consistent with studies based on the ECA data, this study reinforces the importance of substance abuse disorders in distinguishing the violence rates of patients and nonpatients.

Summary. Studies involving measures of violence other than arrest data address some of the difficulties surrounding arrest-rate studies. In terms of criminalization, the systematic selection of mentally ill persons for criminal justice processing cannot explain the higher rates of *self-reported violence not involving arrest* found in the ECA data. Similarly, the results reported by Swanson and colleagues cannot be accounted for by the medicalization/psychiatrization process, as these results were based on representative samples of community residents drawn from the general population who had *not been selected for mental health treatment.*

Finally, these studies seem to suggest that the higher rates of violence among persons with mental illnesses is not due solely to their greater propensity to be drawn from violence-prone segments of society. Link et al. (1992) controlled for many of the sociodemographic variables believed to explain patient-nonpatient differences, as well as for the rates of violence of the communities in which subjects lived. Steadman et al. (1998) confronted this issue by drawing their nonpatient sample from the same neighborhoods as their patient sample. And, Swanson and colleagues controlled for individual demographics, such as SES, thought to be associated with neighborhood setting. Taken together, these efforts diminish the possibility that exposure to violence-prone neighborhoods alone explains the higher rates of violence exhibited by persons with mental illness.

It is difficult to underestimate the importance of these studies - in combination with arrest-rate studies - in providing evidence for an association between mental disorder and violence (Monahan, 1992b, 1997a). Establishing the association among a large representative sample from the general population that was not selected for treatment provides convincing evidence that a fundamental relationship exists. In addition, finding an association between patient status and violence that was not explained away by demographic and neighborhood controls provides further convincing evidence. However, due to the their comparative nature (e.g., the effect of mental illness is assessed in relation to nonmentally ill samples), these studies have been of limited utility to psychiatrists and psychologists who must regularly provide assessments of future violence. The emergence of dangerousness as a criterion for commitment has influenced the environment within which clinicians work, in part, by increasing the percentage of individuals with histories of violence in the mental health system. In addition, the widespread policy of deinstitutionalization described earlier has made it increasingly difficult to manage dangerous patients simply by committing them to psychiatric facilities for long periods of time.

For the purposes of assessing and managing violence risk, it is less important to know whether a certain type of patient has more or less potential for violence than a nonpatient, or whether the rates of violence of patients are higher than nonpatients after certain characteristics are controlled. The important question in terms of risk assessment is how to identify, *from among a population of patients*, those who, due to their high risk for violence, represent a threat to the public's safety if discharged to the community. For example, it has been found that when the comparison population is the general population, symptoms of schizophrenia modestly increase the risk of violence (Swanson et al., 1990). However, when the comparison population is a group of former patients, symptoms of schizophrenia are found to be associated with a reduction in violence risk (Lidz, Mulvey, & Gardner, 1993; Rice & Harris, 1992, 1995). The need for systematic data on the correlates of violence among persons with mental disorder has led *risk assessment research* to become one of the fastest growing areas in the filed of mental health law.

The following section of this chapter reviews this body of research focusing first on studies of specific risk factors and then on the development of actuarial prediction tools that attempt to statistically combine such factors. Particular attention is paid to the wide range of risk factors measured by the MacArthur Violence Risk Assessment Study, as these will become the focus of analyses reported in subsequent chapters of this book.

Risk Assessment Research

A great deal of recent research has addressed the relationship between specific cues or risk factors and the occurrence of violent behavior among persons with mental illnesses. In these studies, psychiatric patients have been assessed according to one or more potential risk factors, such as diagnosis, demographics, or symptomatology, and these measures have been correlated with the occurrence of violence in the community. A recent comprehensive review of the literature on risk factors (Webster et al., 1997) revealed a great many variables that have significant correlations with patient violence (see Chapter One). The overarching purpose of risk assessment research is to establish a set of reliable and valid predictors of future violent behavior that can be used to support clinical assessments of violence risk (Monahan, 1997; Borum, 1996).

Risk Factors for Violence: The MacArthur Violence Risk Assessment Study. One of the most significant contributions of the MacArthur Violence Risk Assessment Study has been to measure - in a single research design - a more comprehensive array of risk factors for violence than has ever before been measured among persons with mental disorder. Risk factors were selected to be measured if they had been validated in existing research (e.g., demographic factors; Klassen and O'Conner, 1994), if they had been mentioned in the clinical literature as potential predictors of violence (e.g., delusions; Taylor and Gunn, 1984), and if they were named in mid-range theories of aggression and violence (e.g., anger; Novaco, 1994, or psychopathy; Hart, Hare and Forth, 1994). Using these criteria to select risk factors for study, the MacArthur Project explicitly acknowledges that there currently exists no fully articulated, comprehensive theory of violence from which to draw hypotheses regarding specific risk factors. Thus, a broader, more inclusive approach to variable selection was taken.

At the time the study was designed, a number of risk factors of interest to the MacArthur project were either unavailable due to lack of established measurement instruments or had not previously been analyzed systematically as risk factors for violence *among the mentally disordered.* For these, the project refined existing measures, including instruments to assess violent fantasies, delusions, hallucinations, social support networks, impulsivity, anger control, and psychopathy.

The risk factors measured by the MacArthur Study have been categorized by Steadman et al. (1994) into 4 substantive domains: dispositional or individual, historical, contextual, and clinical. A complete listing of these risk factors is displayed in Table 2.1. The dispositional domain refers to demographic factors, such as age, race, gender, and social class, as well as to personality characteristics and neurological dysfunction. Due in part to methodological difficulties, biological risk factors, such as cerebrospinal fluid serotonin metabolite level, were not measured. Properly measuring cerebrospinal fluid would have required spinal taps to be conducted on patients who were kept medication-free for at least one week, a strategy that was considered infeasible. In addition, empirical evidence in support of serotonin as a risk factor for violence was determined not to be sufficient (Monahan, 1998: personal communication). The historical domain includes significant life events experienced by the subjects in the past (e.g., family history, work history, treatment history, and criminal history). The contextual domain includes current social supports, social networks, and perceived stress, as well as environmental factors such as access to weapons. Finally, the clinical domain includes types and symptoms of mental disorder, personality disorder, alcohol and drug abuse, and levels of functioning.

Steadman et al. (1994) note that this scheme is not without its difficulties. In particular, the theoretical status of many of the chosen variables has not been resolved. For example, anger is included as a dispositional factor (e.g., trait measures). However, if one believed anger to be highly changeable (e.g., state measures), then it could easily be classified as a clinical factor. In reviewing the research on risk factors for violence among persons with mental illnesses (below), particular attention is paid to those risk factors measured by the MacArthur Risk Assessment Study.

<u>Risk Factor Research</u>. A good deal of research on violent behavior has involved Hare's (1991) Psychopathy Checklist, which was developed as an alternative to the DSM-IIIR antisocial personality disorder diagnosis. Psychopathy

(operationalized as a dichotomous variable indicating a psychopathic personality type) has been found to be a robust predictor of future violence in a wide range of high-risk populations (Hart, Cox, and Hare, 1995; Harris, Rice, and Quinsey, 1993; Forth, Hart & Hare, 1990; Quinsey, Rice & Harris, 1995; Rice & Harris, 1992). For example, Hare and McPhearson (1984) reported that 104 criminals assessed as psychopaths by the Psychopathy Checklist were significantly more likely than 139 other criminals to have engaged in physical violence. Harris, Rice, and Cormier's (1991) study of the recidivism rates of 169 adult male mentally disordered offenders released from a maximum security psychiatric hospital over an average 10-year follow-up period revealed that, over and above the effect of past criminal behavior, psychopaths (as measured by the Hare Psychopathy Checklist, Hart & Dempster, 1997; Hart, Hare & Forth, 1994) exhibited much higher rates of violent recidivism than those who were not psychopaths. A meta-analysis of 18 studies which had investigated the relationship between psychopathy and violence (and other forms of antisocial behavior) revealed, on average, a large effect-size (d=.79) between psychopathy and these outcome measures (Salekin, Rogers, & Sewell, 1996). Psychopathy's defining characteristics, such as impulsivity, criminal versatility, callousness, grandiosity, lack of empathy or remorse, and a tendency to violate social norms make the conceptual link between violence and psychopathy straightforward (Webster et al., 1997; McCord and McCord, 1964; Hare, 1991).

However, at the time of designing the MacArthur Study, a brief version of the PCL validated among mentally disordered samples was not available. Thus, with support from the MacArthur Foundation Research Network on Mental Health and the Law, Hart, Hare, and Forth (1994) developed and pilot-tested a shortened version of the PCL.

This instrument was administered to all MacArthur Study subjects.

Another risk factor for violence that has been emphasized in the literature is impulsivity (Barratt, 1994). According to Barratt (p.71), impulsive aggression is characterized by a "hair trigger" temper. That is, the impulsive aggressive person "usually responds aggressively without thinking and...often expresses guilt and remorse...but lacks the self-control to refrain from doing it again." Although the Barratt Impulsivity Scale (BIS) is the most reliable and valid instrument available for measuring impulsivity (Steadman, et al., 1994), the BIS had not been validated using mentally disordered samples. Again, with support from the MacArthur Network, the BIS was revised and incorporated into the MacArthur Study.

Anger has also been proposed as an important factor in assessing violence risk among persons with mental disorders (Novaco, 1994). Craig (1982) examined the cases of 1,033 patients (virtually all of the admissions in one county for one year) and found that 11% had engaged in violent behavior before admission and that anger was the factor most strongly associated with assaultiveness. Anger was also found by Segal, Watson, Goldfinger, and Averbuck (1988) to be the strongest predictor of physical aggression in the clinical profiles of 208 psychiatric inpatients. More recently, (with support from the MacArthur Network), Novaco (1994) revised a previously developed measurement scale - the Novaco Anger Scale (NAS) - for use in assessing anger among mentally disordered populations. This instrument was used to assess anger among the subjects of the MacArthur Violence Risk Assessment Study.

Several studies of the relationship between symptomatology and violence have been conducted. In a study of 127 inpatients, Lowenstein, Binder, and McNiel

(1994) found that hallucinatory behavior (e.g., the experience of sensory stimuli not shared by others) was significantly higher in patients who later physically attacked others during hospitalization. The association between hallucinations and assaults occurred in the context of a general tendency for other symptoms of psychosis to be associated with violence. Specifically, patients who became physically assaultive also scored higher on certain subscales of the Brief Psychiatric Rating Scale (BPRS): thinking disturbance, hostile-suspiciousness, and agitation-excitement. Similar findings have been reported by Yesavage et al. (1981). In addition, it has been suggested that violence in patients with temporal lobe seizures is more common among the subgroup of such patients who have hallucinatory and paranoid symptoms (Lewis, Pincus, Shanok, and Glaser, 1982). A dimension of hallucinatory behavior typically considered important in evaluating a patient's risk of violence is whether or not the hallucinations command the patient to act in a certain manner such as to behave violently. However, little empirical evidence has been found to support this claim (McNiel, 1994). An instrument measuring hallucinations and command hallucinations was developed and administered by the MacArthur Study.

Delusions are among the most common symptoms experienced by people with schizophrenia and there is evidence that among people with schizophrenia, the violent are more likely to have ever experienced delusions than the nonviolent (Taylor et al., 1994). Hafner and Boker (1982) compared people with a psychotic illness who had been homicidal with psychotic inpatients who had not been violent and found a significant difference in the prevalence of delusions between the two groups. Among patients with schizophrenia, 89% had been deluded at the time of killing or attempted killing compared with 76% of the nonviolent patients. In addition, 70% of homicidal patients with schizophrenia were rated as being in a delusional relationship with their victim at the time of the offense, for example perceiving the victim as an enemy. In addition, Taylor et al. (1994) suggested that between 25% and 40% of the mentally ill who committed violent acts were motivated by delusional thinking. However, the precise characteristics of delusions that relate to violence (e.g., the type and intensity) and how those characteristics might best be measured were unclear at the time the MacArthur Study was designed. In response to this need, Taylor et al. (1994) developed and pilot-tested a more clinically sensitive measure of delusions that was revised by the MacArthur Study group and incorporated into its battery of measures.

A number of recent studies have highlighted the importance of substance abuse disorder as a predictor of violence among persons with mental disorders. Consistent with findings reported by Swanson et al. (1990), a recent study by Steadman et al. (1998) of the violent behavior of 951 psychiatric patients released to the community found that subjects with both a major mental disorder and a substance abuse disorder were more violent during the year following discharge than subjects with a major mental disorder only (31.1% vs. 17.9%). They also found that subjects with a substance abuse disorder and no major mental disorder were more violent than subjects with both types of disorders (43.0% vs. 31.1%). Similarly, Swartz et al. (1998) found that the combination of alcohol or substance abuse and medication noncompliance was significantly associated with serious violent acts among a sample of 331 involuntarily hospitalized inpatients. Instruments measuring drug use and abuse (e.g., the Michigan Alcoholism Screening Test (MAST) (Pokorny, Miller, and Kaplan, 1972) and the Drug Abuse Screening Test; DAST (Skinner, 1982)) were incorporated into the

MacArthur Study.

Persons with personality disorders have long been considered to constitute a considerable proportion of the violent mentally ill population (Widiger and Trull, 1994; Krakowski, Volovka, and Brizer, 1986). This observation is rooted in the notion that violence stems largely from enduring personality traits. Violent behavior is in fact a defining feature for two of the personality disorders included in the American Psychiatric Association's (APA) Diagnostic and Statistical Manual of Mental Disorders (DSM-IIIR; American Psychiatric Association, 1987): the borderline and antisocial personality. Robins, Tipp, and Przybeck (1991) reported that 85% of the 628 persons diagnosed with antisocial personality disorder in the NIMH Epidemiological Catchment Area study had a history of violence. In addition, Bland and Orn (1986) found that among 1,200 randomly selected residents of a large Canadian city, the diagnosis of antisocial personality disorder was a significant risk factor for violent behavior toward a spouse or child, particularly when combined with an alcohol or depressed mood disorder. Data regarding diagnosed personality disorders were gathered by the MacArthur Study from individual patient hospital records.

Discharged patients living in chaotic family environments where there is alcohol or substance abuse and an ongoing history of conflict among family members have been found to be at greater risk for committing violence (Hill, 1982; Klassen and O'Conner, 1988), suggesting the importance of social networks and social supports in understanding the occurrence of violent behavior. However, existing measures of social networks were extremely lengthy and not geared for use in mentally disordered samples. Thus, with support from the MacArthur Network, Estroff and Zimmer (1994) developed a streamlined version of their instrument for measuring affective and instrumental support.

Using this instrument on a sample of 169 individuals with severe mental disorders followed in the community over an 18-month period, they found that having a higher concentration of relatives in the social network increased the odds of threatening others, as did the overall size of the social network. Subjects who threatened violence were more likely to perceive their significant others as attacking and hostile, while perceiving themselves to be friendly. Mothers were the most frequent targets of violence. Based on these results, Estroff and Zimmer (1994) conclude that interpersonal social networks and relationship quality, in addition to clinical condition are important considerations in assessing risks for violence. The streamlined instrument was part of the MacArthur battery of measures.

Finally, research on the relationship between demographic and historical characteristics and violent behavior was reviewed by Klassen and O'Conner (1994). They reported a number of consistent findings: Positive correlations have been found between adult crime and violence and subsequent crime and violence among persons with mental illness (Steadman and Cocozza, 1974; Thornberry and Jacoby, 1979). Life stress has been found to be predictive of future violence among patient samples (Steadman and Ribner, 1982). Studies of mixed gender psychiatric patients have found males to be disproportionately violent in the community compared to females (Craig, 1982). Age has also been found to be predictive of violence (Steadman and Cocozza, 1974; Thornberry and Jacoby, 1979), as has lower educational or occupational status (Harris and Varney, 1986). Being black has been shown to have a significant correlation with violence, however, this effect has been shown to diminish when individual SES is controlled (Swartz et al., 1998; Swanson et al., 1990). As indicated in table 2.1, a wide array of demographic variables were measured by the MacArthur Study.

Actuarial Prediction Tools. There is a long tradition in criminology of using actuarial techniques to predict violent recidivism among released prisoners (e.g., an actuarial instrument developed by INSLAW Incorporated was used to assist U.S. Federal prosecutors in the risk assessment of offenders, and the Salient Factors Score has similarly been used as a risk assessment scale by the U.S. Parole Commission). Actuarial techniques have also been recommended as an important element in improving the reliability and validity of clinical risk judgements (Borum, 1996; Monahan, 1997b). Actuarial instruments are designed to provide actuarial data on the probability of violence among people with a given set of characteristics. The development of such instruments for use in mentally ill populations constitutes a vital part of current mental health law research.

Menzies, Webster, and Sepejak (1985) were among the first researchers to construct a multi-item rating system for assessing violent behavior among mentally disordered offenders. They called their instrument the Dangerous Behavior Rating Scheme (DBRS). The DBRS consisted of 22 items (later reduced to 11, Webster and Menzies, 1993) rated on a 7-point Likert system. The items were grouped into 5 dimensions of dangerous behavior: (1) personality factors, including hostility, anger, rage, capacity for empathy, etc.; (2) situational factors, including environmental stress and social support; (3) facilitating factors, including alcohol and drug use; (4) global estimates of the likelihood of dangerous behavior by clinical staff; and (5) the rater's confidence in the judgements made, including the perceived honesty of the patient in answering questions.

A total of 203 patients referred from the Metropolitan Toronto criminal courts in 1979 were assessed using the DBRS and followed for two years. Information on violent recidivism was obtained via record searches of six major psychiatric hospitals in the region and the Ontario Ministry of Correctional Services Central Registry. The average period of risk in the community was 17.3 months. Menzies, Webster, McMain, Staley, and Scaglione (1994), found that less than 12% of the dangerous behavior manifested by subjects during the follow-up period had been successfully anticipated by the DBRS and, based on these results, advocated caution in using such instruments to predict future violence. They advised that researchers pay greater attention to the many competing forces that determine violent behavior, as well as to the social ecology and interpersonal dynamics of individual violence.

Recent work by Harris, Rice and Quinsey (1993) has focused on developing an actuarial prediction instrument that could be used more effectively to assist clinicians in making assessments of violence risk. Their data were drawn from records amassed over many years at the Oak Ridge Division of the Penetanguishene Mental Health Center. Oak Ridge is a secure hospital providing assessment and treatment services to violent offenders with mental health problems received from the courts, correctional services, and other psychiatric hospitals. Their sample consisted of 618 males admitted to Oak Ridge between 1965 and 1980, who, as of 1988 were either maintained in an open psychiatric ward, halfway house, or discharged to the community. The data were gathered from official hospital records. A total of 191 subjects committed a violent offense during the follow-up period.

Using stepwise discriminant analysis, Harris, Rice and Quinsey (1993) selected variables to be included in their risk assessment instrument. The analysis yielded 12 variables which together best predicted the dichotomous (violent/not violent) outcome variable; they called their instrument the Violence Risk Appraisal Guide (VRAG). The 12 risk factors and their bivariate correlations with violence were as follows: Hare Psychopathy Checklist score (.34), elementary school maladjustment (.31), diagnosed personality disorder (.26), age at index offense (-.26), separated from parents before age 16 (.25), failure on prior conditional release (.24), non-violent offense history (.20), never married (.18), diagnosis of schizophrenia (-.17), victim injury (-.16), alcohol abuse (.13), female victim - index offense (-.11). The overall correlation between the 12 risk factors and the criterion measure was .45, higher than any previous actuarial prediction instrument. A cross-validation study of the Violence Risk Appraisal Guide was performed on a sample of 159 child molesters and rapists followed for an average of 10 years at risk (Rice and Harris, 1997). The performance of the instrument was also examined on a 10-year follow-up of 288 sex offenders that included both those in the original construction sample for the VRAG and the validation sample. The VRAG was found to perform as well as it had on the original construction sample in predicting violent recidivism among the validation samples.[2]

Finally, Gardner, Lidz, Mulvey, and Shaw (1996) demonstrated the utility of using a recursive partitioning methodology to produce a tree-based actuarial tool to identify persons with mental disorder who are at risk for frequent incidents of physical violence. Using Classification and Regression Tree (CART) software (Breiman, Freidman, Olshen, and Stone, 1984), Gardner and colleagues

---

[2]A third instrument, the HCR-20, consists of three domains of predictive factors chosen on the basis of a comprehensive literature review (Webster et al., 1997). As noted in Chapter One, the three domains are: historical, clinical, and risk management. However, as indicated by Borum (1996), the HCR-20 has not yet been tested for reliability and validity and is therefore not currently considered as a usable actuarial tool.

constructed a hierarchical decision tree with four yes/no questions that classified patients into one of five categories, each with a predicted rate of violence. The four questions were: (1) Is the Brief Symptom Hostility Inventory - Hostility Scale score greater than 2?; (2) Are there more than three prior violent acts?; (3) Is age less than 18?; and (4) Is the patient a heavy drug user? A comparison of predictive accuracies showed the decision tree to perform as well as a more traditional main effects model built on a similar array of variables.[3]

Limitations of Risk Assessment Research. Clearly, a good deal of research has been conducted on the prediction of violence among persons with mental disorders and a wide range of risk factors have been identified. However, this research suffers from a number of limitations, many of which have been reviewed by Monahan and Steadman (1994). First, despite the multifaceted nature of violence by people with mental disorder, most studies in this area have employed a very narrow range of risk factors chosen without reference to any theory of violent behavior or of mental disorder. Second, with rare exception (Lidz, Mulvey, and Gardner, 1993), prior studies have used weak markers for the occurrence of community violence. The reliance in many studies on official records such as arrest and rehospitalization, in addition to selection bias issues in terms of who gets arrested or hospitalized, completely overlooks violence that did not precipitate formal intervention by a government agency. As recently reported by Steadman et al. (1998), this practice

---

[3]Recursive partitioning approaches have also been used by the MacArthur Study to produce tree-based actuarial prediction tools (Steadman, Silver, Monahan, Appelbaum, Robbins, Mulvey, Grisso, Roth, and Banks, 2000; Monahan, Steadman, Appelbaum, Robbins, Mulvey, Silver, Roth, and Grisso, 2000).

results in an underestimation of the actual rates of community violence by persons with mental disorder by a factor of 6.

Third, with rare exception, prior studies have tended to enroll only subjects who were presumed to have a high baserate of violence (e.g., males with a history of violence), in order to obtain a sufficient level of violence during the follow-up period to permit statistical analysis. Restricting the sample to one gender, however, precludes an analysis of gender effects related to patient violence. And, given that different factors may be associated with repeat violence than are associated with the first occurrence of violence (Mulvey, Blumstein, and Cohen, 1986), making prior violence a criterion for inclusion in research may yield findings inapplicable to persons who have not yet been violent. Finally, prior research has tended to involve samples drawn from a single facility. Until very recently (Steadman, et al., 1998), it has remained unknown to what extent many of the findings in the field are robust across sites or are the result of local factors that are without general applicability. The fact that research done at different sites has tended to use idiosyncratically defined variables and rarely to replicate the measures used at other sites has impeded the cumulative development of knowledge in the field. It has also meant that data from several sites can almost never be pooled into larger samples for more powerful statistical analyses.

The Importance of Community-Level Risk Factors

An additional limitation of research in the area of mental disorder and violence is that it has focused primarily on the characteristics of individuals (but, see Silver, Mulvey, and

Monahan, 1999; Silver, 2000a, 2000b). This focus derives largely from an assumption that the symptoms and correlates of mental illness (e.g., including aggression) are rooted in the pathology of individuals and from the individual-case-processing nature of the mental health system. Estroff and Zimmer (1994) point out that persons with mental disorders are generally depicted as "ahistorical, socially and interpersonally decontextualized subjects, devoid of life histories apart from their psychiatric or legal careers" (p.261). This depiction implies that patient violence occurs with a high level of cross-situational consistency. Violence researchers have tended to downplay the situational embeddedness of mental illness and to ignore the possibility that symptomatology (and aggressiveness) may vary in type and severity depending on the conditions inherent in the surrounding environment.

This focus makes pragmatic sense, since risk assessment research is designed to be used in clinical settings in which assessment relies almost exclusively on individual interviews and case record reviews (Mulvey and Lidz, 1995). However, to the extent that situational variables contribute to the violent behavior of mentally ill patients, an exclusive focus on individual characteristics limits the degree of predictive accuracy that can be attained. For example, Swanson (1994) emphasized that the ECA data underscore the importance of contextual and life course approaches to the study of violence and mental illness; while serious mental disorder emerged as one significant factor that contributed to the occurrence of violence, it was one of many determinants. "Variables such as age, gender, marital history, economic status, and position in the social structure all define conditions under which mental disorder may be more or less likely to engender assaultive behavior" (p.132). In addition, Swanson and colleagues (1996) caution that because the ECA studies focused largely on individual symptoms, the data tend to reinforce individual-level explanatory models. They conclude that definitive causal inferences regarding psychotic symptoms such as paranoid delusions and violence must await a better understanding of contextual risk factors.

Similarly, Novaco (1994, p.33) argues that the study of anger as a risk factor for violence has much to gain from adopting a contextual perspective emphasizing "anger's embeddedness within physical and social environments." Novaco further argues that "by giving nearly exclusive attention to intrapsychic variables, clinical models impose unnecessary boundaries on our understanding of anger...we ought to give greater attention to the enduring contextual factors that shape anger experiences." In discussing the relationship between personality disorders and violence, Widiger and Trull (1994) suggest that violent behavior results from a complex interaction among a variety of social, clinical, and environmental factors whose relative importance varies across situations and times. They go on to state that "the complexity of this interaction raises the issue of the extent to which one should conceive of violent behavior as resulting from a personality disorder rather than a situational, environmental, or other factor" (p.216). They urge future researchers to "carefully disentangle the interactive factors that contribute to a specific violent act."

However, as a result of the individual-clinical emphasis traditionally adopted by risk assessment researchers, there has been a striking lack of empirical data collected to describe the community contexts in which persons with mental disorders reside. Although most studies conducted to date have therefore not explicitly tested the impact of community-level risk factors, evidence consistent with a contextual argument has been reported. For example, Link, Andrews, and Cullen (1992) found a significant association between neighborhood violence and individual violence, controlling for patient status. In addition, it has been reported that people with mental illness are more likely than nonmentally ill people to become victims of violence (Jacobson, 1989), suggesting that they are more likely to find themselves in violence-prone contexts. A similar line of reasoning is expressed by Hiday (1997) when she posits a theoretical link between mental disorder and violence that operates through a contextual factor she calls "tense situations."

Unfortunately, without data on community-level risk factors, most studies are unable to measure the true magnitude of the associations between individual-level risk factors (e.g., mental illness, substance abuse, etc.) and violence. When we consider, for example, that persons with mental illness may often reside in disorganized communities that have higher rates of drug use, crime, and violence (e.g., due to the placement of halfway houses and other community facilities, or to their lack of economic resources), it is plausible to propose that controlling for such environmental factors may greatly offset the observed associations. Further, due to their perceived "differentness" and vulnerability, persons with mental illness may be more often drawn into conflicts in communities in which violence is a common approach to dealing with threats and resolving disputes (Link and Stueve, 1995; Hiday, 1995, 1997).

A noteworthy exception to the almost exclusive focus on individual characteristics in research on violence and mental disorder can be seen in the study reported by Steadman et al. (1998) (described above). By matching patient and community groups in terms of their aggregate distribution of neighborhood locations in order to compare their aggregate rates of violence, these authors explicitly acknowledge the role of neighborhood contexts in influencing violent behavior. However, they did not measure the specific characteristics of the neighborhood contexts experienced by individual subjects (e.g., poverty, disadvantage) that could be related to violence. Their data therefore do not shed light on the characteristics of neighborhoods that may exacerbate or protect against violent behavior among patients and community members; nor do they shed light on the extent to which the risk factors associated with violent behavior in both groups (i.e., substance abuse) are evenly distributed across neighborhood settings. Similarly, although the study by Link, Andrews, and Cullen (1992) (described above) measured the murder rates of the census tracts in which their patient and nonpatient samples resided (in order to control for the criminality of the neighborhood context), they did not attempt to understand how and for whom the neighborhood context matters.

A recent multi-level study conducted by Silver, Mulvey, and Monahan (1999) using data from the MacArthur Violence Risk Assessment Study goes further than previous efforts in attempting to disentangle individual- and community-level factors related to patient violence. In this study, the authors replicate the results of prior studies of individual-level risk factors for violent behavior among persons with mental disorder and then systematically examine the influence of concentrated neighborhood poverty on these relationships. Concentrated poverty was operationalized to include census tracts in which 30 percent or more of residents lived below the poverty line. Among the risk factors analyzed were: sex, age race, SES, prior arrests for serious crimes, psychopathy, and substance abuse.

The study demonstrates the utility of employing a multi-level approach to the problem of assessing violence risk among persons discharged from a psychiatric hospital. Results indicate that (1) concentrated poverty within the neighborhoods where patients reside after discharge has a significant impact on the overall amount of violence committed by these patients over and above individual-level characteristics; (2) that the socioeconomic status of individual patients is less predictive of violent behavior than concentrated neighborhood poverty; and (3) that due to the strong correlation between race and concentrated poverty, neither had a significant effect when entered into the model together, although both were significantly associated with violence when entered separately. Silver, Mulvey, and Monahan (1999:248) conclude that "research efforts aimed at assessing violence risk among discharged psychiatric patients may benefit from specifying a role for the neighborhood contexts into which patients are discharged, in addition to measuring individual-level characteristics."

A fundamental limitation of the Silver, Mulvey, and Monahan study is that it relied on a single indicator (i.e., percent of individuals below the poverty line) to operationalize a single dimension of the neighborhood context, namely, concentrated poverty. Although their analyses establish neighborhood poverty as an important factor in predicting violence by discharged psychiatric patients, the study does not provide systematic insight into the mechanism by which this association occurs. More importantly, no research has been done to date to determine what other aspects of the neighborhood context matter in the association between mental disorder and violence.

Summary of Literature on Violence and Mental Disorder

Mulvey's (1994) comprehensive review of the literature on mental disorder and violence derives six conclusions which aptly characterize the current state of knowledge: (1) mental illness appears to be a risk factor for community violence in the general population; (2) the size of the association between mental illness and violence, while statistically significant, does not appear to be very large. In addition, the absolute risk for violence posed by mental illness is small; (3) the combination of a serious mental illness and a substance abuse disorder seems to significantly increase the risk of involvement in a violent act; (4) the association between mental illness and violence seems to be significant even when demographic characteristics are taken into account; however, the relative strength of mental illness as a risk factor for violence compared with other characteristics such as socio-economic status, is still not known; (5) active symptoms of mental illness are probably more important as risk factors than is simply the presence of an identifiable disorder; and (6) no clear information about the causal paths that produce the association between mental illness and violence is currently available.

Finally, to this general summary I would add that *we currently do not understand how the neighborhood contexts in which persons with mental disorders reside influence their propensity to engage in violence*; the possibility that neighborhood factors may be involved in the "causal paths that produce the association between mental disorder and violence" has gone largely untested. Filling this gap in our knowledge is the fundamental purpose of this book. To accomplish this purpose requires a coherent theoretical framework for understanding how contextual factors may be implicated in the relationships among patient characteristics and violent behavior. In the following two chapters a theoretical framework is developed along with a set of testable research hypotheses.

Table 2.1. Cue Domains in the MacArthur Risk Assessment Study (Adapted from Steadman et al., 1994: p. 303).

1. Personal/ Dispositional Factors

Demographics
- Age
- Gender
- Race
- Social Class

Personality
- Personality Style
- Anger
- Impulsiveness
- Psychopathy

Cognitive
- IQ
- Neurological Impairment

2. Historical Factors

Social History
- Family History
  - Child rearing
  - Child abuse
  - Family deviance
- Employment History
- Educational Attainment

Mental Hospitalization History
- Prior Hospitalizations
- Treatment Compliance

History of Crime and Violence
- Arrests
- Incarcerations
- Self-reported Violence
- Collateral Reports of Violence
- Violence Toward Self

3. Contextual Factors

Perceived Stress

Social Support
- Living Arrangements
- Activities of Daily Living
- Perceived Support
- Social Networks

Means for Violence (i.e., weapon availability)

4. Clinical Factors

Axis I Diagnosis

Symptoms of Mental Illness
- Delusions
- Hallucinations
- Symptom Severity
- Violent Fantasies

Axis II Diagnosis

Level of Functioning

Substance Abuse
- Alcohol
- Other Drugs

CHAPTER 3

The Importance of Neighborhood Context

> "Defects of the brain,...disorders due to use of drugs, to biochemical disturbances, and the like, all interfere with normal function and behavior. Breaks in the essentials on the social level, because of the complexities of the processes, are more difficult to study. Progress in this field is...slower because the realization of significant social factors is more recent" (Faris and Dunham, 1939, p.155).

Faris and Dunham's statement rings as true today as it did 60 years ago. Indeed, recent studies of the violent behavior of persons with mental illnesses have, with rare exceptions, focused almost exclusively on the explanatory power of individual-level variables. This is due, in part, to the difficulty of collecting relevant social context measures and, in part, to the belief that violence risk is individually determined. From the standpoint of clinical risk assessment, this focus seems reasonable since the data available in clinical settings are typically gathered through face-to-face diagnostic interviews and case record reviews, which tend to emphasize individual attributes. However, from the standpoint of understanding why persons with mental illness commit violent acts, limiting the range of explanatory variables to individual descriptors does not seem justifiable.

The importance of the neighborhood context in understanding patient violence was recently demonstrated by Silver, Mulvey, and Monahan (1999). These researchers found that discharged mental patients living in neighborhoods with high rates of poverty were more likely to engage in assaultive behavior than patients living in neighborhoods with less poverty, holding constant individual-level predictors of patient violence, such as sex, race, age, SES, drug abuse, prior arrests, and psychopathy. This finding suggests that the causes of patient violence may be rooted in both individual-level and community-level factors. However, to date, there have been no comprehensive studies of the neighborhood contexts in which mental patients live and the effects these contexts may have on their violent behavior. By emphasizing explanatory variables that can be measured at the individual-level and de-emphasizing potentially predictive community-level variables, mental health researchers have artificially limited their ability to fully explicate the causes of patient violence.

The purpose of this chapter is to set the stage for the development of a model of violence by persons with mental illness that incorporates community and individual-level risk factors. In order to develop such a model, two issues must be addressed. First, a methodological approach for analyzing the effects of community and individual risk factors must be outlined; for this I draw on recent advances in the area of multilevel data analysis. Second, a coherent rationale for relating community-level risk factors to the violent behavior of mentally ill individuals must be presented; for this I draw on the social disorganization perspective in sociology. Finally, the chapter concludes with a detailed discussion of recent studies of crime victimization focusing on the combined effects of community and individual-level risk factors (Simcha-Fagan and Schwartz, 1986; Sampson and Woolredge, 1987; Miethe and McDowall, 1993; Rountree, Land, and Miethe, 1994). These studies are particularly relevant to the present study because they draw upon social disorganization theory to derive neighborhood-level measures of disadvantage and relate these to the experiences and behaviors of individuals.

The Multilevel Approach: Integrating Community- and Individual-Level Effects

Sociologists have long emphasized that a complete understanding of the lives of individuals requires not only an understanding of their personal characteristics, but also an understanding of the social contexts in which they live. This viewpoint reflects the fundamental assumption that social contexts manifest properties that can not be derived from a summation of the individual characteristics and behaviors that constitute them (Durkheim, 1938). Sociologists further assume that these emergent macrol-level properties structure and constrain individual behavior. Consequently, in order to fully understand individual behavior, it is necessary to analyze not only the characteristics of individuals but also those of the social contexts in which they live.

The study of the effects of macro-level characteristics on individual-level outcomes has been termed multilevel analysis (Bryk and Raudenbush, 1992). Empirically, multilevel analysis involves the incorporation of macro-level variables into equations appropriate for the study of individual-level outcomes. Multilevel effects have been documented for a variety of individual outcomes, including voting behavior (Przeworski, 1974), educational attainment (Garner and Raudenbush, 1991), attitudes toward education (Robson, 1969), life satisfaction (Fernandez and Kulik, 1981), residential mobility (South and Crowder, 1997), community attachment (Sampson, 1988), and violent victimization (Miethe and McDowall, 1993; Rountree, Land, and Miethe, 1994). Yet, most of the more than 2,000 studies of violence published since 1945 were found to focus on either individual-level correlates of violent offending or, to a lesser extent, on community-level correlates of violence rates (Sampson and Lauritsen, 1994). Although these studies have contributed a great deal to our understanding of both the individual-level factors that affect violent behavior and the community-level factors that affect violence rates, they present methodological and interpretive difficulties that have prevented researchers from achieving a full understanding of the causes of violent behavior. The following section describes these difficulties.

Methodological Difficulties in Single-Level Studies. Table 3.1 summarizes the types of studies that have been used in research on violence. Types 1 and 2 are referred to as single-level studies; Type 3 as multilevel. Two types of fallacies are common in single-level designs. These are: (1) fallacies of inference and (2) fallacies of specification. Fallacies of inference occur when conceptual relationships at one level are inferred based on data from another level. Because social scientists have, for the most part, been concerned with drawing inferences at the individual-level, the ecological fallacy (Robinson, 1950; Firebaugh, 1978) has received far more attention than its counterpart, the atomistic fallacy (Diez-Roux, 1998). The ecological fallacy is the fallacy of drawing inferences at the individual level based on macro-level data. For example, suppose a researcher finds that at the country level high per capita income is associated with high rates of murder. If the researcher infers that within countries, individuals with higher incomes have a greater propensity to commit murder than lower-income individuals, he or she may be committing an ecological fallacy (i.e., murder offenses may always be more prevalent among lower income persons, even in richer nations). The atomistic fallacy is the fallacy of drawing inferences at the group level based on individual-level data. For example, even if within countries, higher individual income is associated with lower propensity to commit murder, at the country level high per capita income may be positively associated with murder rates. It would thus be incorrect to use the individual-level association between income and murder to infer an analogous macro-level relationship.

Ultimately, inferential fallacies are methodological problems that can be overcome by ensuring that the inferences drawn from data correspond to the level at which the data were collected. A more substantial problem, however, is whether a study focused on a single level of analysis ignores information that is crucial to understanding the problem being investigated - that is, whether the mechanisms operating at one level can be adequately understood without reference to other levels. Although the data analyzed may properly correspond to the inferences drawn, important data from other levels of explanation may be ignored. This problem has been referred to as cross-level misspecification (Sampson and Lauritsen, 1994).

Ignoring relevant macro-level variables in a study of individual-level associations may lead to what has been termed the "individualistic fallacy" (Valkonen, 1967; Sampson and Lauritsen, 1994; Silver, 2000b), that is, assuming that individual-level outcomes can be explained exclusively in terms of individual-level characteristics. This is a problem with most criminological research on violence, and is especially prominent in the research literature on mental disorder and violence. To the extent that neighborhood conditions can influence a person's potential for violence, studies of violent behavior that ignore their effects are susceptible to mis-representing the effects of individual-level factors (Silver, Mulvey, and Monahan, 1999; Sampson, 1993; Sampson and Lauritsen, 1994). For example, the study by Silver, Mulvey, and Monahan (1999) found that the significant effect of racial status on patient violence was attenuated (i.e., rendered nonsignificant) when neighborhood poverty was included in the model. These researchers further found a high correlation between being African American and living in concentrated poverty. These findings were interpreted to indicate that, due to housing discrimination, African Americans are differentially exposed to neighborhood conditions of extreme poverty where violent behavior is generally more prevalent (see also Sampson, Raudenbush, and Earls, 1997:923). Had neighborhood poverty not been measured, the significance of race as a cause of violence may have been overstated. The problem of cross-level mis-specification cannot be solved by simply comparing poor whites with poor blacks in terms of violence due to the fact that poor whites tend to reside in less disadvantaged areas than do poor blacks and therefore have greater access to jobs, marriage opportunities, and exposure to conventional role models (Wilson, 1987). Operating within an individualistic framework not only obstructs our understanding of the causes of violence, but can lead to policy recommendations inappropriately aimed at the characteristics of individuals rather than at the characteristics of the communities in which they live.

Analogously, assuming that rates of violence are fully explainable in terms of macro-level characteristics may lead one to ignore important compositional differences within macro-level units related to violence rates. This can result in what has been referred to as a "sociologistic fallacy" (Riley, 1963; Diez-Roux, 1998). For example, suppose a researcher finds that communities with higher rates of population turnover have higher violence rates and concludes that high population turnover leads to social disorganization which increases the risk of violence for all community inhabitants. Suppose it is subsequently shown using individual-level data that most violent acts are committed by transient residents. This would suggest that higher rates of community violence were inappropriately attributed to social disorganization affecting all community members (i.e., both transient and permanent residents) rather than to compositional differences across communities in the percentage of transient residents (who may be more likely to commit violent acts due to individual-level factors). In thinking theoretically about the effects of macro-level factors, careful consideration must be given to the fact that "individuals commit the crimes that constitute the rates" (Sampson and Lauritsen, 1994: 81).

Similarly, rates of violence may be higher in disadvantaged neighborhoods not because these neighborhoods promote violent behavior, but because of compositional differences that result from the selective migration into such neighborhoods of individuals prone to violent behavior, and/or selective migration out of such neighborhoods by individuals less prone to violence (Tienda, 1989; Sampson and Lauritsen, 1994). By assuming that macro-level characteristics are all that matter (e.g., without collecting data on individual characteristics, such as SES), individual-level selection processes may be easily confused with neighborhood effects. As Tienda (1989:23) has argued:

"If systematic selection processes are the primary mechanism bringing together individuals with similar socioeconomic characteristics and behavioral dispositions within defined spatial areas, then neighborhood effects may represent little more than an aggregation of the selection process."

Finally, a sociologistic fallacy may be committed whenever individuals are assumed not to differ in their susceptibility to macro-level influences; macro-level approaches cannot explain why most individuals who reside in high-deviance neighborhoods refrain from deviant behavior (Glueck and Glueck, 1950; Wilson and Herrnstein, 1985). Such differences in susceptibility to neighborhood factors may be particularly important for persons with mental disorders who vary in terms of perceptual impairments (i.e., in the form of delusions and hallucinations) that may exacerbate or minimize neighborhood influences. Thus, assuming that macro-level factors are all that matter can obscure an understanding of individual-level causal processes and lead to ineffective social policy.

In general, the level at which a causal relationship occurs can not be determined by the selection of variables from a particular level of analysis. Indeed, both individual and macro-level causal factors may underlie relationships observed at both levels. This is because the actions of individuals feed back to influence the collective environment (Tienda, 1989). Therefore, the unit of analysis does not define the level of causal explanation. In attempting to overcome these difficulties, researchers have recently turned to multilevel models (e.g., models that incorporate data on both individual and community-level risk factors to account for individual-level outcomes) (Bryk and Raudenbush, 1992). However, multilevel models are not without their own set of methodological issues - issues that must carefully be addressed before attempting to draw conclusions from multilevel data. The following section discusses these issues.

Issues in Multilevel Analysis. One of the most difficult aspects of multilevel analysis has been referred to as the "mis-specification of the model at the individual level" (Diez-Roux, 1998). This is when the association between a macro-level variable and an individual-level outcome is actually due to the omission of individual-level variables related to both the outcome and to the macro-level characteristics investigated. For example, one of the issues of concern in the Silver, Mulvey, and Monahan (1999) study was that the observed effect of concentrated neighborhood poverty on individual patient violence was actually due to the systematic discharge of more dangerous patients into high-poverty neighborhoods (i.e., a selection bias introduced by hospital clinicians making discharge-planning decisions). This issue was addressed by including in the multilevel analysis those individual-level variables typically used by hospital clinicians to predict dangerousness. That the effect of concentrated neighborhood poverty emerged after controlling for known individual-level predictors of patient violence (i.e., those most likely related to this sort of selection bias), supports the conclusion that the effect of concentrated poverty on violence was not due a mis-specification of the model at the individual level.

Analysts of multilevel data must also be aware of the possibility that omitted macro-level factors may manifest themselves in relationships found at the individual level. For example, if living under conditions of social isolation causes the development of subcultural values and those values are related to violent outcomes, then it is possible to explain away the effect of neighborhood isolation by including measures of 'individual values' in a multilevel model. In an extreme sense, if enough individual-level factors are included in a model, each of which partially manifests a macro-level factor, the causal influence of the macro-level factor may become statistically masked. However, this would not imply that individual-level variables, rather than macro-level variables, were the true causes of an outcome. The issue of deciding whether a given variable (such as value orientation) is an independent cause of violence or is an intermediate link in a causal chain involving less proximate variables (such as neighborhood isolation) cannot be resolved by statistical methods alone, but must be addressed at the theoretical level.

Another issue that arises in multilevel analysis is the selection of an appropriate unit of aggregation. This process depends, in part, on the theoretical question being addressed and, in part, on the availability of data. In principle, selecting an appropriate unit of aggregation is problematic because "contexts" are often not clearly conceptualized and often have imprecise boundaries. For example, if neighborhoods are the unit of interest, the researcher must specify exactly what constitutes a neighborhood in operational terms. The boundaries of a neighborhood, as perceived by its inhabitants, do not always coincide with the geographical units (i.e., census tracts or block groups) for which data are available. In addition, individuals may form part of a variety of nested or overlapping contexts (Bryk and Raudenbush, 1992), and teasing apart their independent effects (both conceptually and empirically) may be extremely difficult. The current study will focus on neighborhood effects, operationalized in terms of census tract units (see Chapter 5).

Finally, an important statistical issue that arises in multilevel analyses is that individual-level measurements taken within macro-level units may be correlated. This issue was of great concern in the recent study by Sampson, Raudenbush, and Earls (1997) in which collective efficacy was evaluated as a mediating factor in the relationship between neighborhood characteristics and crime rates. Since their measure of neighborhood collective efficacy was derived by aggregating up to the neighborhood level individual responses to five Likert-type questions, Sampson and colleagues were legitimately concerned that subjects' responses to the these five questions varied systematically within neighborhoods as a function of shared individual characteristics (such as age, gender, SES, and ethnicity, homeownership, marital status, etc.). If such within-unit correlations were not accounted for statistically, "then variation across neighborhoods in the composition of the sample of respondents along these lines could masquerade as variation in collective efficacy" (p.921). A similar concern was raised by Rountree, Land, and Miethe (1994) in their recent study of victimization risk in Seattle in which it was argued that traditional regression techniques "do not account for the idea that individuals clustered in the same social groups are often likely to be more similar regarding certain characteristics than are individuals grouped differently" (p. 338).

Residual correlations within macro-level units violate the assumption of independent observations that underlies standard regression-based techniques. This problem is analogous to the problem that arises in longitudinal data analysis when repeated measures are taken on an individual over time. Statistical methods such as hierarchical linear modeling (HLM, Bryk and Raudenbush, 1992) have recently been introduced to deal with this issue. HLM employs submodels and nested error terms to account for systematic variation at different levels of analysis. By allowing the researcher to control for compositional differences that may exist within macro-level units, these methods attempt to remedy the problem of residual correlation. HLM was used in the studies by Sampson, Raudenbush and Earls (1997) and Rountree, Land, and Miethe (1994; see also Elliot et al.,

1996).

Unfortunately, in the current study - which involves the nesting of discharged psychiatric patients within neighborhoods - use of HLM will not be possible. This is because almost two-thirds (61.4%) of the census tracts into which patients were discharged contained only one discharged patient. Without an adequate number of observations nested within neighborhood units, HLM is unable to estimate within neighborhood (e.g., Level 1) models and is thus unable to assess and control for systematic variation within macro-level units. Fortunately, the fact that so many subjects are unique in terms of their census tract location minimizes the risk that observed results will be due to compositional differences within macro-level units. The current study will therefore rely on a variety of traditional linear modeling techniques (i.e., logistic, proportional hazards, and negative binomial regression) combining both individual- and neighborhood-level variables (see Miethe and McDowall, 1993 for a recent example of this approach).

In summary, single-level approaches to the study of violent behavior tend to overlook the influence of variables from the omitted level of analysis and are therefore susceptible to the fallacies of inference and specification discussed above. Consistent with recent work in criminology (Miethe and McDowall, 1993; Bursik, 1988; Farrington, Sampson, and Wilkstrom, 1993; Jencks and Mayer, 1990; Sampson, 1993; Sampson and Lauritsen, 1994; Sampson, 1997; Elliot et al., 1996; Ellen and Turner, 1997; Miles-Doan, 1998), the current study takes the position that a complete understanding of violent behavior requires an analytic approach in which individual characteristics are evaluated in conjunction with the characteristics of the communities in which individuals reside. However, as mentioned earlier, a key element in the development of a multilevel explanatory model that would link the macro-level characteristics of neighborhoods to the violent behavior of mentally ill patients is the operationalization of theoretically relevant neighborhood-level risk factors. Fortunately, many decades of research on the effects of community social disorganization (Faris and Dunham, 1939; Shaw and McKay, 1942; Sampson and Groves, 1989; Sampson and Lauritsen, 1994; Sampson, Raudenbush, and Earls, 1997; Sampson, 1997) have yielded important insights into these neighborhood factors.

The Social Disorganization Perspective: Identifying Community-Level Risk Factors

The purpose of this section is to introduce the social disorganization perspective on crime and deviance. Specifically, the literature on social disorganization is reviewed to gain insight into the relationship between neighborhood characteristics and violent behavior. It should be emphasized that this study will not attempt to *test* the social disorganization perspective as this would require the operationalization of mediating factors such as collective efficacy (Sampson, Raudenbush, and Earls, 1997) and/or community-level friendship networks and organizational participation (Sampson and Groves, 1989) - none of which is available in the current study. Rather, the social disorganization perspective will be reviewed to provide insights into the relevant structural and cultural characteristics of communities that may affect the opportunities and/or costs associated with committing a violent act, as well as the normative support and/or tolerance for such behavior.

Although social disorganization theory has traditionally been studied from a macro-level perspective, the current study posits that social disorganization also influences individual occurrences of deviant behavior. In addition, although social disorganization has been traditionally studied in relation to crime and delinquency among the general population, the current study extends the perspective by positing that social disorganization also affects the likelihood of violence among persons with mental illnesses. The community-level effects on mentally ill persons and the ways in which they may interact with individual characteristics such as symptoms of mental illness (e.g., the presence of paranoid beliefs and/or persecutory delusions) will be discussed in Chapter 4. Before addressing these specific questions, a general review of the social disorganization perspective is presented.

<u>Community Social Disorganization</u>. The ecological perspective on urban deviance was founded at the turn of this century by Robert Park and Ernest Burgess, both sociologists at the University of Chicago. Their approach focused on the natural ("biotic") aspects of community organization and change. Cities were conceived as dynamic, adapting systems operating according to free-market competition among businesses and individuals competing to occupy affordable and desirable locations within the different areas of the city (Sampson, 1997). Park, Burgess, and McKenzie (1925) emphasized how social order in the city (i.e., the orderly distribution of population subgroups into areas where they were best suited) seemed to transcend the day-to-day competition of the market. Burgess emphasized that the growth pattern of the city displayed a radial pattern of concentric zones emanating outward from the central business district as the overall stability of the ecological system was maintained.

The ecological approach was expanded by Chicago sociologist Louis Wirth who, rather than focus on the stability of the urban ecological system, emphasized its disorganized character. Wirth (1938) described how the basic features of urban areas (e.g., size, density, and heterogeneity) inhibited interpersonal connections among residents, thereby leading to a breakdown in social cohesion. Wirth's emphasis on the negative outcomes associated with urban life were further developed by Clifford Shaw and Henry McKay. Indeed, few works in criminology have been more influential than Shaw and McKay's (1942) *Juvenile Delinquency and Urban Areas* (Bursik, 1988). In this classic work, Shaw and McKay integrated Wirth's theme of social dislocation with Park and Burgess' theory of neighborhood change by identifying specific ecological characteristics associated with high rates of crime and deviance.

Shaw and McKay (1942) argued that three structural factors - low economic status, ethnic heterogeneity, and residential mobility - led to the disruption of local community social organization, which in turn, accounted for variations in (macro-level) rates of crime and delinquency (Sampson and Groves, 1989). In their studies of Chicago's neighborhoods, Shaw and McKay found (1) significant variations in delinquency rates within the city of Chicago (based on referrals to the Cook County Juvenile Court); (2) that delinquency rates were highest in deteriorated areas undergoing invasion from adjacent central business and industrial district activities; and (3) that rates of delinquency decreased as distance from the center of the city increased (except in more distant areas also characterized by industry and commerce). These findings led Shaw and McKay to conclude that delinquency was closely related to the growth processes of the city as outlined by Park, Burgess, and McKenzie (1925).

Most importantly, however, Shaw and McKay (1942) found that high rates of delinquency persisted in certain areas over many years, regardless of ethnic population turnover. This finding, more than any other, led them to reject individualistic explanations of delinquency and focus instead on the macro-level processes by which delinquent and criminal patterns of behavior were transmitted across generations. Shaw and McKay emphasized that the causes of crime were located in the structural context of local communities and in the changes taking place across the urban landscape. They further emphasized that autonomous delinquent subcultures arose in socially disorganized communities and were perpetuated through a process of cultural transmission in which delinquent traditions are passed down to subsequent generations. As Sampson (1997) explains: "according to the social disorganization model, the ecological segregation of communities characterized by low economic status, heterogeneity, and mobility results in ineffective community culture and structure" (p.4). Early studies testing Shaw and McKay's model (Lander, 1954; Bordua, 1958; Chilton, 1964) confirmed their emphasis on the effects of community economic status and residential instability.

The social disorganization model was similarly adopted by Chicago sociologists Robert E. L. Faris and H. Warren Dunham in their pioneering study of the distribution of the rates of mental disorder across Chicago and Providence, Rhode Island neighborhoods. Faris and Dunham (1939) identified the pre-admission neighborhood locations of over 30,000 psychiatric patients treated in public and private hospitals during the two year period between 1930 and 1931. These data were then converted into rates per 100,000 population and mapped according to pre-admission neighborhood. Faris and Dunham (1939) found that (pp.35-37): "High rates of insanity appear to cluster in the deteriorated regions in and surrounding the center of the city, no matter what race or nationality inhabits that region...[which] definitely establishes the fact that insanity, like other social problems, fits into the ecological structure of the city." These findings were interpreted by Faris and Dunham (1939) to indicate that urban areas characterized by high levels of social disorganization were also those with high rates of "mental disorganization." Faris and Dunham's (1939) core findings were later confirmed by Levy and Rowitz (1973) with data on 10,653 city residents admitted to Chicago mental hospitals during 1960 and 1961.

Faris and Dunham's (1939) work is of great theoretical relevance to the research reported in this book; not only did their explanation of the relationship between neighborhood conditions and rates of mental disorder rest on social disorganization theory, but they attempted to relate these elements to the experiences and behavior of individuals. In other words, their theoretical argument spanned multiple levels of explanation and involved both the structural and cultural aspects of neighborhood life. Faris and Dunham (1939:154) suggested that "...the development of normal mentality and normal behavior demands a complicated chain of successfully functioning elements on paths of very different sorts." They go on to suggest that "where there is a lack of harmony between family and community influences, there is likely to be conflict *in the person*" [italics added] and that "normal adult mentality... must be supported constantly by a consistent and fairly harmonious stream of primary social contacts."

The crux of Faris and Dunham's (1939: 158) argument is that socially disorganized communities lack many of the necessary conditions for "normal mental organization." In particular, they suggest that "The slum area populated by heterogeneous foreign-born elements forms a chaotic background of conflicting and shifting cultural standards, against which it is quite difficult for *a person* [italics added] to develop a stable mental organization." This results in "confused, frustrated, and chaotic" expressions of behavior, which subsequently manifest themselves as symptoms of mental disorder. Although Faris and Dunham (1939) did not explicitly focus on the aggressive behavior of persons with mental illness, it is a straightforward extension of their theoretical framework to hypothesize that part of this complex of "confused, frustrated, and chaotic" behavior might include acts of aggression. (This line of reasoning is further developed in Chapter 4).

Despite the groundbreaking nature of Faris and Dunham's (1939) analysis of the spatial and social distribution of mental illnesses, the past several decades of research on neighborhood social disorganization has focused almost exclusively on variations in rates of urban crime delinquency. During this time, a revised social disorganization model has emerged as one of the most frequently researched explanations of the association between neighborhood disadvantage and deviant behavior (Sampson and Lauritsen, 1994). Specifically, social organization has been reconceptualized as the ability of a community to realize the common values of its residents and maintain effective social controls (Kornhauser, 1978; Bursik, 1988; Sampson, 1988), an interpretation that builds upon the approach taken by both Shaw and McKay (1942) and Faris and Dunham (1939).

This view of social disorganization is grounded in what has been termed the systemic model (Kasarda and Janowitz, 1974; Sampson, 1988), in which the local community is viewed as a complex system of friendship and kinship networks, and formal and informal associational ties rooted in family life and ongoing socialization processes. The structural dimensions of the systemic model have been operationalized in terms of the prevalence and interdependence of social networks in a community - both informal (e.g., density of friendship ties and acquaintanceship) and formal (e.g., organizational participation) and in the extent of collective supervision that a community directs toward local problems (Shaw and McKay, 1942, Sampson and Groves, 1989). More recently, collective efficacy (e.g., the willingness of local residents to intervene informally in neighborhood activities to promote public order) has been suggested as the primary mediating factor explaining differential violence rates across neighborhoods. Formulated in this way, social disorganization is not only separable from the processes that may lead to it (e.g., poverty, mobility, etc.), but also from the extent of violent behavior that may result (Bursik and Grasmick, 1993).

Three dimensions of social disorganization theory are relevant to the study of violence. The first involves local friendship networks and the density of acquaintanceship. Systemic theory posits that locality-based social networks constitute the core social fabric of human-ecological communities (Sampson, 1988). When residents form local social ties, their capacity for community social control is increased because they are better able to recognize strangers and are more apt to intervene during victimizations (Skogan, 1986). In addition, the greater the density of friendship networks among persons in a community, the greater is the internal constraint on deviant behavior within the perceived span of the social network. The second component of social disorganization important to understanding violence is the rate of local participation in formal and voluntary organizations. Community organizational participation is conceptualized as the structural embodiment of local community solidarity. Along these lines, Kornhauser (1978) argues that when the links between community organizations are weak so is the capacity of a community to defend its local interests. A third dimension of social organization that has been strongly emphasized in the research literature on gang violence is the ability of a community to supervise and control teenaged peer groups (Sampson and Groves, 1989). Shaw and McKay's (1942) ethnic heterogeneity thesis has received less support - although early studies seemed to confirm its influence (Lander, 1954), more recent studies show that rates of violence are positively related in a linear fashion to percent black in the population (Sampson and Lauritsen, 1994). This change in results reflects changes with respect to patterns of immigration and racial segregation in the U.S. since the 1930's (Liska and Messner, 1999).

Despite the conceptual clarity and intuitive appeal of social disorganization theory, the social disorganization process is quite difficult to study directly (Sampson, 1997). This is largely due to a lack of data bearing on the key mediating elements. However, three recent studies have succeeded in providing empirical support for the theory. First, Taylor et al. (1984) examined variations in violent crime (mugging, assault, murder, rape, shooting) across 63 street blocks in Baltimore in 1978. Based on interviews with 687 household respondents, Taylor et al. (1984) constructed block-level measures of social ties (e.g., the proportion of respondents who belonged to an organization to which co-residents also belonged) and 'near-home responsibilities' (e.g., the extent to which respondents felt responsible for what happened in the area surrounding their home). Both of these dimensions of informal social control were found to be significantly related to community-level variations in violence, supporting the social disorganization perspective.

A second, and perhaps more well-known study was conducted by Sampson and Groves (1989). These researchers analyzed the British Crime Survey (BCS), a nationwide survey of England and Wales conducted in 1982 and 1984. Sixty addresses were sampled within 238 ecological areas in Great Britain, which Sampson and Groves (1989) argued, reasonably approximated the concept of a local community. Survey responses were aggregated within each of these ecological units to construct community-level variables. Sampson and Groves (1989) found that the prevalence of unsupervised peer groups in a community had the largest overall effect on rates of victimization by mugging, street robbery, and stranger violence in Great Britain. Local friendship networks had a significant negative effect on robbery, as did organizational participation. Furthermore, variation in the structural dimensions of community social disorganization were shown to mediate the effects of community SES, residential mobility, ethnic heterogeneity and family disruption in the manner predicted by social disorganization theory. Mobility had significant inverse effects on friendship networks, family disruption was a significant predictor of unsupervised teenaged peer groups, and SES had positive effects on organizational participation.

A more recent study of the social disorganization perspective was conducted by Sampson, Raudenbush and Earls (1997). These researchers analyzed a 1995 survey of 8,782 residents in 343 Chicago neighborhoods. Their results showed that the willingness of local residents to intervene informally in neighborhood activities to promote public order (e.g., collective efficacy) was negatively associated with neighborhood violence rates, controlling for compositional differences across neighborhoods in terms of individual-level characteristics. The association between neighborhood violence rates and both neighborhood disadvantage and residential instability were largely mediated by collective efficacy. Furthermore, Sampson, Raudenbush, and Earls

(1997) found that reductions in violence were more directly attributable to collective efficacy than to other theoretically relevant indicators of social organization (e.g., dense personal ties, organizational participation, and neighborhood services). Taken as a whole, these studies suggest that socially disorganized communities characterized by sparse friendship networks, unsupervised teenage peer groups, low organization participation, and low levels of collective efficacy are also characterized by disproportionately high rates of violent behavior.

Although the social disorganization perspective highlights social *control* as a key mediating factor, Cullen (1994) has recently emphasized the equally important role of social *support* in understanding the relationship between neighborhood disorganization and crime. Indeed, Cullen views informal social control and social support as deriving from the same social sources, such that variables employed in many of the above studies can be viewed as operationalizing either concept. For example, although Sampson and Groves' (1989) research has been widely interpreted in the social disorganization literature as evidence that disorganized communities (i.e., those characterized by family disruption, weak friendship networks, and low participation in local voluntary organizations) are unable to exert informal social control over their residents (Sampson and Lauritsen, 1994; Sampson, Raudenbush, and Earls, 1997), Cullen interprets these findings as indicating the importance of neighborhood social support in explaining crime. High rates of family disruption may operationalize not only surveillance over residents, but also the viability of social support networks and the opportunity to develop intimate relations. Further, in interpreting Sampson, Raudenbush, and Earls (1997) recent results, Cullen, Wright, and Chamlin (1998:10) point out that the "construct of collective efficacy included not only a measure of informal social control, but also a measure of 'cohesion and trust' among residents -- or what we would term the existence of helpful or supportive relationships in a community." (This line of reasoning is developed more fully in Chapter 4).

In summary, social disorganization theory posits that disadvantaged neighborhoods stimulate high rates of population turnover and family disruption (Bursik, 1988; Kornhauser, 1978; Sampson and Groves, 1989), impede the development of primary and secondary ties among neighborhood residents, and diminish strong institutional affiliations. Sparse social networks and weak social institutions are thought to result in low levels of commitment to conventional norms, low levels of attachment to local institutions among neighborhood residents, and low levels of collective efficacy and supervision over residents' behavior. These factors, in turn, are thought to increase the opportunities and decrease the costs associated with deviating from group norms and, hence, to contribute to high rates of violence.

It is important to point out, however, that although most studies of social disorganization view crime as a dependent (or endogenous) variable, crime can also be viewed as a structural factor with important "feedback" effects that further increase levels of crime (Skogan, 1986; Sampson and Lauritsen, 1994). These feedback effects may include: (1) physical and psychological withdrawal of residents from community life; (2) weakening of the informal control processes that inhibit crime; (3) a decline in the mobilization capacity of neighborhood residents; and (4) relocation to safer neighborhoods by those residents and businesses with the means to do so. To the extent that fear of violent crime leads residents to withdraw from their neighbors, friendship networks and neighborhood organizations are weakened. Thus, violent crime can not simply be viewed as an outcome of the structural ecological processes described above but must also be seen as an important structural factor contributing to the disorganizing aspects of urban life.

Cultural Disorganization. In addition to calling attention to the structural determinants of neighborhood social disorganization, social disorganization theory also posits the emergence of local conduct norms (or subcultures) in disorganized neighborhoods, especially under conditions of social isolation (Sampson and Lauritsen, 1994; Wilson, 1987). According to Sampson and Lauritsen (1994:61), the structural deficits of communities, such as poverty, mobility, and heterogeneity not only weaken neighborhood networks of formal and informal social control but "obstruct the quest for common values." In other words, neighborhood social disorganization sets the stage for the development of alternative norms for conduct, including those governing individual responses to threatening or conflictual situations (Anderson, 1990; Sanchez-Jankowski, 1991; Hiday, 1997).

Indeed, a major component of Shaw and McKay's original theory was that in heterogeneous, low-income communities alternative organizations (e.g., gangs) emerge with their own subcultures and norms perpetuated through cultural transmission.[4] Similarly, Faris and Dunham

---

[4]Sampson and Lauritsen (1994) point out that other cultural explanations of crime and violence have been posited by criminologists. In terms of violence, the most prominent explanation continues to be the subculture of violence theory (Wolfgang and Ferracuti, 1967). The basic tenet of subcultural theory is that violent behavior reflects values that differ from those of the dominant culture. While this theory does not contradict Shaw and McKay's theory, neither does it refer explicitly to community-level causal processes.

(1939:158) argue that "the chaotic background of conflicting and shifting cultural standards" negatively impacts on the mental health of residents. Thus, although social disorganization theory certainly emphasizes the primacy of structural factors in causing communities to become disorganized, it also focuses on how socially disorganized communities give rise to alternative and conflicting normative patterns, particularly under conditions of social isolation. According to Sampson and Lauritsen (1994), the most significant reason for the widespread emphasis on structural determinants in studies of crime may be the availability of structurally-based census variables, rather than the belief that structural factors are all that matter.

The important connection between structural characteristics and cultural manifestations has been repeatedly documented in ethnographic research (Suttles, 1968; Anderson, 1978, 1990; Sanchez-Jankowski, 1991). Yet, ethnographic studies of the cultural values that emerge in socially disorganized communities have received far less attention than quantitative studies of rates of crime and delinquency (Sampson and Lauritsen, 1994; Sampson, 1997). Unlike macro-level research, ethnographic studies are uniquely designed provide insights into culturally patterned, group responses to structurally imposed conditions of neighborhood disadvantage. For example, Sanchez-Jankowski's (1991) depiction of the symbiotic relationship between gangs and their host communities demonstrates how poor, disorganized communities can give rise to alternative systems of values and attitudes, particularly regarding the tolerance of gang violence. He argues that gangs assume a militia-type role in poor neighborhoods using violence to protect the community against outside intruders. Community members come to view gangs as better able to deter non-gang crime and injustice than police and consequently come to tolerate the gang's own illegal and often violent activities. In return for gang protection, the community provides the gang with a safe haven in which noncooperation with the police on behalf of gang activities is strong; provides the gang with a steady stream of new recruits by acknowledging the gang's positive contributions to community life; and provides the gang with much-needed information, such as knowledge of police activities and other goings-on outside of the gang's territorial boundaries. Thus, the tolerance of gang violence among residents of a disadvantaged neighborhood may arise, not because residents value (i.e., approve of) violent behavior per se, but because in the absence of adequate policing, gang violence comes to be viewed as a necessary "price" paid for the "service" of community protection.

The notion of cultural adaptation and differentiation in response to structural isolation and other community-level deficits is further highlighted in Anderson's (1990, 1997) ethnographic research. Anderson (1997) reports that within the inner-city, a "code of the streets" has emerged consisting of "a set of informal rules governing interpersonal public behavior, including violence" (p. 2). According to Anderson (1997), the code of the streets is rooted in a cultural adaptation to a profound lack of faith in the police and the judicial system. Against this backdrop, the person who is believed capable of "taking care of himself" (e.g., able to threaten and use violence) is accorded a certain amount of social status. Anderson (1997) states that knowledge of the code is largely defensive and that "even though families with a decency orientation are usually opposed to the values of the code, they often reluctantly encourage their children's familiarity with it to enable them to negotiate the inner-city environment." These two cultural orientations - "decent" and "street" - combine to socially organize inner-city life which means that "even youngsters whose home lives reflect mainstream values - and the majority of homes in the community do - must be able to handle themselves in a street-oriented environment" (p. 1). In this context, the use of violence is not valued as a primary goal, but is an expected and tolerated part of life (Sampson, 1997). This is consistent with Shaw and McKay's (1942: 180) argument that "the dominant tradition in every community is conventional, even those having high rates of delinquency."

The intimate relationship between structural and cultural forces is similarly reflected in the concept of anomie (Merton, 1938). Anomie was originally described by Durkheim (1897/1951) as a state of normlessness that emerges in the absence of adequate social and moral controls. More recently, anomie has been depicted as "the presence of contradictory norms and the collective sense that moral order is too weak to warrant trusting other people" (Sampson, 1997: 41). According this depiction of anomie, the coexistence of competing systems of cultural values and norms within a society (or neighborhood) undermines mainstream normative practices by fostering a collective sense of uncertainty regarding the behavior of others. This uncertainty weakens a neighborhood's ability to organize itself against unwanted problems, such as crime and violence. Anomie theory thus highlights the important connection between cultural differentiation and social disorder.

The complementary nature of the relationship between social disorganization and cultural adaptation is further developed in the work of Wilson Julius Wilson. In *The Truly Disadvantaged*, Wilson (1987) argues that during the 1970's, the extent of disadvantage experienced by poor residents of inner-city neighborhoods increased relative to both poor residents outside of the inner-city and poor residents of the same inner-city neighborhoods in previous decades. According to Wilson, the exodus of middle- and upper-income black families from the inner-city removed an important social buffer that might have deflected the full impact of prolonged joblessness and deindustrialization that began in the 1970's. The removal of the social buffer from these neighborhoods set the stage for the spiral of social and economic decline that now characterizes the inner-cities of the Northeast and Midwest. Wilson's thesis is based on the assumption that the basic institutions of an area (i.e., churches, schools, etc.) are more likely to remain viable if the core of their support comes from economically stable families in inner-city neighborhoods.

Wilson (1987) argues that as the proportion of poor residents in the inner city increased during the 1970's and 1980's, social isolation deepened, leading to what he called "concentration effects," that is, the negative impact that living in an exceedingly impoverished neighborhood has on individual residents. According to Wilson (1987), concentration effects emerge in response to structural constraints on opportunities for inner-city residents (1) to interact with middle- and upper-income individuals, (2) to gain access to jobs and job networks, (3) to enroll in quality schools, (4) to find economically viable marriage partners, and (5) to gain exposure to conventional role models (Sampson and Wilson, 1994). Concentration effects are hypothesized to lead to an "exponential increase" in the manifestations of social problems in areas characterized by extreme disadvantage (Wilson, 1987:57). Further, the social transformation of the inner-city that has resulted in the emergence of concentration effects appears to stem rather directly from planned governmental policies at the local, state, and federal levels (Massey and Denton, 1993; Sampson and Lauritsen, 1994). As Sampson and Lauritsen (1994: 89) note, "This conceptualization diverges from the natural market assumptions of the earlier social ecologists (e.g., Park, et al., 1925) by considering the role of political decisions in shaping community structure." (See also Logan and Molotch, 1987 and Gottdiener and Feagin 1988)

Concentration effects not only limit access to mainstream social and economic resources, but, in the process, give rise to alternative forms of cultural adaption. This is because social isolation limits exposure to stable, employed individuals from different class and racial backgrounds whose daily routines provide a basis for the types of social learning that promote economic advancement in post-industrial society (Sampson, 1997). With regard to violence, individuals (including mentally ill individuals) living in disadvantaged neighborhoods are more likely to view violence as an expected part of life - they are more likely to witness violent acts and be exposed to role models who do not adequately control their own violent impulses. In discussing these cultural manifestations in the context of social disorganization theory, Sampson (1997: p.20) emphasizes that "social isolation does not mean that ghetto-specific practices become internalized, take on a life of their own, and therefore continue to influence behavior, no matter the contextual environment. Rather, it suggests that reducing structural inequality would not only decrease the frequency of these practices but also make their cultural transmission less efficient." Sampson's comments reflect a fundamental appreciation for the ways in which structural constraints shape and fragment cultural norms.

Consistent with these arguments, the current study views the structural and cultural aspects of neighborhood social disorganization theory as complementary; and posits that although cultural factors are manifested in individual attitudes and behaviors, they arise as individuals and groups adapt to the structural constraints of their surrounding environments. Cultural factor are thus not viewed as fixed, internalized aspects of the individual, but rather as a group-level adaptation to the structural constraints of neighborhood life. Therefore, in the following chapter, both the structural and cultural elements of the social disorganization perspective are drawn upon in developing theoretical hypotheses regarding the relationship between neighborhood conditions and violence by mentally ill neighborhood residents.

Before attempting to delineate specific hypotheses regarding the relationship between neighborhood social disorganization and individual-level predictors of patient violence, one more step remains: to examine how previous researchers have attempted to integrate these ideas and to review their results. The multilevel social disorganization approach outlined here has received a good deal attention from criminologists interested patterns of crime victimization (Simcha-Fagan and Schwartz, 1986; Sampson and Woolredge, 1987; Miethe and McDowall, 1993; Rountree, Land, and Miethe, 1994). These studies are particularly relevant to the present study because they draw upon social disorganization theory to derive neighborhood-level measures of disadvantage and relate these to the experiences and behaviors of individuals. In the following section, these studies are reviewed.[5]

---

[5]Studies using multilevel data to analyze violence by persons with mental disorders were reviewed in Chapter 2 (see Silver, Mulvey, and Monahan, 1999; Link, Andrews, and Cullen, 1992).

Multilevel Studies of Crime Victimization

Recent multilevel studies of criminal victimization have sought to integrate social disorganization theory (Sampson and Groves, 1989) with criminal opportunity theory (Cohen and Felson, 1979), positing that socially disorganized areas should have higher rates of crime victimization than do other areas. This is because motivated offenders are thought to draw upon neighborhood characteristics - such as the extent of formal and informal guardianship - for cues about the accessibility and the attractiveness of targets (i.e., persons and/or property) in the neighborhood (Miethe and McDowall, 1993). Thus, individual risks for victimization are thought to be determined, to some extent, by macro-level factors in the neighborhood environment (Rountree, Land, and Miethe, 1994).

Against this theoretical backdrop, Sampson and Woolredge (1987) studied a sample of 238 political districts in Great Britain and found that personal risks of burglary were affected by the levels of several indicators of social disorganization and criminal opportunity, including family disruption, living alone, and density of ownership of portable consumer goods in the district in which an individual lived. Similarly, Smith and Jarjoura (1988) found that risks for burglary in 57 U.S. neighborhoods were influenced by racial heterogeneity, population instability, and median income. In addition, Kennedy and Forde (1990) found significant main effects of macro-level variables such as unemployment and divorce rates on individual risks for both violent and property crime. Although supportive of the multilevel social disorganization approach, these studies were criticized for relying on "broad or vague" macro-level units (e.g., metropolitan areas and electoral wards) and for limiting the multilevel analysis to the estimation of direct effects of contextual factors (Rountree, Land, and Miethe, 1994).

To overcome these limitations, Miethe and McDowall (1993) used a multi-stage sample of city blocks and individual households in Seattle to examine the relationship between individual risks of victimization and (1) variables reflecting the personal life-styles of residents (e.g., participation in public activities, living alone, leaving home frequently, possessing more expensive goods, taking fewer safety precautions, etc).; (2) variables indicating neighborhood social disorganization (e.g., population mobility, ethnic heterogeneity, low economic resources); and (3) the interactions among them. Pairs of city blocks (consisting of approximately 18 individuals per block-pair) were used to approximate 300 Seattle neighborhoods. The dependent variables were reported burglary or violent crime victimizations in the vicinity of the home during the past two years. Combining individual and neighborhood-level variables in a logistic regression equation, Miethe and McDowall (1993) found individual reports of violent victimization to be significantly enhanced by young age, participation in public activities, lower family income, and living alone. Individual risks for burglary were higher for those who were younger, left home frequently, had higher incomes, possessed more expensive goods, took fewer safety precautions, and lived alone. Including social disorganization variables in the model significantly improved both of the above models over and above the model with only individual-level variables. Residents of disorganized areas showed greater risk of both violent victimization and burglary and the effects of income and living alone on violent victimization were diminished.

Perhaps more importantly, the effects of some individual-level factors were altered with the introduction of social disorganization variables. Specifically, Miethe and

McDowall (1993) found context-specific models for burglary; that is, individual factors such as overall visibility and accessibility to crime and guardianship altered burglary risks for residents of more affluent areas and not for residents of socially disorganized areas. This finding was interpreted by the authors to indicate that the social forces that produce criminal motivation may be so oppressive in disorganized areas that they nullify any positive advantage that routine activities can have in reducing victimization risks. As the authors note, the (paradoxical) implication of this finding is that variations in individual behaviors may be more effective at crime reduction in areas where crime is less prevalent and least effective in high-crime areas where protection is most needed. (For violent victimization, no difference in individual level risks were seen across different neighborhood contexts.)

Miethe and McDowall's (1993) study demonstrates that macro-level social disorganization affects individual risks of crime victimization and conditions the effects of individual behaviors. However, the study has been criticized on methodological grounds for using conventional logistic regression techniques - in which macro-level variables are entered into the same model with individual-level variables - thereby ignoring the hierarchical nature of the data (Rountree, Land, and Miethe, 1994). As discussed above, not taking into account the nesting of individual observations within macro-level units potentially violates the assumption of independent observations on which traditional regression methods are based. To remedy this situation, Rountree, Land, and Miethe (1994) drew upon the same Seattle data set used by Miethe and McDowall (1993), this time using a more statistically appropriate hierarchical logistic regression model (Wong and Mason, 1985; Bryk, Raudenbush, and Congdon, 1996).

Consistent with Miethe and McDowall (1993),

Rountree, Land and Miethe (1994) found that individual factors such as overall visibility and accessibility to crime and guardianship significantly reduced burglary risks for residents of more affluent areas. However, rather than finding no reduction for residents of less affluent neighborhoods, Rountree, Land, and Miethe (1994) report that reductions in burglary risk due to changes in target attractiveness and guardianship were significant albeit of a smaller magnitude than in more affluent areas. Rather than conclude that individual-level factors are overwhelmed in disorganized neighborhoods, they state that "residents in more disadvantaged areas must 'try harder' to obtain the same results as in less disadvantaged areas" (p.411). This reanalysis of the Seattle data suggests that explicitly accounting for the nested nature of multilevel data (e.g., with procedures such as HLM) can increase statistical power in identifying significant cross-level interaction effects in data sets in which multiple observations are nested within macro-level units.

Taken together, these studies of victimization data have demonstrated the importance of neighborhood-level social disorganization in affecting individual outcomes. This approach is currently being furthered by Janet Lauritsen and Robert Sampson in their analyses of the National Crime Victimization Survey (NCVS) data. Facilitated by the National Consortium on Violence Research (NCOVR), the U.S. Census Bureau has made available to Consortium researchers geo-codes for each of the interviews conducted as part of the NCVS. With these geo-codes, researchers can merge NCVS data with tract-level neighborhood measures from the 1990 decennial census to create a nationally representative, multilevel data set of crime victimization. Consistent with the approach described above, these geo-coded NCVS data will be used to investigate the effects on individual victimizations of individual and neighborhood-level risk factors.

Summary

The goal of this chapter was to set the stage for the development of a multilevel model incorporating individual- and community-level risk factors for violence among persons with mental illnesses. A fundamental premise of this project is that the relationship between individual-level characteristics and violence among persons with mental illnesses is affected, to some extent, by the extent of social disorganization in the neighborhood environments in which they live. In contrast to personality- and psychiatric symptom-based explanations of violence among the mentally ill, the current approach views the relationship between mental illness and violence through a contextual lens that highlights the ecological contexts within which violent behavior occurs. In the following chapter, specific research questions are formulated.

Table 3.1. Types of Studies.

Type of Study	Independent Variable(s)	Dependent Variable
1. Individual-Level	Individual-Level	Individual-Level
2. Macro-Level	Macro-Level	Macro-Level
3. Multilevel	Macro- and Individual-Level	Individual-Level

CHAPTER 4

Extending Social Disorganization Theory

> "Neurobiological factors may be the origin of severe mental illness; but social factors affect its course, manifestations, and connections to violence" (Hiday, 1997:412).

Empirical research generally suggests that neighborhood conditions matter in explaining individual outcomes (Miethe and McDowall, 1993; Bursik, 1988; Farrington, Sampson, and Wilkstrom, 1993; Jencks and Mayer, 1990; Sampson, 1993; Sampson and Lauritsen, 1994; Sampson, 1997; Elliot et al., 1996; Ellen and Turner, 1997; Miles-Doan, 1998). However, efforts to identify which aspects of the neighborhood context matter most for which types of individuals, and to quantify the functional form and relative strength of neighborhood effects have appeared only rarely (see Miethe and McDowall, 1993; Rountree et al., 1994; South and Crowder, 1999). Even more rarely have such questions been addressed regarding the violent behavior of persons with mental illnesses (see Silver, Mulvey, and Monahan, 1999; Link, Andrews, and Cullen, 1992 for exceptions). As a result, the empirical literature on patient violence offers remarkably little help to mental health clinicians and policy makers who must design and implement intervention strategies to help reduce violence among mental patients living in various neighborhood settings.

A fundamental premise of this book is that in order to fully account for the variation in violent behavior committed by persons with mental disorders, their neighborhood contexts must be taken into account. This core idea extends the traditional focus of mental health research by highlighting the *neighborhood* as an important explanatory factor (i.e., in addition to individual characteristics) and extends the traditional focus of social disorganization research by attempting to explain the violent behavior of *individuals with mental illnesses* (i.e., as opposed to aggregate rates of crime and delinquency among the general population). Not since Faris and Dunham's (1939) pioneering study of the spatial and social distribution of mentally ill individuals has the social disorganization perspective been explicitly applied to a mentally ill sample.

However, Faris and Dunham (1939) did not attempt to describe or explain the *violent* behavior of mentally ill persons. Their main interest was in relating various types of mental disorders (e.g., schizophrenia, alcohol and substance abuse, and psychosis) to social conditions in Chicago's neighborhoods. The current study expands upon Faris and Dunham's original thesis by focusing on the relationship between neighborhood conditions and *violence* among mentally ill persons living in and around the city of Pittsburgh. Specifically, this study brings to bear recent reformulations and extensions of the social disorganization model of crime and delinquency (Kasarda and Janowitz,

1974; Bursik, 1988; Sampson, 1988, Sampson and Groves, 1989; Skogan,1990; Sampson and Lauritsen, 1994; Cullen, 1994; Aneshensel and Sucoff, 1996; Anderson, 1997; Cullen, Wright, and Chamlin,1998) to assess the importance of neighborhood social disorganization in explaining the violent behavior of discharged psychiatric patients.

The purpose of this chapter is to specify a set of core research hypotheses examining the relationship between neighborhood social disorganization and individual characteristics in predicting the violent behavior of discharged psychiatric patients. These hypotheses are organized in terms of the following five questions:

1. Does neighborhood social disorganization contribute to models predicting violent behavior among discharged psychiatric patients over and above the effects of known individual-level predictors? If so, which neighborhood characteristics seem to matter most? Does controlling for neighborhood social disorganization explain away (or enhance) the effects of individual-level predictors?

2. What is the relative importance of neighborhood- and individual-level characteristics in terms of the amount of variation in violence explained?

3. What is the functional form of the relationship between neighborhood social disorganization and patient violence (i.e., are there concentration effects)?

4. What other individual-level outcomes (i.e., other than violent behavior) are expected to result from living in a socially disorganized neighborhood? To what extent do such individual-level factors mediate the

social disorganization-violence relationship?

5. Are there cross-level interaction effects? That is, do the effects of individual-level characteristics on violence vary across different neighborhood contexts? If cross-level interactions exist, which individual-level factors interact with which contextual factors?

Before these questions can be answered, however, two issues are addressed. First, a theoretical framework is provided that relates neighborhood social disorganization to the violent behavior of mentally ill persons. For this I draw largely on theoretical arguments provided by the extensive body of literature on social disorganization reviewed in the previous chapter, focusing in particular on the work of Faris and Dunham (1939) and Cullen (1994). Second, a rationale is provided for selecting the specific variables that will be used to represent individual patient characteristics and neighborhood level factors.

Theoretical Framework

The core theoretical question of this book is: How might levels of neighborhood social organization affect the likelihood that persons with mental illnesses will engage in violence? To answer this question, it is useful to first distinguish among three fundamentally important aspects of the social disorganization perspective. The first two represent concepts prominently featured in the published literature on social disorganization, namely, *informal social control* (i.e., the extent to which neighborhood residents monitor and control the behavior of individuals within the neighborhood boundaries) and *cultural differentiation* (i.e., the presence of competing normative systems of behavior within a neighborhood). The third, and less frequently discussed aspect of the theory, draws upon Faris and Dunham's (1939) and Cullen's (1994) work in emphasizing the importance of *social support* in the lives of neighborhood residents. Social support refers to the extent to which neighborhoods provide opportunities to develop and maintain supportive social relationships.

In the remainder of this section, each of these concepts are described in terms of their relevance for hypothesizing a relationship between neighborhood social disorganization and violence among discharged psychiatric patients. The first two factors - informal social control and cultural differentiation - are discussed only briefly, since they were discussed at length in the previous chapter. Discussion of the third factor - social support - is presented in more detail.

Informal Social Control. The social disorganization perspective is typically depicted by criminologists as a macro-level variant of control theory (Liska and Messner, 1999). Messner and Rosenfeld (1994:53) argue that social disorganization "...erodes the capacity of local institutions...to *impose controls* [emphasis added] over the behavior of residents." In discussing neighborhood social disorganization as an indirect cause of violence among persons with mental illnesses, Hiday (1997:402) argues that "socially disorganized communities are unable to *exert control* [emphasis added] over a large proportion of their members." By undermining the processes of informal social control, social disorganization is thought to increase the opportunities and decreases the costs associated with engaging in violence, thereby increasing the likelihood that individual residents will commit violent acts (Sampson and Lauritsen, 1994).

Similarly, Faris and Dunham (1939) argue that the "confused, frustrated, and chaotic" expressions of behavior often exhibited by mentally ill persons, may result, in part, from their location in socially disorganized neighborhoods where they are *"freed from the social control which enforces normality in other people*" (p.174, emphasis added). Although Faris and Dunham do not explicitly focus on the aggressive behavior of persons with mental illness, it is a straightforward extension of their theoretical framework to hypothesize that part of this complex of "confused, frustrated, and chaotic" behavior might include acts of aggression. Based on these arguments, mentally ill individuals living in socially disorganized neighborhoods where there is less informal social control are expected to exhibit higher rates of violent behavior than mentally ill persons living in less disorganized areas, regardless of their personal characteristics.

<u>Cultural Differentiation</u>. Recent elaborations of the social disorganization perspective (Sampson and Lauritsen, 1994; Sampson, 1997; Sampson, Raudenbush, and Earls, 1997) suggest two ways in which cultural differentiation can influence violent behavior. This first is reflected in Sampson and Lauritsen's (1994) discussion of anomie theory. Anomie refers to "the presence of contradictory norms and the collective sense that the moral order is too weak to warrant trusting other people" (Sampson, 1997: 41). According to anomie theory, the coexistence of competing systems of cultural values and norms within a society (or neighborhood) undermines mainstream normative practices by fostering a collective sense of uncertainty regarding the behavior of others. This uncertainty weakens a neighborhood's ability to organize itself against unwanted problems, such as crime and violence, thereby increasing the likelihood that individual residents will engage in such behavior (Sampson,

Raudenbush, and Earls, 1997). Hiday (1997:402) stresses this line of reasoning when she argues that mentally ill individuals living in socially disorganized neighborhoods "often lose their moorings" and "live in a state of anomie." Similarly, Faris and Dunham (1939: 158) argue that socially disorganized areas provide "...a chaotic background of *conflicting and shifting cultural standards* [emphasis added], against which it is quite difficult for a person to develop a stable mental organization."

The second way in which cultural differentiation has been discussed is in terms of the emergence of alternative normative structures for guiding conduct. This line of reasoning is exemplified in Anderson's (1990, 1997) ethnographic research which points to the emergence of a "code of the streets" in inner-city neighborhoods. According to Anderson (1997:2), the code of the streets refers to "a set of informal rules governing interpersonal public behavior, including violence." The code is a manifestation of a cultural adaptation to a profound lack of faith in the police and the judicial system. Against this backdrop, the person who is believed capable of "taking care of himself" (e.g., able to threaten and use violence) is accorded a certain amount of social status. In this context, the use of violence becomes an expected and tolerated part of neighborhood life (Sampson, 1997; Sampson and Lauritsen, 1994). Based on these arguments, mentally ill individuals living in socially disorganized neighborhoods in which there are competing normative structures and in which a code of the streets has taken root, are expected to exhibit higher rates of violent behavior than other similar persons living in less disorganized areas.

Social Support. While the impact of social disorganization on the extent of informal social control and cultural differentiation has received a great deal of theoretical attention in the social disorganization literature (Sampson and Groves, 1989; Sampson and Lauritsen, 1994; Sampson, 1997), far less attention has been given to the importance of social disorganization in conditioning the availability of *social supports* to individual residents (Cullen, 1994; Faris and Dunham, 1939). Yet, social support from primary groups has been cited as essential for a sense of self-unity (Mead, 1934) and lack of it as a prominent cause of suicide (Durkheim, 1897/1951). This point is clearly stated by Cullen (p.528): "...we are missing something important when we reduce [the social disorganization perspective] to the sterile interplay of the concepts of disorganization, control, and cultural values."

Indeed, a considerable amount of research in urban sociology has sought to reveal the factors that interfere with the viability of social support networks (Wirth, 1938; Kasarda and Janowitz, 1974; Wellman, 1979; Sampson, 1988; Logan and Spitze, 1994).[6] Based on research rooted in what Kasarda and Janowitz (1974) referred to as the "systemic model" of local solidarity (see Chapter 3), Sampson (1988) found that the viability of neighborhood friendship networks depended

---

[6]The exact nature of the relationship between neighborhood level factors and the social networks of individual residents is still debated in the literature on urban sociology (Wellman, 1979; Logan and Spitze, 1994). This debate has focused primarily on whether, as a result of modernization and urbanization, social ties between individuals have been suppressed or "lost" due to the size, density, and heterogeneity of modern living environments (Wirth, 1938), whether they have been expanded or "liberated" beyond local spatial boundaries due to advanced communication and travel technology (Wellman, 1979), or whether they have been maintained or "saved" due to the proximity, mutual need, and shared interests of local residents (Logan and Spitze, 1994; Logan and Molotch, 1987; Fischer, 1995).

not only on individual-level factors, but also on macrosocial forces operating at the neighborhood level. This finding is consistent with Lin's (1986:18) definition of social support as the "...perceived or actual instrumental and/or expressive provisions supplied by the community, social networks, and confiding partners." This definition clearly suggests that social support occurs on different social levels and that in addition to individual-level support derived from confiding individuals, such as a spouse or best friend, social support can also be viewed as a property of *the communities* in which individuals reside (see Cullen, 1994:530).

The importance of these arguments for the current study is in providing a strong theoretical rationale for hypothesizing that the extent of social support received by mentally ill people is influenced not just by their individual characteristics (i.e., in terms of their individual ability's to maintain a social network), but also by the social conditions of the neighborhoods in which they live. As Ellen and Turner (1997:840) state, "...people living in a more socially cohesive community are more apt to look out for their neighbors, help them weather bad times, and share information with them about relevant community news." The importance of social support in determining the quality of neighborhood life is further emphasized in recent research on America's inner cities (Wilson, 1987; Massey and Denton, 1993; Anderson, 1997; Ellen and Turner, 1997). This literature documents the large-scale social forces (i.e., deindustrialization, joblessness, persisting racial segregation, migration to the suburbs, etc.) that have increased the social isolation of inner-cities and compromised the capacity of such communities to provide residents with adequate levels of social support. Massey and Denton (1993) attribute high levels of neighborhood social isolation and weak social ties to widespread housing and employment discrimination. For Wilson (1987), neighborhood social isolation is related to the withdrawal of middle- and working-class families from disadvantaged neighborhoods - families that otherwise would serve as a "social buffer" providing neighborhood residents with access to employment information and other social support resources.

The ameliorative effects of residing in a community where supportive relationships are readily available may be especially important to mentally individuals who, due to their mental illnesses, may require periodic assistance from fellow residents. Specifically, the functional limitations that severely mentally ill persons may possess (i.e., in terms of communication and travel) may place additional constraints on their abilities to maintain extensive social networks.[7] Persons with mental illnesses are known to exhibit many of the individual-level characteristics that have been associated with a limited geographic range of social ties, including financial and material dependence, and unstable employment (Estroff and Zimmer, 1994). To the extent that mentally ill residents - particularly those with functional disabilities - must rely on limited social networks to access needed

---

[7]The notion that some types of individuals are less able to maintain extensive social networks is known in the urban sociology literature as the *residual neighborhood* thesis (Logan and Molotch, 1987; Logan and Spitze, 1994). According to Logan and Spitze (1994:457), the term "residual neighborhood" refers to "the hypothesis that neighboring is an alternative form of socializing for people who do not have access to broader networks." Among the personal characteristics that have been shown to limit the spatial range of social networking opportunities are financial need, minority racial status, unemployment, and old age (Campbell and Lee, 1990). Each of these characteristics is thought to decrease social network size and proximity by limiting social contacts to those individuals accessible within the neighborhood bounds.

supports, their vulnerability to the levels of social disorganization within the neighborhood is increased. As a result, the social supports of mentally ill individuals may be especially constrained in disorganized neighborhood environments where opportunities to achieve supportive social relationships are lacking.

Cullen's (1994) emphasis on social support in conceptualizing the effects of neighborhood social disorganization is strikingly similar to arguments posed by Faris and Dunham (1939) almost 60 years earlier. In attempting to account for the clustering of persons with schizophrenia in "zones of transition," Faris and Dunham looked to "the nature of social life and conditions in certain areas of the city" for insight (p.170). Consistent with Shaw and McKay's (1942) finding regarding the distinct spatial patterning of delinquency across neighborhoods, Faris and Dunham observed that certain mentally disordered individuals also seemed to cluster in disorganized neighborhoods of the city where social ties among residents appeared weak. More importantly, Faris and Dunham observed that such neighborhood conditions led to the experience of elevated levels of "social isolation" among mentally ill residents. They wrote: "the conditions producing isolation are much more frequent in the disorganized communities."

Faris and Dunham suggested that "normal adult mentality" must be supported by a "*fairly harmonious stream of primary social contacts*" [emphasis added] and that "any factor which interferes with social contacts with other persons [i.e., such as social disorganization] produces isolation"(p.154). The parallel between Faris and Dunham's emphasis on social isolation and Cullen's emphasis on social support is clear. Both authors express the fundamental premise that supportive social relationships - rooted in the ecology of the neighborhood - are crucial to the emotional and psychological well-being of individual residents.

Cullen (1994) further suggests that the social sources of informal social control and social support are so closely related that the variables employed in many previous studies can be viewed as operationalizing either concept. For example, Sampson and Groves' (1989) research reveals that higher crime rates tend to occur in communities characterized by family disruption, weak friendship networks, and low levels of participation in local voluntary organizations. Sampson and Groves interpret these findings as an indication that such communities are unable to exert informal social control over their residents. However, these measures can easily be seen as indicators of social support. As Cullen (1994) points out, high rates of family disruption may operationalize not only surveillance over residents, but also the viability of social support networks and the opportunity to develop intimate relations. Similarly, the recent study by Sampson, Raudenbush, and Earls (1997:923) emphasized collective efficacy as a robust predictor of low rates of violence. However, as Cullen, Wright, and Chamlin (1998:10) note, "The construct of collective efficacy included not only a measure of informal social control, but also a measure of 'cohesion and trust' among residents -- or what we would term the existence of helpful or supportive relationships in a community." Many prior studies can thus be interpreted as providing support for the control thesis as well as indicating a possible inverse relationship between social support and crime.

In addition, the close association between neighborhood cultural differentiation and social support is evident in Sampson, Raudenbush, and Earls' (1997:919) argument that people are less likely to interact with one another when "...*the rules are unclear* [emphasis added] and people mistrust or fear one another." Aneshensel and Sucoff (1996:295) further state that "residents of [socially disorganized neighborhoods] come to mistrust neighbors, increasingly stay indoors and off the streets, limit social contacts with close friends and family, and generally retreat from public participation in the community" (see also Massey and Denton, 1993; Skogan, 1990; Liska and Warner, 1991). As residents of disorganized neighborhoods withdraw from social interaction fewer opportunities for neighborhood social networking are available to mentally ill residents. As Ellen and Turner (1997:842) argue, "...people living in high-crime areas are likely to lead more sheltered, isolated lives, spending less time outside their homes participating in community activities."

Particularly relevant to this discussion is Cullen's (1994:538) argument that *the more social support a person receives, the less likely it is that he or she will engage in violence.* In support of this proposition, Cullen cites Loeber and Stouthamer-Loeber's (1986) comprehensive meta-analysis of family correlates of delinquency. Loeber and Stouthamer-Loeber found that delinquency was related inversely to child-parent involvement, such as the amount of intimate communication, confiding, sharing of activities, and sharing help. Indeed, social support factors were among the most powerful family factors related to delinquency; their effects exceeded those of parental criminality, marital discord, parental absence, parental health, and family size.

The implication is that when individuals are enmeshed in a network of supportive relationships, the risk of crime, violence, and other individual pathologies is diminished. As Cullen (1994:542) argues, "...social supports may exert independent (main) effects on crime not by facilitating control, but by reducing other sources of crime (e.g., lessening emotional difficulties, relieving strain, transforming deviant identities)." Extending these insights to persons with mental illnesses, it is expected that in communities that contain highly supportive social networks, residents are more likely to get involved when a person with mental illness shows visible signs of decompensation (i.e., when their mental condition deteriorates). To the extent that this occurs, such persons will be more likely receive treatment for their for their symptoms and other needed supports, thereby reducing the risk that they will commit a violent act.

Summary. The theoretical arguments outlined in this section attempt to describe how levels of neighborhood social organization might affect the likelihood that persons with mental illnesses will engage in violence. Consistent with traditional presentations of the social disorganization perspective, the theory emphasizes the central roles of *informal social control* and *cultural differentiation*. In addition, the theory draws upon the works of Faris and Dunham (1939) and Cullen (1994) in emphasizing the importance of *social support* in explaining the relationship between social disorganization and violence. Taken together, these arguments lead to the expectation that mentally ill persons living in socially disorganized neighborhoods where (1) fewer opportunities exist for developing supportive social relationships; (2) there is less informal social control; and (3) there is cultural differentiation - will be more likely to engage in violence, net of the effects of their individual characteristics.

With this theoretical framework as a backdrop, the following sections provide specific hypotheses regarding the effects of neighborhood social disorganization and individual characteristics on patient violence. However, before these hypotheses are formulated, a justification for the selection of particular individual and neighborhood-level risk factors is provided.

Selection of Risk Factors

Individual-Level Risk Factors. The overall purpose of these analyses is to assess the contribution of neighborhood characteristics to the prospective assessment of patient violence. Therefore, individual-level characteristics included in the current study were selected because (1) they have been demonstrated by prior research or theory to be associated with risk for future violence among persons with mental illnesses; (2) they may be used by hospital clinicians in making prospective assessments of patient violence (Quinsey and McGuire, 1986); or (3) they are analogous to measures obtained at the neighborhood level (i.e., SES, racial status) and are thus useful in helping to separate out the effects of the neighborhood context. Controlling for individual-level predictors of patient violence that meet these criteria provides a difficult test of the explanatory power of neighborhood-level factors.

The specific individual-level risk factors that will be assessed in this study consist of five clinically relevant risk factors: psychopathy, anger, impulsivity, substance abuse, and paranoid beliefs; one historical risk factors: prior adult arrests for serious crimes against persons; one social network factor: available social supports; and eight demographic risk factors: gender, race, age, marital status, socioeconomic status, occupational status, and length of residence (operational definitions are provided in Chapter 5).

Exogenous Causes of Social Disorganization. Consistent with much prior research (Sampson, Raudenbush, and Earls, 1997; Brooks-Gunn, Duncan, and Aber, 1997; South and Crowder, 1997; South and Crowder, 1999), this study utilizes census tract data to operationalize neighborhood conditions. Data were extracted from the 1990

Census to reflect neighborhood differences in poverty, race and ethnicity, immigration, the labor market, age composition, education composition, family structure, homeownership, vacant dwellings, and residential stability. Census data were collected independent of, and prior to, the MacArthur Study data, thus allowing for temporal sequencing. Consistent with Sampson, Raudenbush, and Earls' (1997) approach for examining neighborhood effects in Chicago, a factor analysis will be conducted to assess whether a smaller number of linear combinations of census characteristics describe the structure of the 145 neighborhoods in Pittsburgh. Based on prior research and theory, at least two factors are expected to emerge from this analysis: a factor representing neighborhood disadvantage and a factor representing residential instability. However, other factors are also possible (Bellair,1997).

These census tract measures are, of course, not direct indicators of neighborhood social disorganization; rather, they reflect the key structural conditions suggested by a long line of theorists as exogenous causes of social disorganization (Shaw and McKay, 1942; Bursik, 1988; Sampson and Groves, 1989; Sampson and Lauritsen, 1994; Sampson, Raudenbush, and Earls, 1997). Therefore, conclusions drawn from this study regarding the effects of neighborhood-level social disorganization must be inferred from the effects of these structural antecedents (as direct measures of the social disorganization process, i.e., informal social control, cultural differentiation, and social support, are not available from the U.S. Census). However, although *neighborhood*-level indicators of social disorganization are not available, the study does have access to certain *individual*-level measures predicted to intervene between neighborhood social disorganization and individual patient violence. Specifically, data on the social supports received by individual patients are available for empirical analysis. Thus, although the mediating effects of *neighborhood*-level social support networks cannot be assessed in this study, the effects of *individual* social supports (i.e., social support reported by individual patients) may be examined empirically.

Research Hypotheses

In the remainder of this chapter, specific hypotheses regarding the multilevel effects of patient characteristics and neighborhood social disorganization on violence are formulated. This approach to the study of violence among persons with mental illnesses is consistent with the multilevel perspective increasingly advocated by criminologists (Elliot et al., 1996; Miethe and McDowall, 1993, Rountree et al., 1994; Sampson and Lauritsen, 1994; Sampson, 1997) and provides an empirical examination of Faris and Dunham's (1939:154) assertion that "...the development of normal mentality and normal behavior demands a complicated chain of successfully functioning elements on paths of very different sorts."

1. Main Effect of Social Disorganization on Patient Violence. The theoretical arguments presented above lead to the expectation that neighborhood social disorganization (i.e., neighborhood disadvantage, residential instability, etc.) will have an effect on patient violence due to decreased levels of informal social control, increased levels of cultural differentiation, and decreased opportunities for the development of supportive social relationships. This effect is hypothesized to hold across patient groups (i.e., net of the effects of individual characteristics).

Hypothesis 1: Neighborhood social disorganization will have a significant main effect on patient violence, net of the effects of individual-level characteristics.

2. Amounts of Variation in Violence Explained by Social Disorganization and Patient Characteristics. In the majority of empirical studies that find significant neighborhood effects, these effects are generally much smaller than the effects of individual and family characteristics (Ellen and Turner, 1997). Focusing specifically on the effects of neighborhood poverty on patient violence, Silver, Mulvey, and Monahan (1999:248) found that although concentrated poverty contributed significantly to the prediction of patient violence, "the majority of the explained variation in violence belongs to the individual-level risk factors." It is not known whether this same pattern of results will obtain with the more elaborate operationalization of neighborhood factors proposed here. However, consistent with past research, it is hypothesized that, due to the indirect nature of the effects of social disorganization on violence (i.e., via informal control, cultural differentiation, and neighborhood social support networks), individual-level characteristics will account for the majority of explained variation, as they likely reflect more proximate causes of patient violence.

Hypothesis 2: Individual-level characteristics will account for the majority of explained variation in patient violence compared with neighborhood characteristics.

3. Concentration Effects in the Social Disorganization-Violence Relationship. According to South and Crowder (1999), an often overlooked factor in empirical assessments of the effects of neighborhood conditions on

individual behavior is the idea of *concentration effects* (see also Ellen and Turner, 1997). According to Wilson (1987:57), concentration effects are hypothesized to lead to an "exponential increase" in the manifestations of social problems in areas characterized by extreme disadvantage. South and Crowder argue that such exponential increases "lie at the heart of the epidemic or contagion models of social problems...and presumably gives substance to the concept of concentrated poverty, differentiating it from simply high poverty" (manuscript, p.4). They find a significant nonlinear relationship between neighborhood disadvantage and nonmarital fertility among white women, with increasing rates of out-of-wedlock childbearing occurring in especially disadvantaged communities.

Based on these observations, the relationship between neighborhood social disorganization and patient violence is hypothesized to be nonlinear. That is, the magnitude of the effect of social disorganization on patient violence is expected to increase as neighborhoods become more socially disorganized. An assessment of the potential nonlinear effects of social disorganization on patient violence will be conducted by adding exponential terms for the effects of the social disorganization variables to each of the models tested.

Hypothesis 3: The magnitude of the effect of neighborhood social disorganization on patient violence will increase as neighborhoods become more socially disorganized.

4. <u>Social Support as a Mediator in the Social Disorganization-Violence Relationship</u>. Both Faris and Dunham (1939) and Cullen (1994) point to the importance of neighborhood-level social support as a mediating factor in the relationship between neighborhood conditions and individual

outcomes, such as violence. Specifically, neighborhood social disorganization is expected to constrain individual opportunities to develop and sustain supportive social relationships, thereby restricting the availability of social supports experienced at the individual level (Kasarda and Janowitz, 1974; Sampson, 1988). Less social support at the individual level is expected, in turn, to increase an individual's risk for violence (Cullen, 1994). Although a measure of the viability of neighborhood-level social support networks is not available for analysis in the current study, a measure of individual-level social support (based on patient self-report) is available. Based on the theoretical arguments described above and the availability of data, it is hypothesized that the effects of social disorganization on patient violence will be, in part, mediated by the extent of individual-level social support received by patients.[8]

Hypothesis 4: The effects of social disorganization on patient violence will be, in part, mediated by the extent of social support received by patients.

5. Conditioning Effects of Social Disorganization on Effects of Patient Characteristics. Neighborhood social disorganization is hypothesized to increase an individual

---

[8]Partial (as opposed to complete) mediation is hypothesized due to the multiple pathways through which social disorganization is predicted to affect patient violence (i.e., through informal social control, cultural differentiation, and neighborhood-level social supports). In addition, the less than ideal nature of the available measure of social support (i.e., individual-level support as opposed to a more theoretically relevant construct involving neighborhood-level social support networks) also contributes to the expectation of partial, as opposed to complete, mediation.

patient's propensity to engage in violence by decreasing informal social controls, increasing cultural differentiation, and obstructing the development of supportive social relationships. Similarly, patients who exhibit individual-level characteristics known to be associated with violent behavior are expected to exhibit a higher propensity for violence. The question is whether the combined effects of high-risk patient characteristics and socially disorganized neighborhood conditions are additive or interactive.

An additive relationship would indicate that the effects of individual characteristics on increased violence are constant across neighborhood contexts. An interactive effect, on the other hand, would indicate that the effects of individual characteristics on increased violence were greater in socially disorganized neighborhoods, and/or that their effects were diminished in socially organized neighborhoods (i.e., where there are greater social controls, less cultural differentiation, and more active neighborhood-level social support networks).[9] These possibilities are particularly relevant in examining the previously documented effects of two of the more prominent risk factors cited in the risk assessment literature (see Chapter 2): namely, paranoid symptoms and substance abuse. The remainder of this section develops specific hypotheses regarding contextual effects that may be expected to condition the relationship between these risk factors and patient violence.

Paranoid Disorders. Faris and Dunham (1939) were

---

[9]Mathematically, of course, such effects can also be interpreted as the differential effects of social disorganization on violence across different types of patients. However, as the purpose of the current study is to assess *contextual* effects related to social disorganization, such an interpretation, while mathematically feasible, is less theoretically compelling.

among the first to suggest a relationship between social support and paranoid beliefs. In discussing persons who believe they "hear voices," Faris and Dunham (p.174) argued that "many such persons have some basis in their experience for such a belief." They describe examples of a patient who had spent time in jail believing that people were calling him jailbird, and a girl who had been raped believing that people were talking about her behind her back. In both instances, the patients reported hearing voices which, when analyzed further, yielded a basis in the social reality that surrounded them.[10] Further, as indicated in Chapter 2, paranoid symptoms and persecutory delusions have recently been shown to contribute to the violent behavior of persons with mental illnesses (Link and Stueve, 1994; Swanson, et al., 1996, Link et al., 1999).

Faris and Dunham's theoretical argument regarding the relationship between social isolation and paranoid beliefs is consistent with Cullen's (1994) emphasis on the crucial role of social support. Faris and Dunham argued that "for isolated persons who feel they could not know directly what

---

[10]In emphasizing the importance of the social surroundings, however, Faris and Dunham (1939) did not argue that the symptoms of illness were socially determined. Their position on this issue was summed up well in Ernest Burgess' introduction to their work. Describing Faris and Dunham's (1939) theoretical stance, Burgess wrote, "...even if [social factors] play less direct roles [than biological or psychological factors], they may nonetheless be essential" (p. xv). This is consistent with Hiday's (1997) assertion that "neurobiological factors may be the origin of severe mental illness; but social factors affect its course, manifestations, and connections to violence" (p.412). In other words, even if biological factors were to be established as the ultimate causes of mental illness, social factors may still be crucial for understanding how mental illness is manifested in specific symptoms and how those symptoms relate to violence.

persons might be whispering, such thoughts [i.e., those with paranoid content] are not entirely unreasonable." In addition they argued that "the conditions producing isolation are much more frequent in the disorganized communities." Accordingly, discharged psychiatric patients residing in socially disorganized neighborhoods are expected to be more socially isolated (i.e, report fewer social supports) than other patients and that the effects of paranoid symptoms on violence are expected to be stronger among socially isolated patients.

More specifically, the lack of opportunity to develop and sustain socially supportive relationships in socially disorganized neighborhoods is expected to increase the isolation of individuals suffering from paranoid disorders, leading to increases in the likelihood that paranoid beliefs will result in violence. Conversely, the greater opportunity to develop and sustain supportive relationships in social organized neighborhoods is expected to decrease the social isolation of paranoid individuals, thereby decreasing the likelihood that paranoid symptoms will result in violence. Individual social support is thus conceived as a conditioning factor in the relationship between paranoid symptoms, and patient violence. To test these ideas, a product term representing the interaction between presence of paranoid symptoms and the extent of social support received by individual patients will be assessed. It is hypothesized that mentally ill persons with paranoid symptoms who are also socially isolated (i.e., receive little social support) will be more likely to engage in violence than other patients.

Hypothesis 5: Paranoid symptoms and lack of social support are expected to interact in their relationship patient to violence.

Substance Abuse. Numerous studies have found substance abuse to be more prevalent among conditions of poverty and social disadvantage (Anderson, 1990, 1997; Sampson and Lauritsen, 1994) and much research has implicated substance abuse in violent behavior (Bushman and Cooper, 1990; Miczek, DeBold, Haney, Tidey, Vivian, and Weertz, 1993; Phil and Peterson, 1993; Sampson and Lauritsen, 1994). Further, the positive association between abuse of illegal substances and violence among persons with mental illnesses has been well-established (Swanson et al., 1990; Swanson, 1994; Swanson, et al., 1997; Steadman et al., 1998). Swanson and colleagues have shown substance abuse to increase risk for violence among persons with mental disorders by a factor of four, and studies of mentally disordered persons in jails and prisons have found them to be at increased risk for drug abuse problems and to have exhibited higher rates of drug use at the time of their arrests (Abram and Teplin, 1991; Cote and Hodgins, 1990).

As early as 1939, Faris and Dunham noted that "the dispensing and use of drugs" was especially prevalent in the "zones of transition." They attributed this relationship to the "lack of normal social life" that underpinned "the dissatisfactions which cause the use of drugs to be felt as a release..." (p.170). In other words, they believed that social conditions in the neighborhood predisposed residents to "dispense and use" drugs. Indeed, recent research has shown that persons who live in high-poverty neighborhoods where drugs are readily available and where there is a high degree of tolerance for their use, will be more likely to use drugs themselves (Sampson and Lauritsen, 1994; Anderson, 1997; Massey and Denton, 1993). However, the notion that the association between drug abuse *and violence* among persons with mental illnesses may, to some extent, be related to the neighborhood environments in which they live has not been studied.

Two alternative hypotheses may be posited regarding the effect of the neighborhood context on the relationship between substance abuse and violence, both of which are rooted in arguments posed by Faris and Dunham (1939). Specifically, Faris and Dunham (p.122) observed that mentally ill drug abusers in Chicago lived mainly in socially disorganized neighborhoods where "it is of course easier to obtain an in-group solidarity and maintain contacts with other addicts and 'dope peddlers.'" Based on this observation, it is plausible to hypothesize that mentally ill individuals previously diagnosed with drug abuse disorders may be more likely to commit violent acts when they reside in socially disorganized neighborhoods where there are greater opportunities to find drugs via "other addicts and dope peddlers," thereby leading to additional increases in their propensity for violence.

Hypothesis 6: Patients with substance abuse disorders who reside in socially disorganized neighborhoods are expected to exhibit more violence than those who reside in less disorganized neighborhoods.

The alternative hypothesis reflects Faris and Dunham's emphasis on the importance of in-group solidarity in understanding the neighborhood effect. Specifically, it may be hypothesized that it is in socially *organized* neighborhoods (i.e., which contain functioning social networks to facilitate the use, trade, and tolerance of drugs) that mentally ill persons with substance abuse disorders would be more likely to use drugs, thereby increasing their likelihood of committing violence. That is, the trust required to share and deal drugs may be more prevalent in neighborhoods characterized by dense and stable social relationships, leading to increased violence among residents with substance abuse problems. To assess these competing hypotheses, product terms between neighborhood conditions and individual substance abuse disorder will be examined.

Alternative Hypothesis 6: Patients with substance abuse disorders who reside in *socially organized* neighborhoods will exhibit more violence than those who reside in socially disorganized neighborhoods.

Summary

This chapter presents a set of testable research hypotheses - grounded in the social disorganization perspective - that assess the effects of neighborhood conditions and individual characteristics on the prediction of violence among persons with mental illnesses. Taken together, these hypotheses explore the utility of applying a social disorganization perspective to the study of violence among discharged psychiatric patients. In addition, these hypotheses seek to broaden the scope of research on risk factors for violence among persons with mental illness by examining the role played by neighborhood-level factors. The results obtained will determine the relevance of the social disorganization perspective for understanding the violent behavior of discharged patients - a group for whom research has been limited to individual-level explanations. In addition, to the extent that neighborhood social disorganization matters in accounting for the violent behavior of discharged psychiatric patients, and to the extent that cross-level interactions are found, the results of this study will provide important information to mental health policy-makers and clinicians responsible for the prediction and management of patient violence. In the following chapter, the procedures used to generate the study sample and the analytic techniques that will be used to assess the research hypotheses are described.

CHAPTER 5
Data, Measures, and Statistical Procedures

This chapter describes the data sources, measures, and statistical procedures that will be used to assess the core research hypotheses outlined in Chapter 4. This chapter is organized into three sections. The first section describes the two main data sources - the MacArthur Violence Risk Assessment Study and the 1990 U.S. Census Summary Tape Files. The second section provides operational definitions for each of the independent variables. The third section describes how the dependent measures are operationalized and the statistical procedures to be used.

Data Sources

Patient Sample. The primary data source for this study is the MacArthur Foundation's Violence Risk Assessment Study (Monahan and Steadman, 1994; Steadman et al., 1998; Silver, Mulvey, and Monahan, 1999; Silver, 2000a, 2000b). Between 1992 and 1995, the MacArthur Study sampled admissions from the Western Psychiatric Institute and Clinic (WPIC), an acute psychiatric inpatient facility located in Pittsburgh, PA. To be eligible for participation in the study, subjects had to be: (1) acute (i.e., short stay) civil admissions; (2) between the ages of 18 and 40; (3) English-speaking; (4) White or African American; and (5) have a hospital chart diagnosis indicating the presence of a major mental disorder (i.e., schizophrenia, schizophreniform, schizoaffective, depression, dysthymia, mania, brief reactive psychosis, delusional disorder, alcohol or drug abuse or dependence or a personality disorder).

Hospital data collection was conducted in two parts: (1) an initial interview to obtain a wide array of background data; and (2) a second interview by a research clinician (M.S.W.-level) to confirm the subject's hospital chart diagnosis and to administer several other clinical scales. Research clinician diagnoses corresponded to chart diagnoses in 91.8% of the cases. All subjects were asked for written informed consent to participate in the study. The median length of hospitalization for enrolled patients was 15 days.

Five attempts were made to re-interview enrolled patients in the community (approximately every 10 weeks) over the one-year period following discharge from WPIC. A collateral informant was also interviewed using the same interview schedule. A collateral was the person who was most familiar with the patient's behavior and functioning in the community through direct contact, usually at least weekly. Collateral informants were nominated by patients during each follow-up interview. If the collateral nominee did not have at least weekly contact with the subject, the interviewer suggested a more appropriate person based on a review of the subject's social network data. Collateral informants were most often family members (47.1%), but were also friends (22.0%), professionals (16.1%), significant others (11.8%), or others (e.g., co-workers; 3.0%). All subjects and collateral informants were paid for each completed interview.

Official records provided a third source of information about the patients' behavior in the community. During the follow-up interviews, patients were asked whether they had been readmitted to a psychiatric facility. If a patient was readmitted and gave approval for release of information, the hospital was contacted to obtain information regarding the rehospitalization, including dates of hospitalization, diagnosis, and reasons for admission. Arrest records for all patients were obtained at the end of the one-year follow-up.

Of the 4,069 admissions to WPIC that occurred between 1992 and 1995, 2,532 met the study's eligibility criteria. A total of 629 patients were approached to participate in the study. The refusal rate was 33.2% (n=209).[11] Twenty-nine patients who agreed to participate were discharged before the hospital interview could be completed. The final sample given a hospital interview was 391, 312 of whom completed the first follow-up interview. Post-discharge census tract locations were identified for 270 of these 312 subjects. There were no significant differences

---

[11]A major concern in any observational study of patient violence is that patients who consent to participate will consist only of cooperative (i.e., less dangerous) patients who are less likely to exhibit violence in the community. However, the patients who consented to participate in this study were, as a group, significantly younger, less likely to have a medical record diagnosis of schizophrenia, and more likely to have a medical record diagnosis of alcohol or drug abuse. These sample biases point in the direction of the enrolled sample being more likely to be violent than other eligible patients (see Steadman et al., 1998). The natural result of these biases would be to increase the overall rate of violence observed during the follow-up period, but is not likely to influence the relationships between violent behavior and the particular risk factors considered.

between enrolled subjects who did not complete the first two follow-up interview (n=79) and those who did (n=312) in terms of sex, age, race, or admission diagnosis. Nor were there any significant differences between subjects for whom post-discharge neighborhood location was known (n=270) and those for whom it was not known (n=42).

Tract-Level Data from the U.S. Census. Prior research suggests that most people regard their neighborhood as larger than one block but smaller than an entire sector (i.e., the North side of a city) (Lee, Oropesa, and Kanan, 1994; Lee and Campbell, 1997). Census tract boundaries lie between these two extremes and are drawn to encapsulate relatively homogeneous populations in terms of demographic and economic characteristics. Tract boundaries are delineated with the advice of local committees working under Census Bureau guidelines and therefore typically reflect important physical features that define neighborhoods, such as major streets or railroads, as well as important ethnic and social divisions (Duncan and Aber, 1997).

Census tracts are small, relatively permanent statistical subdivisions of a county which typically contain between 2,500 and 8,000 persons and vary in geographic size depending on population density. For the purpose of statistical comparison and reporting, census tract boundaries are formulated to be maintained over a long period of time; however, physical changes in street patterns and new construction require occasional boundary revisions. The data provided by the decennial census at the tract level come from the census forms that the population is asked to fill out on April 1 of the first year of every decade. Census tracts are identified by a four-digit number and are unique within a county. Although census tracts are perhaps imperfect operationalizations of neighborhoods (Tienda, 1991), they come closer than any commonly available geographic entity in approximating the usual conception of a neighborhood (South and Crowder, 1997; Elliot et al., 1996; Hill, 1992; Ricketts & Sawhill, 1988; Gramlich, Laren, & Sealand, 1992; Lee, Oropesa, & Kanan, 1994; Massey, Gross, & Shibuya, 1994; Robert, 1998; Silver, Mulvey, and Monahan, 1999).

Similar to most other data collection efforts involving psychiatric patients, the MacArthur Risk Assessment Study was not designed to collect objective indicators of the qualities of the neighborhoods in which discharged patients resided. Thus, a significant contribution of the current study involves adding neighborhood measures to this extensive patient data set. Census tract identifiers for each subject were obtained by the University of Pittsburgh's Center for Social and Urban Research using mapping methods to geo-code each subject's post-discharge address into its respective census tract. Census tract locations were based on the addresses at which subjects reported residing most often during the first 10 weeks after discharge from WPIC. Following treatment at WPIC, the 270 subjects in this study were discharged to 145 census tracts in Allegheny County, PA.

Using census tract identifiers, patient records were matched to census tract records from the 1990 U.S. Census to create a multi-level analysis file consisting of both neighborhood and patient level characteristics. Thus, objective data on the characteristics of Pittsburgh area neighborhoods are available for analysis along with the extensive array of individual risk factors gathered by the MacArthur Study.

Explanatory Variables

Neighborhood Measures. Three general strategies have been used in prior studies to select specific neighborhood measures for empirical analysis (Sampson and Morenoff, 1997). One approach has been to estimate multivariate models with a broad range of neighborhood and individual characteristics and present trimmed models that include only variables with significant effects (Billy and Moore, 1992; Brewster, Billy, and Grady, 1993). A second approach has been to examine the main effects of a large number of neighborhood variables (without considering the effects of individual-level variables) and retaining in subsequent analyses only those neighborhood variables with the strongest, independent effects on the criterion measure. The effects of these neighborhood variables are then assessed controlling for individual-level characteristics (Brooks-Gunn et al., 1993; Crane, 1991). A third approach, often used to minimize the multicollinearity typically found among neighborhood measures, has been to create one or more composite measures based on a factor analysis of several neighborhood characteristics and estimate the effects of these composite measures (see Sampson, Raudenbush, and Earls, 1997 for a recent example; Elliot et al., 1996; Sampson and Morenoff, 1997; South and Crowder, 1999; Duncan and Aber, 1997).

The current study will follow Sampson, Raudenbush, and Earls (1997) and Duncan and Aber, (1997) in adopting the latter approach to developing neighborhood-level variables for analysis. Specifically, the organization of community risk factors will be examined both empirically (through factor analysis) and theoretically (by ensuring that the empirical dimensions identified with factor analysis map onto theoretical constructs related to social disorganization). This strategy is adopted because of the significant overlap typically observed among neighborhood-level measures and because multivariate indices of underlying dimensions of neighborhood conditions are generally more reliable than single-index measures (Duncan and Aber, 1997). In addition, this approach allows for the specification, both conceptually and empirically, of neighborhood dimensions that are relatively independent, rather than simply relying on the most significant single predictor.

The following variables were constructed from data elements extracted from the U.S. Census Summary Tape Files: neighborhood poverty (e.g., percentage of all persons in households with income below federal poverty level, percentage of households that have public assistance incomes), neighborhood wealth (mean family income, mean household wage income, percentage of families with income greater than $50,000 per year), neighborhood family structure (e.g., percentage of families headed by a female), neighborhood employment (adult unemployment rate, percentage of employed persons with executive or managerial positions), and neighborhood residential stability (percentage of residents who lived the same housing unit five years earlier), neighborhood racial composition and immigration (percentage black, percentage foreign-born), and neighborhood housing stock (percentage of housing units that are vacant).

Individual-Level Variables. The vast majority of published research on patient violence focuses on the identification and assessment of individual-level risk factors (Mulvey, 1994; Silver, Mulvey, and Monahan, 1999). The main purpose of this study is to evaluate the extent to which factors associated with neighborhood social disorganization contribute to the prediction of violent outcomes over and above the effects of known individual-level predictors. In addition, this study is designed to assess the extent to which neighborhood characteristics condition the effects of known individual-level predictors of patient violence. The following criteria were therefore used to select specific individual-level risk factors for analysis: (1) they have been demonstrated by prior research or theory to be associated with risk for future violence among persons with mental illnesses; (2) they may be used by hospital clinicians in making prospective assessments of patient violence; or (3) they are analogous to measures obtained at the neighborhood level (i.e., SES, racial status) and are thus useful in helping to separate out the effects of the neighborhood context. Controlling for individual-level predictors of patient violence that meet these criteria will provide a conservative test of the explanatory power of neighborhood-level factors. The specific patient-level variables selected for analysis are described below (see Table 5.1 for a summary of concepts and measures).

Demographic Characteristics. Four demographic characteristics are assessed. Gender is represented by an indicator variable called Male, where 1 = male and 0 = female. Age is the number of years between birth and target hospitalization. Race is represented by a variable called African American, where 1= African American and 0= white.[12] Socioeconomic status (SES) is operationalized using the Hollingshead and Redlich (1958) two-factor (education and occupation) method. The respondent's occupation was used (if he or she had an occupation), or, if not, the respondent's parents' occupation was used. Respondents fell into five groups, with SES=1 the lowest group and SES=5 the highest. Employment status is

[12]Due to the relatively small number of Hispanic admissions to WPIC, only non-Hispanic whites and non-Hispanic African Americans were approached for participation in the study.

measured by a dichotomous variable called Work in which 1 = employed (either full or part time) at the time of hospital admission. Marital status is measured by a dichotomous variable called Married in which 1 = married (or living with someone as if married) at the time of hospital admission). Finally, Residential Stability will be measured in terms of the number of months the patient had been residing at the address at which he or she lived at the time of hospital admission.

Clinical Characteristics. Five clinically relevant characteristics will be assessed. The presence of a substance abuse diagnosis was determined by research interviewers using the DSM-IIIR Checklist (Janca and Helzer, 1990) as part of the in-hospital diagnostic interview. Subjects diagnosed with a substance abuse disorder include those who demonstrate (1) continued use of substances despite having a persistent social, occupational, psychological, or physical problem caused or exacerbated by such use; or (2) recurrent use in situations in which use is physically hazardous (e.g., driving while intoxicated). A variable indicating the presence of a substance abuse disorder is used.

Anger levels were measured using a modified version of the Novaco Anger Scale (NAS), specifically revised for use in assessing anger among mentally disordered populations (Novaco, 1994). The total score of the NAS is constructed from two parts. Part A includes three clinically oriented scales: Cognitive, Physiological Arousal, and Behavioral Response. Each scale consists of 16 items rated on a 3-point scale from 1=Never True to 3=Always True. Part B provides an index of anger intensity and generality across a range of potentially provocative situations and consists of 25 items rated on a four-point scale from 1=Not at All Angry to 4 = Very Angry.

The Cognitive component of the NAS is based on the premise that "there is no direct relationship between external events and anger," but that "the maintenance of anger is a function of our perceptions and the way in which we process information" (Novaco, 1994:35). This cognitive mediation of anger heightens the relevance of anger as a risk factor for violence as mental disorder is known to affect cognitive functioning. The Physiological Arousal component of anger reflects "physiological activation in the cardiovascular, endocrine, and limbic system, as well as other autonomic and central nervous system areas, and by tension in the skeletal musculature" (Novaco, 1994:37). The role of Behavioral Response in anger formation is emphasized by the cognitive labeling perspective: the inclination to act in an antagonistic manner toward the source of provocation "partly defines the emotional state as anger as opposed to some other state or emotion" (Novaco, 1994:39). The Intensity or Generality of anger "assesses the degree of anger experienced with regard to various situations of provocation" (Novaco, 1994:39). Unpublished results from the MacArthur Study have shown the Behavioral Response component of the Novaco Anger Scale to be most predictive of violent behavior. The Behavioral subscale will therefore be used in these analyses. The internal reliability (i.e., Cronbach's α coefficient) for the 16 items that comprise the Behavioral subscale of the NAS (for the MacArthur Study subjects) is .89, well above acceptable limits.

Barratt (1994) argues that the personality trait of impulsiveness is significantly related to aggression. Impulsivity is measured in the current study using the Barratt Impulsiveness Scale (BIS-11) which consists of 30 items rated on a four-point scale (1 = Rarely/Never and 4 = Almost Always/Always). The BIS-11 scale consists of three factors: Ideo-Motor, Non-Planning, and Coping Stability (Barratt, 1994). The Ideo-Motor factor includes motor items (e.g., "I do things without thinking") and cognitive items (e.g., "I am a careful thinker"). The Non-Planning factor includes such items as "I plan tasks carefully" and "I plan trips well ahead of time." The Coping Stability factor includes such items as "I like to think about complex problems" and " I finish what I start." Unpublished results from the MacArthur Study have shown the Non-Planning component of the Barratt Impulsiveness Scale to be more predictive of violent behavior than any of the other BIS-11 subscales. The Non-Planning subscale will therefore be used in these analyses. The internal reliability (i.e., Cronbach's α coefficient) of the 12 items that comprise the Non-Planning subscale of the BIS-II (based on the MacArthur Study data) is .63.

There a number of ways to operationalize paranoid symptoms within a mentally disordered sample. The key issue lies in (1) the separation of paranoid beliefs that result from mental illness (i.e., those that are the product of a personality disorder, or are enmeshed within a delusional framework) from those that accurately reflect a threatening reality (e.g., reality-based beliefs). In discussing this issue, Link et al. (1999) refer to Lemert's (1962) finding that when the people around a paranoid person conspire and plot in an effort to control the afflicted person's behavior, they simultaneously reinforce and provide a reality base for the person's paranoid beliefs. Therefore, a measure of paranoid belief must be used that does not confound these two interpretations.

Another key issue in measuring paranoid beliefs is reflected in recent analyses by the MacArthur Research Project focusing on the effects of threat/control-override (TCO) symptoms in which it has been found that delusions are *negatively* related to violence and that threat/control override symptoms are not related to violence (Appelbaum, 2000). This finding contradicts those of other studies but may be explained by the observation that patients with many delusions are simply more disabled (i.e., more likely to suffer from serious disorders such as schizophrenia) than other patients, regardless of the paranoid content of their delusions, and therefore are less likely to engage in violence.

To avoid these measurement difficulties, the current study will rely neither on the number of paranoid delusions nor on the subjects' self-report of harmful intentions from others. Rather, this study will focus on *paranoid personality disorder* as diagnosed by project interviewers using the Structured Interview for DSM-III-R Personality (SIDP-R, Pfohl, et al., 1989). The SIDP-R is a semi-structured interview designed for use by non-clinicians to diagnose a wide range of personality disorders, including paranoid disorders. In rating the SIDP-R, information from a number of sources is used, including self-report, chart material, and first-hand experience with the patient. When there is conflicting information, the rater must independently assess the validity of the various sources to decide which to consider as the basis for diagnosis.

To be diagnosed with a paranoid personality disorder, subjects must be rated as positive on four of the following seven dimensions: (1) "expects to be exploited or harmed by others"; (2) "questions loyalty or trustworthiness of friends or associates"; (3) "reads hidden demeaning or threatening meanings into benign remarks or events"; (4) "bears grudges or is unforgiving of insults or slights"; (5) "reluctance to confide in others"; (6) "is easily slighted and quick to react with anger or to counterattack"; or (7) "questions fidelity of spouse or sexual partner." In addition, to scoring positive on four of these seven items, it must also be established by the rater that their "occurrence is not exclusively during the course of schizophrenia or a delusional disorder." This latter criterion eliminates the confound described above associated with the number of paranoid delusions and overall mental disability. A variable indicating the presence of a paranoid personality disorder will be analyzed.

Finally, psychopathy was measured by the Hare Psychopathy Checklist: Screening Version (Hare PCL-SV). The Hare PCL-SV consists of two main factors. Factor 1 focuses on affective-interpersonal traits and Factor 2 focuses on behavioral traits. Psychopathy's defining characteristics, such as impulsivity, criminal versatility, callousness, and lack of empathy or remorse make the conceptual link between violence and psychopathy straightforward (Webster et al., 1997). The psychometric properties of the PCL-R have been well-established (Hart & Dempster, 1997; Hart, Hare & Forth, 1994). Following Hart, Cox, and Hare (1995), subjects scoring 13 or higher on the 12 items of the Hare PCL-SV were categorized as probable or definite psychopaths; all other subjects are categorized as nonpsychopaths (see also Harris, Rice and Quinsey, 1994).[13] The reliability of these 12 items was well within the acceptable range (Cronbach's α=.89).

History of Violence. Prior arrest histories were obtained from officially recorded rap sheet data provided by the Pennsylvania State Police Central Repository. The rap sheets for each subject were reviewed by project staff for information on whether or not the subject had been arrested for any serious adult offenses (i.e., murder, manslaughter, aggravated assault, and rape) prior to their enrollment in the study. A dichotomous variable was constructed indicating a past history of violent offenses.

Social support. Social support was measured using a

---

[13]According to Harris, Rice and Quinsey (1994), psychopathy is appropriately conceptualized as a "taxon," i.e., an attribute or condition such as pregnancy that is either present or absent in the individual, rather than as a dimensional factor.

modified version of an instrument developed by Estroff and Zimmer (1994) to assess the social networks of mentally ill individuals. The instrument measures social network size and composition as well as the amount of support available to individual subjects. Support (e.g., having people one can turn to in times of need) was assessed by asking subjects to name specific individuals they talk to about (and who help them with) things that are important to them (i.e., whom they tell their problems to, whom they consider to be important people in their lives, and whom they share special occasions with, such as holidays. Individuals named in response to these questions were considered as providers of social support for the patient. From these items a unique tally of individuals will be constructed eliminating duplicate mentions of specific individuals. The total number of unique supporters will be used to measure the level of support available to individual patients.

Dependent Measure and Statistical Procedures

Measurement of Patient Violence. Questions about violence were adapted from the Conflict Tactics Scale, as expanded by Lidz, Mulvey, and Gardner (1993). Subjects and collaterals in both the patient and collateral samples were asked whether the subject had committed each of eight categories of violent behavior in the past 10 weeks, including: (1) pushing, grabbing or shoving; (2) kicking, biting, or choking; (3) slapping; (4) throwing an object; (5) hitting with a fist or object; (6) sexual assault; (7) threatening with a weapon in hand; and (8) using a weapon. If a positive response was given, the subject or collateral was asked to list the number of times the behavior occurred and to provide details about the incidents (e.g., place, other participants, level of injury).

Only the most serious act for each discrete incident was coded. Incidents of child discipline without injury were excluded.

For the purposes of this study, the following acts were categorized as Violence: acts of battery that resulted in physical injury; sexual assaults; assaultive acts that involved the use of a weapon; or threats made with a weapon in hand. Violent acts reported by any of the three data sources -- subject self-report, collateral report, or official records -- were reviewed by a team of trained coders to obtain a single "reconciled" report of violence. This triangulation of information sources was accomplished by having two coders independently review each case where a violent act was reported by any of the information sources. The codes assigned to the case were then discussed. Discrepancies in coding were resolved through extensive group meetings until a single reconciled report of the violent act was determined.[14]

This study will examine acts of violence that occurred during the first 20 weeks following discharge from WPIC. A 20 week risk period was chosen because it represents the period during which post-discharge violence rates are at their highest (Steadman et al., 1998), and because a majority (62.8%) of the subjects who committed a violent act during the one-year follow-up had done so by the end of this 20-week period. In other words, the 20 week period immediately following discharge from the hospital appears to be the period of greatest risk for violence among this sample of psychiatric patients, and therefore represents the period likely to be of greatest concern to mental health clinicians and policy makers (Steadman et al., 1998; Silver, Mulvey, and

---

[14]The hierarchy of the coding rules used for this reconciliation process is shown in Appendix A.

Monahan, 1999.

Three Operationalizations of Patient Violence. A significant contribution of the proposed study to the field of violence risk assessment is to examine violent outcomes using a multiplicity of methodological approaches. Specifically, this study will operationalize patient violence during the first 20 weeks following hospital discharge in three ways: as a dichotomy, as the time to a first violent act, and as a count of violent incidents. Each of these operationalizations corresponds to a different notion of risk. Measuring prevalence implies a concern with aggregate rates of violence among discharged patients; measuring the time to a first violence incident implies a concern with the imminence of violent outcomes; and measuring counts of violent incidents implies a concern with the overall amount of violence that occurs within a certain period. Clearly, each of these measures reflects a different aspect of what is generally referred to as violence risk. Approaching the study of patient violence using these three measures should shed considerable light on the nature of the relationship between individual-level risk factors, neighborhood conditions, and risk of violence among discharged psychiatric patients.

Violence as a Dichotomous Outcome. The vast majority of recent studies of violence among persons with mental illnesses have operationalized violence as a dichotomous outcome (Steadman et al., 2000; Monahan et al., 2000; Silver, Mulvey, and Monahan, 1999; Steadman et al., 1998; Tardiff, Marzuk, Leon, and Portera, 1997; Lidz, Mulvey, and Gardner, 1993; Link, Andrews, and Cullen, 1992; Swanson et al., 1990; Link et al., 1999). This operationalization is consistent with one of the main purposes of risk assessment research, which has been to isolate individual risk factors that may assist in the identification - from among a group of patients - those likely to commit future acts of violence. Consistent with these prior studies, the proposed study will examine a dichotomous outcome variable in which 1 = Any act of violence during the first 20 weeks following hospital discharge.

Time to First Violence Act. By focusing almost exclusively on violent behavior operationalized as a dichotomous outcome measure, the literature on mental illness and violence offers little insight into the timing of violent incidents. Although specific risk factors have been shown to be associated with increases in the *prevalence* of violence during a given time period (i.e., using a dichotomous outcome measure), little is known about whether and, if so, how these risk factors relate to the *imminence* of violent behavior (i.e., propensity for violence to occur early in time following hospital discharge). It is reasonable to argue that a patient who committed a violent act immediately after hospital discharge had a higher risk of violence (i.e., either due to individual or contextual factors) than a patient who did not commit a violent act until the twentieth week after discharge. It is therefore reasonable to expect that mental health clinicians and policy makers concerned with assessments of violence risk would be concerned not only with the prevalence of violence among certain types of persons, but also with the imminence in time of such behavior. Thus, in addition to examining violence as a dichotomous outcome, this study will also examine the effects of individual and neighborhood level risk factors in terms of the time that lapses before a first violent act of violence.

Counts of Violent Acts. Another important, albeit seldom examined aspect of patient violence, is the number of violent acts committed by patients within a specified time period after hospital discharge. It is reasonable to argue that a patient who committed 10 violent acts following hospital discharge had a higher risk of violence (i.e., again, either due to individual or contextual factors) than a patient who committed only one act of violence during that period. It is therefore reasonable to expect that mental health clinicians and policy makers concerned with assessments of violence risk would be concerned not only with the prevalence and timing of violence among certain types of persons, but also with the *amount* of violent behavior likely to be exhibited by such persons. Yet virtually no studies of violence among mentally disordered persons have focused on counts of violent acts (for a rare exception, see Gardner, Mulvey, and Shaw, 1995). Therefore, in addition to examining violence as a dichotomous outcome and as a time to first violent event, this study will also examine the effects of individual and neighborhood level risk factors in terms of the number of violent acts committed by patients during the first 20 weeks following hospital discharge.

Since the actual time during which subjects were at risk of committing violence in the community may vary, i.e., due to variation in follow-up periods resulting from missed interviews or because subjects were removed from the community (i.e., rehospitalized or incarcerated) for some portion of the 20 week observation period, the models examining violence as either a dichotomous outcome or as a count of violent incidents will be estimated controlling for the number of days at risk in the community. (This issue is handled automatically in the event history analysis).

Statistical Procedures. In accord with the operationalizations of patient violence described above, three statistical procedures will be used to assess patient violence contextually - standard logistic regression (Maddala, 1983), a type of event history analysis known as proportional hazards regression (Allison, 1984; Yamaguchi, 1991), and a form of Poisson regression known as negative binomial regression (Greene, 1993; Gardner, Mulvey, and Shaw, 1995).[15] Logistic regression will be used to analyze violence as a dichotomous outcome; proportional hazards regression will be used to analyze the time to the first violence act; and negative binomial regression will be used to analyze counts of violent incidents. Logistic regression will not be described in detail here as it is fairly well-used in sociological and mental health research. Proportional hazards regression and negative binomial regression, on the other hand, are utilized less frequently in these areas and therefore will be described in some detail.

Event History Analysis. Event history analysis is designed to assess the patterns and correlates of events in time (Yamaguchi, 1991; Allison,1984). It is based on the observation that a certain time period of nonoccurrence must precede an occurrence for it to be recognized as an event. A central concept in event history analysis is the *risk set*, which is the set of individuals who are at risk of event occurrence at each point in time. At the end of each time period, the risk

---

[15]Hierarchical statistical models, such as HLM (Bryk and Raudenbush, 1992), are available which take into account the hierarchical nature of multilevel data and provide more stable estimates of the parameters and standard errors associated with such models. As described in Chapter 3, however, the current study will not make use of HLM. This is because almost two-thirds (61.4%) of the census tracts into which patients were discharged contained only one discharged patient. Without an adequate number of observations nested within neighborhood units, HLM is unable to estimate within neighborhood (e.g., Level 1) models and is thus unable to assess and control for systematic variation within macro-level units. Fortunately, the fact that so many subjects are unique in terms of their census tract location minimizes the risk that observed results will be due to compositional differences within macro-level units (for a recent discussion of this issue, see Robert, 1998).

set is diminished by the number of individuals who experience an event during that period. The rate of the occurrence of events usually varies over time and among subgroups of cases. This rate of occurrence, when attached to a particular moment in time, is referred to as a hazard rate, which is defined as *the probability that a violent event will be committed at a particular point in time by a particular individual given that the individual is at risk at that time.*[16] Note that because the risk set steadily diminishes over time as events occur, it is possible for the hazard rate to increase even when the number of cases which experience events declines. The hazard rate is the fundamental dependent variable in an event history model.

There are two possible advantages to analyzing violent outcomes as event data using a hazard model as opposed to relying solely on a logistic regression model. First, the dichotomization of the dependent variable, violence, may involve a loss of information in terms of the variability of the timing of the violent event. Second, and perhaps more serious, when the effects of covariates on the hazard rate of violence vary with time - that is, when the hazard rate is related to an interaction between the covariates and the timing of violent incidents - the results of a dichotomous analysis become conditional upon the length of the arbitrary fixed observation period (Yamaguchi, 1991). In such a case, the effects of covariates on the dichotomous outcome using a logistic regression model may change significantly if, for example the period of observation is 2 weeks instead of 20 weeks. By explicitly taking into account the timing of violent

---

[16]The term hazard rate comes from biostatistics, where the typical event is death. However, the hazard rate is easily conceived of as a transition rate in which the transition between discrete states, such as nonviolent and violent, is modeled.

events, these potential problems can be avoided.

1. Censored Data Points. One major advantage of hazard-rate models for the analysis of duration data, compared with conventional methods such as linear regression in which the duration is used as the dependent variable, is its capacity to deal with censored observations. Censoring exists when incomplete information is available about the duration of the risk period up to an event because of a limited observation period (i.e., such as when the recall period for a subject is not long enough to include the occurrence of an event, or when the subject drops out of the study before an event is observed). In the current study, the true date of exit from the risk period (i.e., the period during which the subject is at risk for committing a violent act) cannot be known for subjects who have not committed a violent act by the time of their last interview (i.e., the censoring time), or who dropped out of the study prior to the end of the 20 week observation period (i.e., did not complete a second follow-up interview). In addition, subjects may be rehospitalized or incarcerated (i.e., removed from the community) after their discharge from the initial WPIC hospitalization. Such subjects will be treated as censored observations.

In situations such as this in which censoring times vary across individuals in ways that are not under the control of the investigator, censoring is considered as random (Allison, 1984). When censoring is random, event history methods assume that the censoring times are independent of the times at which the events occur, controlling for the explanatory variables in the model. This assumption would be violated if, for example, individuals who were more likely to be violent were also more likely to become censored before they commit a violent act.

Allison (1984) recommends testing this assumption

using a sensitivity analysis consisting of a re-estimations of the event history model treating the censored observations in an extreme way. Specifically, the re-estimation involves recoding the censoring times to equal the longest time observed in the data (regardless of whether that time is censored or uncensored). This recoding has the effect of holding constant the timing of censored cases in the analysis while maintaining the pattern of censored observations and observed events, thereby directly addressing the issue of whether the obtained results depend on the censoring pattern found in the data. According to Allison, if the parameter estimates resulting from the standard analysis are similar to those obtained from this extreme re-estimation, one can be confident that violations of the independence assumption are not serious.

2. Cox Proportional Hazards Regression Model. The Cox proportional hazards model is a semi-parametric event history technique that accounts for censored data points while producing logistic regression-like parameter estimates (Allison, 1984; Yamaguchi, 1991; see Silver, 1995 for a recent application of this procedure). In addition to its superiority over linear regression for data involving censored cases, this procedure provides interpretable parameter coefficients. Specifically, for two predictor variables, the model may be written as:

$$Log\ h(t) = a(t) + b_1x_1 + b_2x_2$$

where h(t) is the hazard rate and a(t) can be any function of time. Because a(t) does not have to be specified, the model is often described as partially parametric or semi-parametric. It is called the *proportional hazards* model because for any two individuals at any point in time, the ratio of their hazards is assumed to be constant. Formally, for any time t, $h_i(t)/h_j(t) = c$, where i and j refer to distinct individuals and c may depend on explanatory variables but not on time. As Allison

(1984:38) points out, "even when the proportional hazards assumption is violated, it is often a satisfactory approximation."

Similar to the odds ratio produced by a logistic regression, the parameter estimates that result from a proportional hazards regression model indicate the multiplicative change in the hazard rate for each unit change in a predictor variable. For dummy coded covariates such as MALE this parameter would be the ratio of the estimated hazard of violence for male patients compared to that of female patients. This can also be understood as the relative risk of violence associated with being male, keeping in mind that a high risk of violence implies shorter lengths of time to the first violence act. A coefficient of 1 indicates that the covariate had no affect on the risk of violence, values greater than 1 indicate a greater risk of violence, and values less than one indicate a reduced risk of violence.

An important issue in any event history analysis is the timing of the measurement of the explanatory variables and whether to treat them as time-constant or as time-varying. Many of the explanatory variables described above are, by definition, time-constant (e.g., gender, race, arrest history). However, others may change over the course of the first 20 weeks following discharge (e.g., neighborhood location, social support, SES). Unfortunately, in the current study, the only variable for which detailed data on timing is available is the violence variable. However, as described above, the purpose of this analysis is to examine the effects of neighborhood characteristics on the relationship between patient violence and *those individual-level risk factors typically used to make prospective predictions of violent behavior prior to discharge from the hospital*. Therefore, treating the explanatory variables as time-constant best reflects the real-world prediction situation in which most mental health clinicians and policy makers find themselves; that is, a prediction of future violence must be made based on what is known at present, given that some of that information may change over time. Thus, all explanatory variables will be treated as time-constant in these analyses. While this approach may introduce error into the estimation of the effects of specific parameters, it is well-suited for addressing the proposed research question involving prospective risk assessment.

Negative Binomial Regression. Analyses of counted data that do not take into account the unique distribution of values across the count scale may produce misleading results. For example, one approach to analyzing counted data is to begin by reducing the counts to a smaller number of categories (i.e., 0-5, 6-10, etc.) or to a dichotomy (i.e., 0-2, 2+). However, reducing counts to categories wastes information and may dilute statistical power. In addition, results may be influenced by the choice of cut-points used to define categories (Gardner, Mulvey, and Shaw, 1995).

Another approach that has been used is to analyze counted data using ordinary least squares regression. However, it has been shown that the linear model can produce nonsensical, negative predicted values and that the hypothesis tests in linear regression depend on assumptions about the variance of scores that are unlikely to be met by counted data (Fox, 1984; Gardner, Mulvey, and Shaw, 1995). Specifically, in ordinary linear regression, the validity of statistical tests are premised on the assumption that the variances of the residuals are the same for all cases (Fox, 1984). However, in Gardner, Mulvey, and Shaw's (1995) study of counts of violence among a mentally disordered sample, the correlation between the predicted counts of violent acts and the absolute values of the residuals produced by the regression model was found to be .32. This problem -

often referred to as heteroscedastisicity - distorts the estimated variances of the parameter estimates causing the standard errors of the regression coefficients to be smaller than their true values, thus inflating the probability of a Type I error.

One typical response to this problem is to seek a transformation of the counted data to eliminate the correlation between the expected counts and the residuals. However, transformations of counted data tend not to produce the desired result because the modal value tends to remain at the bottom of the distribution (e.g., in the data to be analyzed here, 96.0% of all cases had fewer than two violent incidents). Therefore the variance typically remains small at or near the transformed lower-count values relative to other transformed points on the count scale. Perhaps more important, the count integers (i.e., 0, 1, 2, etc.) are the natural and meaningful scale for counted data and should therefore be retained when possible. In other words, instead of transforming the data to meet the assumptions of the ordinary least squares regression model, it is preferable to adopt a regression model that captures the natural features of the data.

The negative binomial regression model is a form of Poisson regression designed for use in counted data. The model has two main advantages over ordinary least squares regression: (1) it incorporates the fact that predicted counts must be non-negative; and (2) it incorporates probability distributions for the dispersion of the dependent variable scores around the expected value that are appropriate given the skewness typically found in counted data. The simplest such regression model is the Poisson regression model. However, unless extremely restrictive assumptions are met (i.e., for all i individuals in the data, the variance of the expected value of y_i is assumed to equal the mean of y_i), the Poisson model produces incorrect estimates of the variance terms and misleading inferences about the regression. In addition, a common problem with assuming that count data based on individual behavior fit a Poisson distribution is that more individuals tend to fall at the high end of the count scale than is expected under the Poisson model. When this happens the observed counts have larger variance than implied by the Poisson distribution and the data are said to be overdispersed (Greene, 1993). Gardner, Mulvey and Shaw (1995) recommend the use of negative binomial regression in which a random term reflecting uncertainty about the true rates at which events occur for individual cases is included in the model. This enables the model to take into account that the variances of the dependent measure for each subject may vary, thus providing a better account of the probability distribution of individual cases (i.e., allowing a larger variance estimate than the Poisson model).

Due to the logarithmic transformation involved in estimating the negative binomial model, interpretation of the parameters produced by the model are comparable to those of the logistic regression and proportional hazards regression models. Specifically, in the negative binomial regression model, a one unit increase in an independent variable multiplies the expected incident count by a factor of $\exp(\beta_j)$, where β_j is the parameter estimate for the jth variable, and a one unit decrease divides the expected incident count by the same amount.

Limitations

A number of limitations are inherent in the proposed study design. First, the study relies on census tract variables to operationalize neighborhood conditions. Although census tracts are well-defined spatial units, they may fail to accurately capture those aspects of "neighborhood" that matter most to individual patients. To the extent that the neighborhood is measured at an improper level of aggregation (i.e., do not correspond to individuals' conceptions of their neighborhoods), results will underestimate the importance of neighborhood conditions in predicting patient violence. Second, this study measures neighborhood location at a single point in time. However, it is reasonable to expect that some subjects will change neighborhoods (i.e., relocate) prior to the end of the 20 week follow-up period. Thus, a point-in-time measure of neighborhood location may not accurately reflect the environment to which a mentally ill person is actually exposed over the observation period.

Third, this study is not able to assess the overall length of residence in a particular neighborhood during a subject's life course; certainly, greater neighborhood effects would be expected for those individuals living in a neighborhood for 20 years as opposed to 20 weeks. Fourth, to the extent that neighborhood-based measures drawn from the Census are tenuously linked to the theoretical processes suggested by social disorganization theory, neighborhood effects may be further underestimated. Finally, the geographic range of neighborhoods represented by the patient sample may be restricted leading to reduced variability in neighborhood measures, thus resulting in an underestimation of neighborhood effects. Given these concerns, caution must be exercised in drawing conclusions regarding the size and nature of the effects of neighborhood conditions on patient violence, as the study may underestimate such effects. These observations are particularly important in assessing the relative contribution of individual- and neighborhood-level factors based on this study (i.e., in terms of variation in violence explained).

Another set of concerns that emerge in any study that

attempts to simultaneously analyze individual and contextual variables is selection bias. Selection bias results from the fact that individuals are not randomly distributed into neighborhoods, but have some degree of choice regarding the neighborhoods in which they live, or are constrained to live in certain neighborhoods due to their individual characteristics (for rare exception, see Rosenbaum, 1991). If, for example, important unmeasured characteristics lead mentally ill individuals both to reside in certain kinds of neighborhoods and to engage in violence, then the apparent effects of neighborhood conditions on patient violence may overestimate the true effects. Selection bias can thus be thought of as a case of omitted variables (Duncan, Connell, and Klebanov,1997). Failure to include such variables may lead to biased parameter estimates of the effects of neighborhood conditions. Such concerns are especially important in studies such as this in which the majority of aggregate units (i.e., census tracts) contain only a single individual case-observation (i.e., discharged patient).

In terms of discharged psychiatric patients, an important omitted variable might be the hospital clinicians' inclination to systematically discharge more dangerous (i.e., potentially violent) patients to disadvantaged neighborhoods. This issue was specifically addressed by Silver, Mulvey, and Monahan (1999) in their recent study of the effects of neighborhood poverty on patient violence (using the same data on which the current analyses will be conducted). They argued that if neighborhood effects were "due to the systematic discharge of more dangerous (i.e., potentially violent) patients to neighborhoods with more concentrated poverty, then we would expect that controlling for factors related to perceived dangerousness would explain away the concentrated poverty effect." Their approach was to assess the effects of neighborhood poverty controlling for individual risk factors typically used by clinicians to assess dangerousness (i.e., gender, age, race, SES, arrest history, substance abuse and psychopathy). These factors were thus considered as a proxy for the omitted selection bias variable. That these factors did not explain away the effect of neighborhood poverty on patient violence suggested that the effect was, to a considerable degree, independent of selection biases related to dangerousness. Similar variables will controlled in the current study.

A second important omitted variable may be an individual patient's ability to attain residence in a neighborhood of his or her choice. People choose where to reside on the basis of factors (especially SES, but also other unmeasured and unmeasurable ones) that may also be related to violent behavior. To what extent the relationship between neighborhood factors and violence may be determined by such selection effects cannot be fully known. However, this issue will be addressed in the current study by examining the significance of neighborhood variables, holding constant individual-level factors such as SES and employment status - factors that may be related to both an individual's ability to choose his or her neighborhood of residence and to the occurrence of violent outcomes.

Despite these limitations, the proposed research represents an important advance in the study of patient violence. Specifically, this research improves upon prior research on patient violence by including the neighborhood context as an explanatory variable and by using multiple analytic strategies to assess a variety of operationalizations of violence. In addition, the proposed research extends the scope of social disorganization research by assessing its relevance for understanding the violent behavior of mentally ill persons.

Table 5.1. Concepts and Measures.

Concepts	Measures
Social Disorganization	Factor solution based on U.S. Census tract-level data
Demographics	
Gender	1 = Male; 0 = Female
Age	Number of years between birth and target hospitalization
Race	1 = African American; 0 = White
Marital Status	1 = Married or living with someone as if married at the time of hospital admission
SES	Weighted combination of education and occupation [Hollingshead and Redlich, 1958]
Employment Status	1 = Employed either full or part-time at the time of admission to the hospital
Length of Residence	Number of months resided at address where subject lived upon admission to hospital
Clinical Factors	
Substance Abuse Diagnosis	1 = Yes; 0 = No [DSM-IIIR Checklist: Janca and Helzer, 1990]
Anger	Behavioral component of Novaco Anger Scale (NAS) [Novaco, 1994]
Impulsiveness	Non-Planning component of Barratt Impulsiveness Scale (BIS) [Barratt, 1994]
Paranoid Personality Disorder	1 = Yes; 0 = No [Structured Interview for DSM-IIIR Personality (SIDP-R): Pfohl et al., 1989]
Psychopathy	1 = Probable/Definite Psychopath; 0 = Not [Hare Psychopathy Checklist: Screening Version (PCL-SV, Hart, Cox, and Hare, 1995)]
History of Violence	1 = Any prior adult arrests for serious crimes against persons; 0 = No such history [measured from official arrest data]
Social Support	Number of supporters [instrument developed by Estroff and Zimmer, 1994]

CHAPTER 6

Descriptive Results and Bivariate Relationships

In previous chapters, a theoretically grounded set of research hypotheses was proposed to assess the utility of employing a social disorganization perspective in predicting violence among persons with mental illnesses. In addition, rationales were provided for the selection of specific variables for analysis. In this chapter, descriptive statistics and bivariate relationships are presented for all variables included in the study.

The chapter is organized into three sections. The first section describes the census tract measures that were obtained from 1990 U.S. Census Summary Tape Files to characterize the neighborhoods into which patients were discharged after treatment at the Western Psychiatric Institute and Clinic (WPIC). These data are factor analyzed to arrive at a smaller number of theoretically relevant underlying dimensions and compared with neighborhood data representing the living environments of the general population.

The second section describes the individual-level risk factors that will be examined. These variables will serve as controls in assessing neighborhood effects and will be used to analyze cross-level interactions. Bivariate associations among these variables are presented and discussed.

The third section outlines the various operationalizations of the dependent measure that will be used in subsequent analyses to draw inferences about the relationship between neighborhood factors and patient violence. These include the prevalence of violence (i.e., dichotomous outcome), the imminence of violence (i.e., time to first violent incident), and the amount of violence (i.e., number of incidents) committed by psychiatric patients during the first 20 weeks following hospital discharge. The section concludes with an assessment of the bivariate associations between these operationalizations of risk for violence and the explanatory variables included in the study.

In approaching these analyses, it is important to keep in mind that the main purpose of this study is to assess *neighborhood effects* and not to conduct an in-depth analysis of individual-level risk factors.[17] Thus, many of the individual-level predictor variables in this study (i.e., gender, age, race, substance abuse disorder, anger, impulsiveness, paranoid disorder, and psychopathy) were selected because they have been found to be significantly associated with patient violence (i.e., in this and/or other studies; see Chapter Two). Other individual-level variables were selected because they help to isolate the effects of analogous neighborhood-level measures (i.e., SES, employment status, marital status, length of residence). One variable (i.e., number social supporters) was selected because it is hypothesized to be a

---

[17]Such analyses constitute the main focus of ongoing work by the MacArthur Foundation's Violence Risk Assessment Study (Steadman, et al., 2000; Monahan et al., 2000).

partial mediating factor in the neighborhood-violence relationship (see Chapter 4). Finally, since this study is focused exclusively on violent behavior that occurred in the community (i.e., not during a hospitalization or incarceration), a variable representing the number of days at risk in the community is included to control for *time* as an opportunity factor that may affect the occurrence of community violence.[18] It should be added that controlling for these variables also minimizes the likelihood that observed neighborhood-level effects are due to selection bias (see chapter 5).

The Neighborhoods in which Patients Live

The 270 patients in this study were discharged into 145 census tracts in Allegheny County, PA after receiving treatment at WPIC. For each tract, 11 measures were taken from U.S. Census files to represent the structural antecedents of social disorganization. Table 6.1 provides operational definitions for each of these measures and Table 6.2 provides their means, standard deviations, and quartile values.[19] Although descriptive of the 145 neighborhoods into which

---

[18]This variable is included in the logistic and negative binomial regression models only since the timing of events is handled automatically in the proportional hazards regression models.

[19]As discussed in Chapter 5, these measures were selected because they reflect key structural conditions suggested by a long line of theorists as exogenous causes of social disorganization (Shaw and McKay, 1942; Bursik, 1988; Sampson and Groves, 1989; Sampson and Lauritsen, 1994; Sampson, Raudenbush, and Earls, 1997).

patients were discharged after treatment at WPIC, these data do not enable the reader to compare the neighborhoods in which patients live to those of the general population; nor do they take into account the uneven distribution of patients across neighborhoods. As mentioned in previous chapters, 56 of the 145 census tracts (38.6%) into which patients were discharged received more than one discharged patient; 12 census tracts received more than two discharged patients; and one tract received a total of nine of the 270 discharged patients in this study (see Table 6.3). Treating each neighborhood as equally weighted in the computation of summary statistics (as do the figures in Table 6.2) does not provide adequate descriptive information about the neighborhood contexts into which the typical patient was discharged after treatment. To ascertain this information requires that each census tract be weighted in proportion to the number of discharged patients residing within the census tract boundaries before calculating summary statistics. Taking this approach allows us to answer the question: In what types of neighborhoods are we most likely to find the typical discharged psychiatric patient; and are these neighborhoods better or worse off than what we observed assuming an even distribution of patients across neighborhoods.

In addition, although not central to these analyses, it is also informative to compare the types of neighborhoods into which patients were discharged to the types of neighborhoods in which the general population of Allegheny County, PA tends to live.[20] Such a comparison provides perspective in terms of how different the neighborhood

---

[20]Allegheny County includes all of the areas into which it was at least theoretically possible for treated patients to have been discharged.

contexts of discharged patients are from those of the general population. This comparison is provided in Table 6.4. The figures in the Patient column are weighted according the actual distribution of the 270 patients within the 145 census tracts; the figures in the GP column are weighted according to the actual distribution of the 1,334,196 individuals counted by the 1990 Census as residing within the 467 census tracts of Allegheny County, PA.

Overall, Table 6.4 suggests that discharged patients tend to live in neighborhoods that are more disadvantaged than those of the general population of Allegheny County. For example, the typical discharged patient lives in a neighborhood in which 24.4% of the population falls under the poverty line compared to 11.7% for the general population - a greater than 2-fold difference; similarly, the typical patient lives in a neighborhood where 31.7% of the households are female-headed compared to 18.7% for the general population; further, the typical patient lives in a neighborhood that is 31.2% black compared to 11.2% for the general population - an almost 3-fold difference. Indeed, all of the differences reported in Table 6.4 point in the direction of discharged patients residing in less advantaged neighborhoods. These differences are also seen by examining the quartile values listed in the right side of the table. For example, looking at the 75th percentile column, we see that whereas one-quarter of the neighborhoods in which discharged patients lived had poverty rates above 40.0%, the comparable figure for the general population is 15.0%.

Furthermore, by comparing the figures in Table 6.4 to those of Table 6.2, we can observe the effect of weighting according to the number of discharged patients in each census tract. For example, comparing the poverty rates in these tables shows that the effect of weighting was to increase the poverty rate (from 18.7% to 24.4%), indicating that even among the 145 census tracts in which discharged patients are represented, they tend to concentrate in those neighborhoods with higher rates of poverty. Indeed, consistent with the results of the patient-general population comparison reported above, all of the comparable figures in these two tables point in the direction of discharged patients clustering in less advantaged neighborhoods.

The relationship between disadvantaged neighborhood conditions and mental status observed for this sample of patients is consistent with a large number of previous studies reporting a relationship between individual SES and mental status among the general population (Dohrenwend, 1990; Holzer et al, 1986; Dohrenwend et al., 1980; Dohrenwend, 1983; Jarvis, 1971; Leighton et al., 1963; Srole et al., 1962; Hollingshead and Redlich, 1958; Odegaard, 1956; Faris and Dunham, 1939). This association has generally been explained in terms of two processes: social stress and social selection. The social stress explanation holds that rates of mental disorder are higher among lower-SES persons because of the greater environmental adversity they experience, which facilitates mental disturbance among them (Faris and Dunham, 1939; Hollingshead and Redlich, 1958; Leighton et al., 1965; Srole et al., 1962; Dohrenwend, 1990; Aneshensel and Sucoff, 1996). The social selection explanation argues that rates of mental disorder are higher among lower-SES groups because persons with mental disorders drift downward or fail to rise out of lower SES groups (Jarvis, 1971; Odegaard, 1956; Dohrenwend, 1990). Others have argued that both processes are at work (Dohrenwend, 1990). After reviewing evidence bearing on this relationship over the course of recent decades, Dohrenwend (1990:41) concluded that "this issue has remained unresolved to this day." Nor will this issue be resolved in the current study. The comparisons provided above merely confirm the results of these prior studies for this sample of discharged patients using neighborhoods as the basis for comparison.

Factor Analysis of Neighborhood Variables. Consistent with prior research (Land, McCall, and Cohen, 1990; Sampson, Raudenbush, and Earls, 1997), a considerable degree of inter-correlation was found among these 11 neighborhood measures (see Table 6.5). Out of a total of 55 bivariate correlations, 45 were statistically significant and 11 showed bivariate correlations above .70. Overall, these correlations suggest that social problems tend to concentrate within neighborhoods. For example, neighborhood poverty was significantly correlated with public assistance income (r=.79), female-headed households (r=.76), unemployment (r=.81), vacant dwelling (r=.68), and percent black (r=.65).

According to Land, McCall, and Cohen (1990:942), simultaneously analyzing measures with high levels of intercorrelation (such those described here) may lead to what Gordon (1968) called the "partialing fallacy." The partialing fallacy refers to a situation in which all of the explained variance in a regression model is attributed to the particular regressor (among a highly correlated set of regressors) that possesses the (possibly very slightly) higher correlation with the dependent variable - even though there may be no theoretical or substantive basis for making such an attribution. To solve this problem, Land, McCall, and Cohen recommend developing a factor analytic solution which reduces the multicollinearity problem by extracting from the highly correlated measures a unifying, conceptually meaningful empirical factor.

To assess whether these neighborhood measures could be reduced to a smaller number of underlying factors, a principal components factor analysis was conducted (Kim and Mueller, 1978). In the first part of the analysis, a

Varimax (i.e., orthogonal) rotation was used to identify the simplest set of independent (i.e., uncorrelated) factors. However, given prior research in this area (Land, McCall, and Cohen, 1990; Sampson and Lauritsen, 1994) and given the inter-correlations described above, this approach makes the somewhat unjustifiable assumption that the underlying structure of the patient neighborhoods can be summarized by factors that are completely unrelated (i.e, uncorrelated) to one another. Based on prior research in the area of social disorganization (Sampson and Lauritsen, 1994), it is reasonable to expect a certain degree of association between the underlying structural dimensions of urban neighborhoods. Thus, in the second part of the analysis, the orthogonality restriction was relaxed by re-estimating the underlying factors using an oblique rotation (i.e., allowing the resulting factors to correlate). This approach makes the less restrictive assumption that the factors describing the structure of patient neighborhoods are at least somewhat related to one another. Factor solutions obtained using these two approaches were virtually identical (i.e., in terms of factor loadings, number of factors identified, and explained variance). Thus, given the significant inter-correlations among the constituent variables (Table 6.5), the oblique rotation solution is presented, allowing the underlying factors to be correlated.

Consistent with prior theory and research, the poverty-related variables given in Table 6.3 were highly associated and loaded on the same factor (see Table 6.6). With an eigenvalue equal to 6.2 (explained variance = 56.6%), the first factor was dominated by high loadings for public assistance (.92), female-headed households (.91), poverty rate (.87), unemployment rate (.87), percent black (.81), high income (-.80), vacant dwellings (.76), managerial employment (-.75), and mean household wage (-.73). Clearly, the predominant interpretation of this factor is as a measure of neighborhood disadvantage. The second factor depicted in Table 6.6 (eigenvalue equal to 1.8, explained variance = 16.4%) was dominated by two variables, residential stability (-.90) and percent foreign born (.86), suggesting an interpretation in terms of residential movement and mobility in and around a neighborhood.[21] Together, these 2 factors accounted for 73% of the variation in the data.[22] To represent these factors parsimoniously, factor regression scores were calculated by weighting each measure by its factor loading and summing the resulting products. The Pearson correlation between the two factors based on the oblique solution was a modest -.06 (p=.49), indicating that the factors were largely distinct.[23]

In terms of social disorganization theory, it may seem somewhat surprising that this analysis did not yield a

---

[21]The correspondence between percent foreign-born in a neighborhood and neighborhood residential mobility is believed to occur in the following ways. First, due to the need to obtain housing upon arriving in the U.S., foreign-born persons are expected to be more likely to find their way into neighborhoods with a fair amount of residential turnover - as it is in such neighborhoods that they are more likely to find available housing. Second, foreign-born persons are expected, on average, to have been residing in the U.S. (and therefore at their current location) for less time that than their U.S.-born counterparts due to their more recent arrival to the U.S..

[22]A third factor was initially identified but was too weak to interpret substantively (eigenvalue = 1.07 and no factor loading greater than .58). The factor solution was therefore limited to a two factors.

[23]Comparable results were obtained from a factor analysis of all 467 census tracts in Allegheny County, PA suggesting that these results adequately reflect the structure of neighborhoods in the larger area and are not the result of having analyzed only the 145 neighborhoods in which patients were found to reside.

population heterogeneity factor, which might have combined percent black and percent foreign born, but rather found percent black to correspond with overall neighborhood disadvantage. However, there is a fair amount of current research suggesting a strong association between percent black and neighborhood disadvantage (Massey and Denton, 1993; Wilson, 1987; Sampson and Lauritsen, 1994). Massey and Denton attribute high levels of racial segregation to widespread housing and employment discrimination. They argue that this type of discrimination has touched off a cycle of disadvantage, leading to decreased access to jobs and adequate schools among individual residing in largely black areas, thereby reinforcing the significant association between neighborhood racial composition and disadvantage. Indeed, Sampson and Lauritsen (1994) argue that this result has a long history in criminology. They point out that despite the strong emphasis on ethnic heterogeneity as a structural determinant in social disorganization theory, Shaw and McKay's (1942) original research showed a tendency for rates of delinquency (i.e., one indicator of neighborhood problems) to be higher in predominantly black/foreign born areas than in areas of maximum heterogeneity.

Patient Characteristics

As described in the previous chapter, 14 measures reflecting individual patient characteristics are examined in these analyses (see Table 6.7). Descriptive statistics for each of these measures is provided in Table 6.8.[24] As shown, 55.2%

---

[24]Five of these variables were found to contain missing data: SES (1 case), anger (1 case), impulsiveness (7 cases), psychopathy (17 cases), and paranoid

of the patients were males; the mean age was 30.4 (sd=6.2); 33.7% were black; 32.6% were married or living with someone as though married at the time of hospitalization; the mean 5-category SES score was 1.7 (sd=1) indicating a tendency for patients to fall at the lower end of the SES range of 1 to 5; 41.5% were employed either full- or part-time at the time of hospitalization; and the mean length of residence (at the address at which patients lived prior to hospitalization) was 42.4 months (sd=78.6). These figures are representative of the larger population of acute psychiatric admissions from which this sample was drawn (Steadman et al., 1998).

In terms of clinically relevant risk factors, 32.6% of patients had substance abuse disorders, consistent with a rate of 33.8% recently reported by Swartz et al., (1998) for a sample of 331 involuntarily admitted psychiatric inpatients awaiting outpatient commitment treatment in North Carolina. The mean anger score was 29.5 (sd=7.2), consistent with findings previously reported for a sample of 158 psychiatric patients selected from three hospitals in California (Novaco, 1994). The mean impulsiveness score was 24.0 (sd=7.9), consistent with findings previously reported for other samples of psychiatric patients (Barratt, 1994). A total of 17.4% of patients were diagnosed with paranoid personality disorders; 20.0% scored as psychopaths; and 23.3% had histories of

---

personality disorder (34 cases). For the non-dichotomous measures (SES, anger, and impulsiveness), missing data were handled using mean-substitution. For the dichotomous measures (psychopathy and paranoid personality disorder), mode-substitution was used in order to maintain the original metric of the measure. To further assess the impact of missing data, all multivariate analyses will also be run including dummy variables representing those cases for which missing values were substituted. To the extent that these analyses yield similar results, parameter estimates based on the former (i.e., simpler) strategy will be reported.

adult arrests for serious crimes against persons. In addition, the mean number of social support providers (i.e., persons reported by subjects as providing assistance during times of need) was 5.5 (sd=2.1).

Table 6.9 provides bivariate correlations for these measures. These results conform, in large part, to what might be expected regarding the characteristics of U.S. citizens in general and discharged psychiatric patients, in particular. For example, we see that black patients were more likely than white patients to have substance abuse disorders (r=.44) and paranoid disorders (r=.23), more likely to be angry (r=.23), more likely to score as psychopathic (r=.35), more likely to have histories of violent arrests (r=.35), less likely to be employed (r=-.16) and less likely to receive social support (r=-.18). These associations are consistent with recent depictions of the dire conditions of urban life among African Americans (Massey and Denton, 1993; Wilson, 1987). Male patients in this sample were more likely than female patients to have a violent arrest history (r=.29), more likely to exhibit symptoms of psychopathy (r=.17), and more likely to be employed (r=.20).

Patients with substance abuse disorders were more likely than those without substance abuse disorders to be impulsive (r=.26), more likely to score as psychopathic (r=.32), more likely to have violent arrest histories (r=.44), and less likely to receive social support (r=-.21). Patients diagnosed with paranoid personality disorders were more likely than those without paranoid disorders to be angry (r=.20), impulsive (r=.20), and psychopathic (r=.28). Patients scoring as psychopaths were more likely than those not scoring as psychopaths to be black (r=.35), less likely to be employed (r=-.18), more likely to have substance abuse diagnoses (r=.32), and more likely to be angry (r=.16) and impulsive (r=.24). Finally, persons who resided in their residences for longer periods of time tended to be employed (r=.16), less angry (r=-.12), and less impulsive (r=-.19) compared to those with shorter residential tenures. In general, these associations confirm for psychiatric patients what is well-known for other members of the general population, namely that individual problems tend to cluster within specific groups of individuals.

Next, we assess whether individuals with such characteristics tend to cluster within certain neighborhood environments. To address this question, bivariate associations between the patient characteristics and Neighborhood Factors were computed (Table 6.10). As shown, the Neighborhood Disadvantage Factor correlates positively (at the p<.05 level) with African American race (r=.66), diagnosed substance abuse disorder (r=.32), psychopathy (r=.31), history of violent arrest (r=.29), anger (r=.21), and paranoid personality disorder (r=.19). In addition, the Neighborhood Disadvantage Factor correlates inversely with employment (r=-.24), individual SES (r=-.15), and social support (r=-.23). The Neighborhood Mobility Factor correlates inversely with length of residence (r=-.25), marital status (r=-.20), psychopathy (r=-.12), anger (r=-.13), and African American race (r=-.13).

These bivariate associations are important for two reasons. First, they represent the first systematic attempt to relate individual-level risk factors for violence among persons with mental illnesses to the neighborhood environments in which they live. Second, they yield results largely consistent with what may be expected based on prior research and theory. For example, the strong correlation between patient race and neighborhood disadvantage is consistent with current research on residential segregation that has documented a strong association between minority racial status and disadvantage within U.S. metropolitan areas

(Massey & Denton, 1993); and the significant association between neighborhood disadvantage and individual substance abuse and violence histories is consistent with ethnographic research recently reported by Anderson (1990, 1997). The significant negative correlations between individual SES, employment status and neighborhood disadvantage is consistent with human capital models of residential attainment (Logan, Alba, McNulty, & Fisher, 1996; South & Deane, 1993). Further, the negative correlation between social support and neighborhood disadvantage is consistent with Cullen's (1994) suggestion that neighborhood social disorganization fosters individual social isolation by undermining supportive relationships. Finally, the strong correlation between neighborhood residential mobility and individual length of residence is consistent with the systemic model depicted by Kasarda and Janowitz (1974) and Sampson (1988).

Somewhat surprising are the negative associations found between the Neighborhood Mobility Factor and levels of anger and psychopathy among discharged patients, given the positive associations between these patient characteristics and the Neighborhood Disadvantage Factor. However, an examination of the bivariate associations between the Neighborhood Mobility Factor and the census tract measures used as inputs in the factor analysis suggests that high-mobility neighborhoods in these areas of Allegheny County also tend to score as less disadvantaged on a number of dimensions. For example, high-mobility neighborhoods tend to have fewer families receiving public assistance income ($r=-.21$, $p<.001$), have lower unemployment rates ($r=-.14$, $p<.05$), and contain a smaller proportion of black residents ($r=-.17$, $p<.01$). Thus, the negative associations between anger and psychopathy and neighborhood mobility are not inconsistent with the positive associations found between these individual-level measures and neighborhood disadvantage.

Post-Discharge Violence

As mentioned above, the criterion measure for this study is operationalized in three ways: as a dichotomous outcome measure indicating the occurrence of any violent incident during the 20 week follow-up period; as an event-history consisting of the time to the first act of post-discharge violence; and as a count of violent incidents over the follow-up period. In constructing these measures, only violent incidents that occurred prior to a subsequent rehospitalization or incarceration were counted as valid incidents. This criterion resulted in the exclusion of two recorded violent incidents because they occurred after the subject had been rehospitalized or incarcerated. Because no violent incidents had occurred for these 2 cases prior to rehospitalization, they were treated as non-violent and censored at the date of rehospitalization. This was done in order to ensure that the dependent measure focused specifically on post-discharge community violence and was not confounded with subsequent treatment in a mental health or jail facility.

For all cases, a variable indicating the number of days at risk for violence was computed. For cases for whom no rehospitalization or incarceration occurred, this measure includes the number of days between hospital discharge and the time of the last community interview. It is during these days that a subject may have committed an act considered as violent by this study. For cases for whom a rehospitalization or incarceration did occur, the measure of time at risk includes the number of days between hospital discharge and their first rehospitalization or incarceration. This period was chosen in order to focus the analysis on patient violence occurring after the target hospitalization at WPIC. For the proportional hazards model, the time to a first violent incident was computed as the number of days between hospital discharge and the date of the first violent incident; cases for whom no violent incident occurred were coded as censored and given a time measure equal to the number of days at risk as described above.

Of the 270 discharged patients in this study 33 (12.2%) were involved in at least one act of violence toward others during the 20 week period following hospital discharge. This rate of violence is consistent with that reported for the larger (3 site) MacArthur Study (Steadman et al., 1998). Together, these subjects committed a total of 88 separate violent incidents (Table 6.11 displays the distribution of violent incidents). The median time between hospital discharge and a first violent incident (for the 33 subjects who had a violent incident) was 36.0 days (sd=47).

Before addressing the core research hypotheses using the multivariate models described in Chapters 4 and 5, the bivariate associations between violence and each of the individual- and neighborhood-level risk factors are examined (Table 6.12). Documenting bivariate associations provides an important backdrop to the interpretation of multivariate results. In order to examine these relationships, each of the three statistical models described in Chapter 5 (logistic regression, Cox proportional hazards regression, and negative binomial regression) were estimated with each risk factor separately. This strategy, as opposed to that of bivariate Pearson correlations, was adopted to take into account the unique distributional qualities of the various dependent measures.

Displayed in Table 6.12 are the exponentiated parameter coefficients from each of the models. For the logistic regression models, these coefficients may be interpreted as odds ratios representing the multiplicative difference in the odds of committing a violent act for each unit change in the independent variable (where the odds of committing a violent act is the probability of committing an act divided by the probability of not committing an act). For example, the odds of committing a violent act for black patients was 2.7 times greater than the odds for white patients. For the Cox model, the exponentiated parameter coefficient may be interpreted as the multiplicative difference in the hazard of committing a violent act associated with a unit change in the independent variable (where the hazard of committing a violent act is the probability of committing an act given that one has not been previously committed). For example, the hazard of committing a violent act for black patients was 2.5 times greater the hazard for white patients. For the negative binomial model, the exponentiated parameter coefficient is interpreted as the multiplicative difference in the number of violent acts expected for a unit change in the independent variable. For example, that black patients are estimated to commit 3.6 times more violent acts than white patients.

Overall, these bivariate analyses yielded strikingly consistent results. The following characteristics were found to be significantly associated with all three operationalizations of violence risk: black racial status, substance abuse disorder, anger, paranoid disorder, psychopathy, history of violent arrests, and neighborhood disadvantage. Discharged patients with these characteristics tended exhibit higher rates of violence, sooner after discharge, and with greater frequency. For male gender and married status, significant positive associations were found for violence prevalence and timing but not for numbers of incidents. For social support, a significant negative association was found with the number of violent incidents only. No significant associations with violence were found for age, SES, employment status, length of residence, and neighborhood mobility. It is particularly interesting to note that whereas the Neighborhood Disadvantage Factor was significantly related to violence for all three models, the individual SES measures was not. This finding raises substantive questions about the use of individual-SES as a proxy measure for a patient's neighborhood setting when assessing violence risk.

It is also important that, in contrast to the theoretical arguments laid out in previous chapters, no significant effect of neighborhood mobility on patient violence was observed; nor was there an effect for individual length of residence on patient violence. Yet, as observed above, neighborhood mobility and individual length of residence were significantly associated with one another in the theoretically predicted direction ($r=-.25$, $p<.001$). Thus, although there is an association between neighborhood mobility and patient mobility, neither variable seems to affect patient violence. All of the effect of neighborhood conditions on patient violence seems, based on these bivariate associations, to be attributable to neighborhood disadvantage.

Conclusion

The bivariate analyses provided in this chapter suggest: (1) that discharged psychiatric patients tend to reside in more disadvantaged neighborhood settings than other members of the general population; and (2) that there is a significant bivariate association between residence in a disadvantaged neighborhood and violence among mentally ill persons. Indeed, the second finding appears all the more striking given the first. That is, the fact that discharged psychiatric patients tend to reside in less advantaged neighborhoods implies less variation overall in the neighborhood contexts into which patients are discharged. From a statistical standpoint, this restricted range of variation in patient neighborhood contexts renders the association between neighborhood conditions and patient violence more difficult to achieve. Thus, it might be anticipated that with a larger variation in neighborhood contexts the association between neighborhood context and patient violence would be stronger. Given the restricted range of patient neighborhoods, the finding reported here can be interpreted as a conservative test of the association between neighborhood conditions and patient violence.

The next step in this study is to examine the multivariate models that address the specific research questions raised in the previous chapters. These models will focus specifically on assessing the overall importance of neighborhood factors in predicting patient violence including an assessment of mediating and cross-level interaction effects. In the following chapter, the results of these analyses are presented.

Table 6.1. Neighborhood Measures.

Variable	Description
% Poverty	Percentage of all households with incomes below federal poverty line
% Public Assistance	Percentage of households with public assistance income
Mean Household Wage	Mean household wage and salary income among households with such income
% High Income	Percentage of families with annual income greater that $50,000
% Female-Headed Households	Percentage of families headed by females
% Unemployment	Percentage of persons 16 years or older that are unemployed
% Executive/Managerial Jobs	Percentage of employed persons 16 year or older that are in executive or managerial positions
% Residentially Stable	Percentage of persons age 5 or older living in the same housing unit five years earlier
% Vacant Dwellings	Percentage of housing units that are vacant
% Black	Percentage of residents who are black
% Foreign Born	Percentage of residents who are foreign born

Table 6.2. Descriptive Statistics: Pittsburgh Patient Neighborhoods (n=145).

				Percentiles	
Variable	Mean	Standard Deviation	25th	50th	75th
% Poverty	18.7	16.7	5.0	14.0	26.0
% Public Assistance	11.9	12.2	3.8	8.0	16.0
Mean Household Wage	$31.8k	$16.7k	$23.1k	$29.4k	$37.7k
% High Income	24.5	18.2	10.5	20.0	36.5
% Female-Headed Households	26.8	19.2	12.5	21.0	34.0
% Unemployment	9.2	8.1	4.0	7.0	11.0
% Executive/Managerial Jobs	11.2	6.0	7.0	11.0	14.0
% Residentially Stable	60.3	14.4	54.8	64.0	70.0
% Vacant Dwellings	8.9	6.2	4.0	8.0	13.0
% Black	22.6	32.0	1.0	6.0	31.0
% Foreign Born	4.6	5.3	2.0	3.0	5.3

Table 6.3. Distribution of Patients Across Census Tracts.

Number of Tracts	Number of Discharged Patients Per Tract	Cumulative Percentage of Census Tracts
89	1	61.4
28	2	80.7
12	3	89.0
4	4	91.7
7	5	96.6
1	6	97.2
1	7	97.9
2	8	99.3
1	9	100.0
145 Total	270 Total	

Table 6.4. Comparison of Pittsburgh Patient (n=270) and General Population (GP) Neighborhoods (n=1,334,196).

Variable	Mean		Standard Deviation		Percentiles 25th		50th		75th	
	Patients	GP	Patients	GP	Patients	GP	Patients	GP	Patients	GP
% Poverty	24.4	11.7	20.3	12.8	8.0	4.0	18.0	7.0	40.3	15.0
% Public Assistance	14.7	7.9	14.8	9.1	5.0	3.0	9.0	5.0	19.0	10.0
Mean Household Wage	$28.7k	$37.0k	$15.0k	$16.1k	$20.3k	$25.5k	$25.9k	$33.8k	$34.6k	$41.6k
% High Income	21.4	29.2	17.9	18.0	9.0	15.0	16.0	25.0	30.3	41.0
% Female-Headed Households	31.7	18.7	22.6	13.9	14.8	10.0	24.0	14.0	40.0	22.0
% Unemployment	12.0	6.9	11.3	6.0	4.0	4.0	9.0	5.0	13.0	8.0
% Executive/Managerial Jobs	10.3	12.8	5.8	5.9	6.0	9.0	10.0	12.0	13.0	16.0
% Residentially Stable	57.0	65.3	14.9	11.5	44.0	60.0	60.0	67.0	69.0	73.0
% Vacant Dwellings	10.5	6.3	6.7	4.9	5.0	3.0	10.0	5.0	14.0	8.0
% Black	31.2	11.2	36.5	23.0	3.0	1.0	12.0	2.0	53.0	6.0
% Foreign Born	5.1	3.1	5.7	3.1	1.0	1.0	3.0	2.0	8.0	4.0

Table 6.5. Bivariate Pearson Correlations: Pittsburgh Patient Neighborhoods (n=145).

Variable	1	2	3	4	5	6	7	8	9	10
1. % Poverty										
2. % Public Assistance	.79***									
3. Mean Household Wage	-.58***	-.52***								
4. % High Income	-.58***	-.62***	.84***							
5. % Female-Headed Households	.76***	.89***	-.55***	-.62***						
6. % Unemployment	.81***	.86***	-.49***	-.58***	.78***					
7. % Executive/Managerial Jobs	-.55***	-.59***	.63***	.77***	-.60***	-.55***				
8. % Residentially Stable	-.35***	.05	.09	-.14	-.10	-.01	-.03			
9. % Vacant Dwellings	.68***	.63***	-.47***	-.53***	.65***	.58***	-.47***	-.21**		
10. % Black	.65***	.79***	-.40***	-.48***	.81***	.75***	-.49***	-.07	.55***	
11. % Foreign Born	.03	-.33***	.15	.34***	-.27***	-.29**	.29***	-.56***	-.06	-.27**

* p<.05   ** p<.01   *** p<.001

Table 6.6. Principal Components Factor Loadings: Pittsburgh Patient Neighborhoods (N=145).*

Variable	Factor Loading
Disadvantage	
% Public Assistance	.92
% Female-Headed Households	.91
% Poverty	.87
% Unemployment	.87
% Black	.81
% High Income	-.80
% Vacant Dwellings	.76
% Executive/Managerial Jobs	-.75
Mean Household Wage	-.73
Mobility	
% Residentially Stable	-.90
% Foreign Born	.86

* Explained Variation = 73.2%
Rotation = Oblimin with Kaiser Normalization
Factor Correlation = -.06

Table 6.7. Individual Characteristics: Concepts and Measures.

Concepts	Measures
Demographics	
Gender	1 = Male; 0 = Female
Age	Number of years between birth and target hospitalization
Race	1 = African American; 0 = White
Marital Status	1 = Married or living with someone as if married at the time of hospital admission
SES	Weighted combination of education and occupation [Hollingshead and Redlich, 1958]
Employment Status	1 = Employed either full or part-time at the time of admission to the hospital
Length of Residence	Number of weeks resided at address where subject lived upon admission to hospital
Clinical Factors	
Substance Abuse Diagnosis	1 = Yes; 0 = No [DSM-IIIR Checklist: Janca and Helzer, 1990]
Anger	Behavioral component of Novaco Anger Scale (NAS) [Novaco, 1994]
Impulsiveness	Non-Planning component of Barratt Impulsiveness Scale (BIS) [Barratt, 1994]
Paranoid Personality Disorder	1 = Yes; 0 = No [Structured Interview for DSM-IIIR Personality (SIDP-R): Pfohl et al., 1989]
Psychopathy	1 = Probable/Definite Psychopath; 0 = Not [Hare Psychopathy Checklist: Screening Version (PCL-SV, Hart, Cox, and Hare, 1995)]
History of Violent Arrests	1 = Any prior adult arrests for serious crimes against persons; 0 = No such history [measured from official arrest data]
Social Support	Number of supporters [instrument developed by Estroff and Zimmer, 1994]

Table 6.8. Individual Characteristics: Descriptive Statistics.

Variable	Mean	(s.d.)
Demographics		
Male (0/1)	55.2%	
Age (in years)	30.4	(6.2)
Black - Race (0/1)	33.7%	
Married or Live as married (0/1)	32.6%	
SES (5 category)	1.7	(1.0)
Employed (0/1)	41.5%	
Length of Residence (in months)	42.4	(78.6)
Clinical Factors		
Substance Abuse Diagnosis	32.6%	
Anger	29.5	(7.2)
Impulsiveness	24.0	(7.9)
Paranoid Personality Disorder	17.4%	
Psychopathy	20.0%	
History of Violent Arrests	23.3%	
Social Support	5.5	(2.1)

Table 6.9. Bivariate Pearson Correlations: Pittsburgh Patients (n=270).

Variable	1	2	3	4	5	6	7	8	9	10	11	12	13
1. Male													
2. Age	-.03												
3. Black - Race	.01	.08											
4. Married	-.06	.14*	.09										
5. SES	.09	.23***	-.10	.06									
6. Employed	.20**	-.12	-.16*	-.01	.31***								
7. Length of Residence	.10	-.10	-.11	-.10	.03	.16**							
8. Substance Abuse d/o	.12	.13*	.44***	.01	-.09	-.02	-.10						
9. Anger	-.04	-.13*	.23***	.09	-.22***	-.08	-.12*	.13*					
10. Impulsiveness	.04	.10	.09	-.01	-.25***	-.13*	-.19**	.26***	.27***				
11. Paranoid PD	.01	-.04	.23*	.10	-.07	-.09	-.07	.24	.20**	.20**			
12. Psychopathy	.17**	.02	.35***	.05	-.13*	-.18**	.06	.32***	.16**	.24***	.28**		
13. Violence Arrest Hx	.29***	.18**	.35***	.12*	-.07	-.04	-.11	.44***	.19**	.23***	.14*	.38***	
14. Social Support	-.12	-.12*	-.18**	.03	.12	.20**	.11	-.21***	-.13*	-.21**	-.10	-.09	-.25***

* p<.05 ** p<.01 *** p<.001

Table 6.10. Pearson Correlations between Patient and Neighborhood Characteristics.

Patient Characteristic	Neighborhood Disadvantage	Neighborhood Mobility
Male	.03	.06
Age	.15*	.01
Black - Race	.66***	-.13*
Married	.02	-.20**
SES	-.15*	.04
Employed	-.24***	-.08
Length of Residence	-.05	-.25***
Substance Abuse d/o	.32***	-.07
Anger	.21**	-.13*
Impulsiveness	.05	.09
Paranoid PD	.19**	.03
Psychopathy	.31***	-.12*
History of Violent Arrests	.29***	-.09
Social Support	-.23***	-.07

* p<.05 ** p<.01 *** p<.001

Table 6.11. Numbers of Incidents Committed by Discharged Patients During 20 Week Follow-Up.

Number of Violent Incidents	Number of Discharged Patients
0	237
1	15
2	8
3	4
5	3
6	1
7	1
17	1
Total	270

Table 6.12. Bivariate Associations with Violence.

Variables	Logistic Regression Exp(b)	Cox Model Exp(b)	Negative Binomial Exp(b)
Male	2.8*	2.8*	1.8
Age	0.9	1.0	1.0
Black	2.7**	2.5**	3.6**
Married Status	2.5*	2.2*	1.6
SES	0.8	0.9	0.8
Employed	0.8	0.8	0.6
Length of Residence	1.0	1.0	1.0
Drug Disorder	3.3**	3.0**	4.0**
Anger	1.1**	1.1**	1.1**
Impulsiveness	1.1*	1.1*	1.1
Paranoid Disorder	4.6***	3.7***	7.9***
Psychopathy	5.7***	5.0***	8.6***
Prior Violent Arrests	3.3**	3.0**	3.9**
Social Support	0.9	0.9	0.8*
Neighborhood Mobility	0.7	0.8	0.6
Neighborhood Disadvantage	1.7***	1.6***	1.8**

* p<.05 ** p<.01 *** p<.001

CHAPTER 7

Multivariate Results

In the previous chapter, two neighborhood-level factors were derived - a Neighborhood Disadvantage Factor and a Neighborhood Mobility Factor, and bivariate associations between these Factors and each of the individual-level measures and control variables were presented. In addition, bivariate associations between all of these measures and each of the three operationalizations of patient violence (i.e., prevalence, imminence, and amount) were examined.

This chapter examines more closely the relationships among the individual-level risk factors (e.g. Male, Age, Black, Drug Diagnosis, Anger, Impulsiveness, Paranoid Disorder, Psychopathy, Prior Violent Arrests, Spouse/Partner, SES, Employed, Length of Residence, and Social Support) and the Neighborhood Mobility and Neighborhood Disadvantage Factors. Following this examination, each of the research questions posed in Chapter 4 are addressed. These questions include: (1) Does neighborhood social disorganization contribute to models predicting violent behavior among discharged psychiatric patients over and above the effects of known individual-level predictors and control variables?; (2) What is the relative importance of neighborhood- and individual-level characteristics in terms of the amount of variation in violence explained?; (3) What is the functional form of the relationship between neighborhood social disorganization and patient violence (i.e., are there concentration effects)?; (4) To what extent does social support mediate the social disorganization-violence relationship?; and (5) Do the effects of individual-level characteristics such as substance abuse and paranoid disorders interact with levels of social support in their relationship patient to violence.

Contextual Effects on Individual-Level Risk Factors for Patient Violence

Before addressing the research questions listed above, it is useful to examine more closely the impact of the Neighborhood Factors on the *bivariate* associations between each of the individual-level risk factors and patient violence. The purpose of such an analysis is to assess the extent to which including neighborhood-level measures alters our understanding of the effects of known individual-level risk factors for violence among discharged psychiatric patients.

A preliminary analysis of this type was recently reported by Silver, Mulvey, and Monahan (1999) using the same data set upon which the current study is based. In that study, however, the neighborhood context was operationalized solely in terms of concentrated poverty (i.e., a dichotomous measure coded 1 for subjects residing in neighborhoods with a greater than 30% poverty rate); violence was operationalized solely as a dichotomous outcome measure; and only a limited number of individual-level risk factors were assessed. Nonetheless, Silver, Mulvey, and Monahan found that (1) concentrated neighborhood poverty added significantly to the prediction of patient violence, over and above the effects of the individual-level predictors; (2) the socioeconomic status of individual patients was less predictive of violence than the level of poverty in the neighborhood; (3) the positive effect of black racial status on patient violence was mediated by the poverty measure; and (4) no evidence of cross-level interaction effects were detected. Although these authors concluded that the implications of these findings lie in emphasizing the importance of assessing contextual conditions, as well as individual characteristics, when predicting risk for violence, they also stated that "...it remains for future research on violence risk to more fully elaborate the theoretical underpinnings of an ecological approach, and to incorporate a wider variety of theoretically derived dimensions and indicators of the neighborhood context" (p.251).

Here, I build upon this initial work in the following ways: (1) by operationalizing two theoretically relevant dimensions of neighborhood structure (i.e., disadvantage and mobility), derived from *multiple* Census measures; (2) by assessing a wider range of individual-level risk factors (i.e., including measures of anger, impulsiveness, paranoid disorder, and social support); and (3) by employing multiple operationalizations of violence. Following Silver, Mulvey, and Monahan (1999), the analyses presented in this section focus on what happens to the relationship between each of the individual-level risk factor and violence after the Neighborhood Factors are held constant. In addition, cross-level interaction effects are assessed.

To conduct these analyses, the following steps were taken. First, each individual-level risk factor was entered into a prediction model to observe its initial coefficient. Then, the Neighborhood Factors were entered into each model. In order to differentiate between the effects of the two Neighborhood Factors (i.e., disadvantage and mobility), each

Factor was entered separately, and then both were entered simultaneously to assess their combined effects. Finally, to check for the presence of cross-level interactions, interaction terms between both Factors and each individual-level variable were entered. Table 7.1 summarizes the results of these analyses, for the logistic, Cox, and negative binomial regression models. (Unless otherwise indicated, the change in model fit associated with the addition of the interaction terms was not significant). The shaded cells in Table 7.1 are meant to draw attention to those individual-level risk factors whose effects were observed to change in the presence of the Neighborhood Factors.

Table 7.1 shows that in most instances in which a change was observed, the result was to diminish the effect size associated with the individual-level predictor. Variables in this category included: Black racial status (Model 3), Drug Disorder (Model 4), Paranoid Disorder (Model 7), Prior Violent Arrests (Model 8), and Psychopathy (Model 9). For these risk factors, the decrease in effect held across all three operationalizations of the dependent measure and was due largely to the inclusion of the Neighborhood Disadvantage Factor. This suggests that part of the bivariate association between each of these risk factors and violence may be related to the fact that scoring as high-risk on these measures is positively correlated with residence in a disadvantaged neighborhood (see Chapter 6). Indeed, it is worth noting that in all but one of the 42 final models presented in Table 7.1 (i.e., controlling for each individual-level risk factor separately), the Neighborhood Disadvantage Factor was found to be significantly related to increased violence. The one exception was for the negative binomial regression with Black racial status (Model 3C) where the effect of Neighborhood Disadvantage attained a significance level of $p=.07$.

For gender (Model 6), the pattern was different. Models 6A and 6B show that the positive effects of Male gender on predicting the transition from a not-violent to a violent status (as measured by the logistic and Cox regression models) was not affected by either of the Neighborhood Factors. In other words, males were more likely to engage in violence sooner after discharge than females across neighborhood conditions. However, this was not the case for the association between Male gender and overall *amounts* of violence committed after discharge. Specifically, a significant, negative interaction effect was detected between Male gender and Neighborhood Disadvantage. In light of the positive coefficient for the main effect of Male in this model, the negative interaction effect indicates that the difference between the amounts of violence committed by males and females decreased at higher levels of neighborhood disadvantage.

To illustrate this effect, the sample was divided into two parts based on the median Neighborhood Disadvantage Factor score. Within the high- and low-Disadvantage groups, the number of violent acts per male and female patient was computed. This analysis revealed that in the high-Disadvantage group, the number of violent acts committed per male and per female was quite similar (0.49 [36 acts for 73 males] compared to 0.42 [26 acts for 62 females]). However, in the low-Disadvantage condition, the difference in the amounts of violence committed by males and females was striking: the number of violent acts per male was 0.33 [25 acts for 76 males] compared to 0.02 for females [1 act for 59 females]. Thus, neighborhood disadvantaged appears to have a stronger effect on the *amounts* of violence committed by females.

In addition, it is important to highlight that the significant positive bivariate association between Black racial status and patient violence was eliminated when the Neighborhood Disadvantage Factor was introduced to Model 3. This suggests significant overlap in the amount of variation in violence explained by both race and Neighborhood Disadvantage, a result that is consistent with the large Pearson correlation of .66 ($p<.001$) previously observed between Black racial status and Neighborhood Disadvantage (Chapter 6). This pattern corresponds with current research on residential segregation that has documented a strong association between minority racial composition and levels of poverty within U.S. metropolitan areas (Massey & Denton, 1993). Neighborhood disadvantage thus appears to be particularly important for understanding the relationship between racial status and violence by discharged patients (Silver, 2000b).

Taken together, these findings underscore the importance of measuring neighborhood-level factors when assessing risk for violence among discharged psychiatric patients. Moreover, these results indicate that in ignoring neighborhood-level factors (as do most studies of violence and mental illness), researchers run the risk of mis-estimating the main effects of individual-level risk factors.

Research Questions

1. Does neighborhood social disorganization contribute to models predicting violent behavior among discharged psychiatric patients over and above the effects of known individual-level predictors and control variables?

To address this question, all of the individual-level risk factors and control variables (e.g. Male, Age, Black, Drug Diagnosis, Anger, Impulsiveness, Paranoid Disorder, Psychopathy, and Prior Violent Arrests, Spouse/Partner, SES,

Employed, Length of Residence, and, for the logistic regression and Poisson models only, Time at Risk) were entered first into each multivariate equation.[25] This allowed the individual risk factors and control variables to explain as much of the variation in patient violence as possible before assessing the main effects of the Neighborhood Factors. The variable Social Support (operationalized as the number of persons reported to provide assistance to individual patients) was not entered at this time, as its role as a mediating factor is assessed below when Question Four is evaluated.

After controlling for the individual-level variables, the Neighborhood Mobility and Neighborhood Disadvantage Factors were entered into each equation, first separately to assess the main effect of each Factor, and then simultaneously to assess their combined main effect.

Neighborhood Effects and the Prevalence of Patient Violence: Logistic Regression Results

Table 7.2 shows the results using logistic regression to analyze the dichotomous outcome, violence in the first twenty weeks following hospital discharge. Model 1 of Table 7.2 shows that when all of the individual-level risk factors and control variables were entered into the logistic regression equation together, only Male, Psychopathy, and Spouse/Partner had significant ($p<.05$) positive main effects on patient violence. The positive effects found for Male and Psychopathy are consistent with much prior research on patient violence in which males have tended to exhibit higher rates of violence than females (Klassen and O'Conner, 1994)

---

[25] As mentioned in previous chapters, these individual-level variables represent risk factors that have been featured in the literature on violence and mental illness as well as control variables important for isolating the effects of the neighborhood context (see Chapter 5).

and psychopaths have tended to exhibit higher rates of violence than non-psychopaths (Hart, Hare and Forth, 1994).

The positive effect of being married (or living with someone as if married) on the occurrence of violence is consistent with current knowledge about the targets of violence by persons with mental illnesses (Steadman, et al., 1998; Estroff and Zimmer, 1994). Specifically, when mentally ill individuals act out violently, they tend to target family members and other know individuals. Hiday (1995, 1997) interprets this pattern of violence as reflecting the propensity for mentally ill persons to be involved in "tense situations" as caretakers attempt to monitor and control their behavior (i.e., by attempting to dissuade them from odd or disruptive behavior or urging them to take prescribed psychotropic medications).

Several of the individual-level risk factors that were reported as significantly related to violence at the bivariate level were not significant when examined in the multivariate logistic regression equation (Model 1). These variables were: Black, Drug Disorder, Anger, Impulsiveness, Paranoid Disorder, and Prior Violent Arrests. Thus, over and above the effects of Male, Psychopathy, and Spouse/Partner, these variables did not contribute significantly to the prediction of patient violence during the first 20 weeks following discharge. However, note that the positive effect of Paranoid Disorder approached statistical significance ($p=.07$). In general, there appears to be a fair amount of overlap in the predictive abilities of these risk factors.

Model 2 of Table 7.2 indicates that adding the Neighborhood Mobility Factor did not significantly increase the amount of variation in violence explained and had only a negligible impact on the coefficients of the individual-level variables in the model. Model 3 indicates that adding the Neighborhood Disadvantage Factor yielded a significant improvement in explained variation in the occurrence of patient violence ($p<.05$) over and above the effects of the individual-level risk factors and control variables already in the model. Specifically, the odds of committing a violent act were significantly greater for discharged psychiatric patients residing in more disadvantaged neighborhoods compared to those residing in less disadvantaged neighborhoods, holding constant all other risk factors. Interestingly, the effect of controlling for Neighborhood Disadvantage in the context of these other risk factors was to cause the small protective effect associated with the variable, Black (see Models 1 and 2), to increase substantially (see Model 3). Specifically, after controlling for Neighborhood Disadvantage and the other individual-level predictors, the effect of black racial status in this multivariate equation was to substantially reduce risk for violence.

Finally, Model 4 indicates that adding both the Neighborhood Disadvantage and Neighborhood Mobility Factors to the equation significantly improved the amount of variation in violence explained. Further, the lack of change in pseudo-R^2 between Models 3 and 4 indicates that most of the model improvement was due to the Neighborhood Disadvantage Factor.

Neighborhood Effects and the Timing of Patient Violence: Cox Regression Results

Table 7.3 presents the results using Cox regression to analyze the time to the first act of violence that occurred during the first twenty weeks following hospital discharge. Model 1 of Table 7.3 shows that when all of the individual-level predictors were entered together, only Male and Psychopathy had significant ($p<.05$) positive effects on patient violence. Specifically, the hazard rate for violence (i.e., the probability of committing a violent act given that one had not been previously committed) was higher for males and psychopaths, controlling for other individual-level predictors.

As above, several of the individual-level risk factors that were reported as significantly related to the time to a first violent event at the bivariate level were not significant when examined in the multivariate Cox regression equation. These variables were: Anger, Black, Drug Disorder, Impulsiveness, Paranoid Disorder, Prior Violent Arrests, and Spouse/Partner. However, note that the positive effects of Paranoid Disorder and Spouse/Partner both approached statistical significance ($p=.07$). Thus, as above, there appears to be a fair amount of overlap in the explanatory power of these measures in terms of the timing of patient violence.

Model 2 of Table 7.3 indicates that adding the Neighborhood Mobility Factor did not significantly increase the amount of explained variation in the hazard rate of violence and had only a negligible impact on the effect sizes of the individual-level variables in the model. Model 3 indicates that adding the Neighborhood Disadvantage Factor yielded a significant improvement in explained variation in the hazard rate of patient violence ($p<.05$). Specifically, the hazard of committing a violent act was observed to be greater for discharged psychiatric patients residing in more disadvantaged neighborhoods compared to those residing in less disadvantaged neighborhoods, holding constant all other risk factors. Interestingly, as was found in the logistic regression results, the effect of controlling for the Neighborhood Disadvantage Factor was to increase the protective effect associated with the variable, Black. Finally, Model 4 indicates, that adding both the Neighborhood Disadvantage and Neighborhood Mobility Factors to the equation significantly improved the amount of variation in violence explained.

<u>Neighborhood Effects and Frequency of Patient Violence:</u>

Negative Binomial Regression Results

Table 7.4 displays the same analyses using negative binomial regression to analyze the amount of violence committed by each subject during the first twenty weeks following hospital discharge. Model 1 of Table 7.4 shows that when all of the individual-level predictors were entered together, Male, Psychopathy, Paranoid Disorder, and Age had significant (p<.05) effects on patient violence. Specifically, the number of violent incidents was found to be higher among younger, more psychopathic, paranoid males, controlling for other individual-level predictors. Interestingly, the effect of Age on the predicted counts of violence was not significant when analyzed at the bivariate level (see Table 7.1 Model 1C) but emerged as a significant protective factor only after holding constant the other individual-level predictors. Further, as above, several of the individual-level risk factors that were reported as significantly related to the frequency of violence at the bivariate level were not significant when examined in the multivariate equation, again suggesting overlap in explanatory power. These variables were: Anger, Black, Drug Disorder, Prior Violent Arrests, and Spouse/Partner.

Model 2 of Table 7.3 indicates that adding the Neighborhood Mobility Factor did not significantly increase the amount of explained variation in the frequency of violence and had only a negligible impact on the effect sizes of the individual-level variables in the model. Model 3 indicates that adding the Neighborhood Disadvantage Factor yielded a significant improvement in explained variation in the predicted counts of patient violence (p<.05). Specifically, the frequency of violent acts was observed to be greater for discharged psychiatric patients residing in more disadvantaged neighborhoods compared to those residing in less disadvantaged neighborhoods, holding constant all other risk factors. Interestingly, as was found in the logistic and Cox regression results, the effect of controlling for Neighborhood Disadvantage was to increase the protective effect of Black. In addition, although gender and Neighborhood Disadvantage were previously found to interact in predicting the frequency of violence (see Model 6C of Table 7.1), this interaction was not significant when entered in conjunction with the other covariates. Finally, Model 4 indicates, that adding both the Neighborhood Disadvantage and Neighborhood Mobility Factors to the equation significantly improved the amount of variation in violence explained.

Summary. The results of these analyses of the effects of neighborhood mobility and neighborhood disadvantage on each of the three operationalizations of patient violence (i.e., prevalence, imminence, and amount) yielded consistent results (see Table 7.5 for a summary comparison of the final models from each analysis). Most importantly, in all three approaches, neighborhood disadvantage was found to have a significant positive impact ($p<.05$) on patient violence over and above the effects of significant individual-level risk factors and control variables. This pattern of results suggests that although the propensity for discharged psychiatric patients to commit violent acts is, in part, related to their individual characteristics (e.g., in all three models Male, Psychopathy, and Paranoid were found to have positive main effects on patient violence), the level of disadvantage in the neighborhood of residence is also an important predictor of subsequent violence, explaining variation in patient violence not accounted for by the individual-level measures. Specifically, mentally ill persons living in disadvantaged neighborhoods were found to be more likely to commit violent acts sooner after discharge and with greater frequency than mentally ill persons living in less disadvantage neighborhoods.

As an illustration of the magnitude of the association between the Neighborhood Disadvantage Factor and patient violence, the final multivariate logistic regression model shown in Table 7.5 was used to compute predicted probabilities of patient violence at varying levels of Neighborhood Disadvantage. For illustrative purposes, the individual-level measures and the Neighborhood Mobility Factor score were first arbitrarily fixed at their respective mean values. Then, the Neighborhood Disadvantage Factor score was made to vary from a low of 2 standard deviations below the mean value for all patients to a high of two standard deviations above the mean, moving in single standard deviation units. The mean values of the individual-level and Neighborhood Mobility measures were then weighted along with each of the Neighborhood Disadvantage values by their respective unstandardized logistic regression coefficients, summed and then exponentiated to produce the predicted odds. These predicted odds were then transformed to probability values using the formula: p=odds/(1 + odds).

The resulting predicted probability values for each of the 5 levels of Neighborhood Disadvantage are presented in Table 7.6. As shown, the probability of violence for discharged patients residing in the lowest Disadvantage condition (i.e., 2 standard deviations below the mean for all patients) was predicted at .03, indicating that for every 100 patients discharged to such neighborhoods, 3 would be expected to engage in violence. By contrast, discharged patients residing in the highest Disadvantage condition (i.e., 2 standard deviations above the mean for all patients) was .21, that is for every 100 patients discharged to such neighborhoods, 21 would be expected to engage in violence. Thus, moving from the lowest to the highest Disadvantage condition resulted in a 7-fold increase in the risk of patient violence.

Interestingly, however, neighborhood mobility was found *not* to have a significant impact on patient violence. This finding, in conjunction with those reported above, suggests that the mechanism by which neighborhood characteristics affect the violent behavior of mentally ill persons in this Pittsburgh sample has less to do with residential movement in and around the neighborhood (and the associated decrements in neighborhood cohesion which such movement has been hypothesized to bring about) and more to do with the overall degree of economic and social disadvantage (i.e., crime, poverty, disorder, social isolation, etc.) inherent in the neighborhood environment.[26]

These analyses also revealed that, after controlling for neighborhood disadvantage and other individual-level measures, the effect of black racial status emerged as protective, achieving its highest level of significance (p=.08) in the negative binomial regression equation. In considering this finding, it is important to point out that prior research on the effects of race have not found uniform effects (Klassen and O'Conner, 1994). For example, although Klassen and O'Conner (1989) found racial differences in patient violence, Rossi et al. (1986) found no differences by race after controlling for diagnosis. Similarly, Tardiff and Sweillman (1980) found an overall difference by race but not when controlling for education. Taken together, these findings suggest that studies of patient violence that include racial status as a predictor but do not control for other relevant measures, such as neighborhood disadvantage, diagnosis, and education, run the risk of not only of overstating the effect of race, but based on the results reported above, perhaps

---

[26]This issue is discussed in more detail in the concluding chapter.

misstating the direction of the effect as well. In light of these results, future research on patient violence should focus more specifically on the effect of racial status, taking into account neighborhood conditions and other relevant predictors.

2. What is the relative importance of neighborhood- and individual-level characteristics in terms of the amount of variation in violence explained?

In the majority of empirical studies that find significant neighborhood effects, these effects are generally much smaller than the effects of individual and family characteristics (Ellen and Turner, 1997). Focusing specifically on the effects of neighborhood poverty on patient violence, Silver, Mulvey, and Monahan (1999:248) found that although concentrated poverty contributed significantly to the prediction of patient violence, "the majority of the explained variation in violence belongs to the individual-level risk factors." Based on these prior findings, it was hypothesized that, due to the indirect nature of the effects of social disorganization on violence (i.e., via informal control, cultural differentiation, and neighborhood social support networks), individual-level characteristics would account for the majority of explained variation, as they likely reflect more proximate causes of patient violence.

To address this question, the pseudo-R^2s produced by a series of logistic regression models were examined. First, comparing the pseudo R^2s from Models 1 and 3 in Table 7.2 we see that 3% out of a total pseudo R^2 of 31% was uniquely attributable to the Neighborhood Factors. That is, after controlling for the individual-level predictors, adding the Neighborhood Factors to the logistic regression equation resulted in a 3% percentage-point increase in the pseudo-R^2 of the model (from 28% to 31%). Second, to ascertain the amount of variation uniquely attributable to the individual-level predictors, these variables were added to a separate logistic regression model controlling for the Neighborhood Factors. Upon adding the individual-level variables, the pseudo-R^2 increased from 9% (i.e., the total amount of variation explained by the Neighborhood Factors alone) to 31% indicating that the individual-level predictors accounted for a total unique contribution of 22%. This leaves 6% (31%-[22% + 3%]) as shared variation.[27]

While computationally simple, the above analyses make a crucial point: Although Neighborhood Disadvantage was found to contribute significantly to the prediction of patient violence, the effects of neighborhood accounted for far less of the explained variation than did the individual-level predictors (unique pseudo-R^2=3% vs. 22%). In addition, these analyses showed that a good amount of the explained variation in patient violence (6% out of a total pseudo-R^2 of 31%) is shared by both individual- and neighborhood-level factors suggesting that studies of patient violence which neglect to specify neighborhood-level factors (as most do) run the risk of overstating the explanatory power of individual-level predictors.

In interpreting these findings, however, it is important to note that only 2 dimensions of the neighborhood context derived from Census data (i.e., disadvantage and mobility) were compared with over a dozen individual-level predictors. To what extent this same pattern of results would have been obtained if it had been possible to measure a more

---

[27]Pseudo R^2s for the Cox and negative binomial models are less well-known and not readily available from existing software packages. However, a similar comparison using the log-likelihood values produced by the Cox and negative binomial regression models yielded a similar pattern of results.

theoretically exhaustive and extensive array of neighborhood factors (i.e., including the strength and interconnectedness of neighborhood social networks, collective efficacy, neighborhood rates of crime and violence, etc. – each of which is featured in the social disorganization literature) can not be determined from these data. It is reasonable to expect, however, that with a more theoretically exhaustive set of neighborhood-level factors, the amount of variation in patient violence accounted for (i.e., relative to individual-level predictors) might increase. Such an analysis, however, must await future research.

3. What is the functional form of the relationship between neighborhood social disorganization and patient violence (i.e., are there concentration effects)?

The question of concentration effects hinges on a determination of the functional form of the relationship between neighborhood conditions and patient violence. To assess functional form in relation to the Neighborhood Disadvantage and Neighborhood Mobility Factors using each of the three operationalizations of violence (i.e., prevalence, imminence, and amount), the same three multivariate techniques were used as above (i.e., logistic, Cox, and negative binomial regression). Using each technique, a series of nested models were estimated. In the first model, the Neighborhood Factor was entered into each equation followed by a term representing this Factor squared. The purpose of entering the squared term into each of the statistical models was to test for non-linearity in the relationship between each Neighborhood Factor and patient violence (South and Crowder, 1999). A significant, positive squared term would indicate that the slope of the relationship between Neighborhood Disadvantage (or Mobility) and patient violence was greater for neighborhoods scoring higher on Disadvantage (or Mobility) than for those scoring lower.

Table 7.7 summarizes these results. As shown, this analysis finds no evidence of concentration effects in the relationship between neighborhood conditions and patient violence. The squared terms in each of the three models (for both Disadvantage and Mobility) were nonsignificant. Thus, for the Neighborhood Mobility Factor, no statistically discernable relationship is found with patient violence, while for the Neighborhood Disadvantage Factor, a linear pattern best describes the relationship with patient violence (i.e., the effect of the linear coefficient was significant and positive using all three statistical approaches; see Tables 7.2-7.4). These analyses suggest that a positive, linear relationship exists between levels of Neighborhood Disadvantage and patient violence with no evidence of concentration effects. For the Neighborhood Mobility Factor, no discernable relationship with patient violence was found.

4. To what extent does social support mediate the social disorganization-violence relationship?

In Chapter 4, it was hypothesized that the effect of neighborhood social disorganization on patient violence might operate, in part, via the amount of social support available to discharged patients. This hypothesis was derived largely from Cullen's (1994) and Faris and Dunham's (1939) arguments that the individual-level social supports available to mentally ill persons are due in part to the degree of support available at *the neighborhood level* and that, therefore, mentally ill persons residing in socially disorganized neighborhoods would have fewer opportunities to develop supportive relationships.[28] It was further argued by Cullen (1994) that the more social support a person received, the less likely it was that he or she would engage in violence. These theoretical arguments led to the hypothesis that social support would mediate the association between neighborhood social disorganization and violence, suggesting that the effect of social disorganization on patient violence operated, in part, indirectly by means of its effect on social supports.

In the following analyses, the extent to which Social Support (i.e., the number of social supporters reported by subjects to have provided assistance during times of need) mediates the relationship between neighborhood conditions and patient violence is examined. In order to assess this hypothesis, coefficients representing the relationship between the Neighborhood Factors and patient violence were observed before and after introducing the social support measure to each of the three statistical models (i.e., logistic, Cox, and negative binomial regression). To the extent that the parameter estimates associated with the neighborhood factors are reduced with the introduction of the social support measure, this would provide evidence of statistical mediation indicating that the effect of the neighborhood operates, at least in part, through the amount of social support available to individual subjects. The results of these analyses are reported in Table 7.8.

A comparison of the models with and without Social Support indicates that adding Social Support had no effect on the relationship between neighborhood conditions and patient

---

[28]Recall that consistent with these arguments, the number of social supporters available to individual patients was reported in Chapter 6 to be significantly lower for those patients living in more disadvantaged neighborhoods (Pearson $r = -.23$, $p < .001$).

violent using all three operationalizations of patient violence. Specifically, the size of the coefficients associated with the Neighborhood Disadvantage and Neighborhood Mobility Factors in all three statistical models remained unchanged when Social Support was introduced to the equations. Thus, although at the bivariate level the Neighborhood Disadvantage Factor was found to be negatively related to the number of social supporters available to patients and positively related to patient violence (both of which are consistent with the theoretical arguments developed in Chapter 4), the effect of Neighborhood Disadvantage on patient violence was not mediated by the level of social support available to individual subjects. While supporting the notion that neighborhood social disorganization constrains the social supports available to individual patients, these findings do not support the argument that social supports are a mediating mechanism by which neighborhood conditions affect the propensity for patients to commit violence.

Indeed, analyses reported in the previous chapter found no significant bivariate association between social support and violence for either the logistic or Cox regression models, and only a modestly significant effect (p=.04) for the negative binomial model - an effect which was rendered non-significant when evaluated in conjunction with each of the following covariates separately: Anger, Black, Drug Disorder, Impulsiveness, Paranoid Disorder, Prior Violent Arrests, Psychopathy, Employed, Neighborhood Disadvantage, and Neighborhood Mobility.

5. Do the effects of individual-level characteristics such as substance abuse and paranoid disorders interact with levels of social support in their relationship patient to violence?

In Chapter 4, it was hypothesized that in addition to affecting the overall amounts of violence committed by discharged psychiatric patients, the conditions found within socially disorganized neighborhoods might also moderate the strength of the association between certain individual-level risk factors and violence. In particular, the theoretical discussion focused on two types of psychiatric disorders diagnosed prior to hospital discharge: substance abuse disorders and paranoid disorders.

Paranoid Disorders. In terms of paranoid disorders, it was argued (based on ideas drawn from Faris and Dunham, 1939) that a lack of opportunities to develop and sustain socially supportive relationships in socially disorganized neighborhoods would increase the isolation of individuals suffering from paranoid disorders, thus leading to increases in the likelihood that paranoid beliefs would result in violence. Conversely, it was argued that the greater opportunities to develop and sustain socially supportive relationships in socially organized neighborhoods would decrease the social isolation of paranoid individuals, thereby decreasing the likelihood that paranoid symptoms would result in violence. Individual social support was thus conceived as a proximate conditioning factor in the relationship between paranoid symptoms and violence.

To evaluate this interaction effect using the three multivariate techniques as above (i.e., logistic, Cox, and negative binomial regression) an interaction term representing the product of Social Support and Paranoid Disorder was entered in to each equation, controlling for the individual-level measures. As shown in Table 7.9, this analysis yielded no significant interaction effect across the equations. In all three models, the interactions between Social Support and Paranoid Disorders was found to be nonsignificant.[29]

Drug Disorder. In Chapter 4, two alternative hypotheses were posited regarding the effect of neighborhood social disorganization on the relationship between substance abuse and violence, both of which were rooted in arguments posed by Faris and Dunham (1939). First, it was hypothesized that mentally ill individuals previously diagnosed with drug abuse disorders may be more likely to commit violent acts when they reside in socially disorganized neighborhoods where there are greater opportunities to find drugs via "other addicts and dope peddlers," thus leading to increases drug use and violence. Alternatively, it was hypothesized that it is in socially *organized* neighborhoods (i.e., those which contain functioning social networks to facilitate the use, trade, and tolerance of drugs) that mentally ill persons with substance abuse disorders would be more likely to use drugs, thereby increasing their likelihood of committing violence. That is, the trust required to share and deal drugs may be more prevalent in neighborhoods characterized by dense and stable social relationships, leading to increased violence among residents with substance abuse problems.

As a first step in the analysis, data are presented in tabular form. For the purpose of presentation, the sample was first divided into two parts based on the median Neighborhood Disadvantage and median Neighborhood Mobility Factor scores. The resulting sample partitions consisted of (1) subjects residing in neighborhoods in the

---

[29]In addition, consistent with the results reported in Model 7 of Table 7.1, non-significant coefficients were obtained when interactions between Paranoid Disorder and the Neighborhood Factors were assessed for all three operationalizations of violence.

upper half of the Neighborhood Disadvantage distribution; and (2) subjects residing in neighborhoods in the lower half of the Neighborhood Disadvantage distribution. The same was done for the Neighborhood Mobility Factor score resulting in two sample partitions consisting if (1) subjects residing in neighborhoods in the upper half of the Neighborhood Mobility distribution; and (2) subjects residing in neighborhoods in the lower half of the Neighborhood Mobility distribution.[30]

A common element in the competing hypotheses outlined above is that drug *use* patterns among persons previously diagnosed with substance abuse disorders would be found to differ across neighborhood environments. Specifically, the first hypothesis implies that drug disordered patients discharged into socially disorganized neighborhoods would exhibit higher rates of drug use compared to similar patients discharged into less disorganized neighborhoods, while the alternative hypothesis suggests that drug disordered patients discharged into socially disorganized neighborhoods would exhibit lower rates of drug use compared to similar patients discharged into less disorganized neighborhoods.

Therefore, before examining the conditioning effects of the Neighborhood Factors on the relationship between diagnosed substance abuse disorders and patient violence, it is essential to examine the patterns of self-reported post-discharge *drug use* across neighborhood conditions for patients previously diagnosed with substance abuse disorders. These data are reported in Table 7.10. As shown in the upper portion of the table, comparable rates of self-reported post-discharge drug use were found among the 88 individuals

---

[30]The median value of each Neighborhood Factor was chosen as a cut-point in order to maximize the size of the samples in both the upper and lower conditions.

previously diagnosed with drug abuse disorders across the two Neighborhood Disadvantage conditions. The rates of drug use for diagnosed subjects were 60.7% and 57.6% in the Below-Median and Above-Median Disadvantage groups, respectively. Similarly, as shown in the lower portion of Table 7.10, comparable rates of self-reported post-discharge drug use were found across the two Neighborhood Mobility conditions. The rates of drug use for diagnosed subjects were 64.6% and 51.3% in the Below-Median and Above-Median Mobility groups, respectively.[31]

These finding call into question both of the hypotheses outlined above. Since both hypotheses hinged on a finding of differential patterns of post-discharge drug use across neighborhoods, neither is supported by these findings regarding drug use patterns. Thus, not surprisingly, when the above hypotheses regarding the interaction between Drug Disorder and neighborhood conditions were tested in terms of patient violence within each of the three statistical models (i.e., logistic, Cox, and negative binomial; see Table 7.11), none of the interaction terms were found to be significant. The relationship between having been diagnosed with a drug disorder and patient violence does not appear to be conditioned by the levels of disadvantage and mobility in the neighborhood environment.

---

[31]Although not reflected in this table, it is also worth noting that a significantly greater proportion of patients diagnosed with substance abuse disorders were discharged into the Above-Median Disadvantage neighborhoods than into Below-Median Disadvantage neighborhoods (44.4% vs. 20.7%; Fisher's Exact Test, $p<.01$). This is consistent with the significant bivariate correlation between Neighborhood Disadvantage and Drug Disorder reported in Chapter 6 (Pearson $r=.32$, $p<.001$).

Summary of Multivariate Results

In summary, the results of these multivariate analyses indicate that Neighborhood Disadvantage enhances the prediction of patient violence over and above the effects of known individual-level predictors and control variables, and that this effect appears to be linear (i.e., no evidence of concentration effects were found). However, although Neighborhood Disadvantage was found to have a significant main effect on patient violence, the individual-level risk factors analyzed in this study were found to account for the lion's share of explained variation in violence based on all three operationalizations of patient violence. The Neighborhood Mobility Factor was found not to be predictive of patient violence.

Analyses of the extent to which individual social supports mediated the relationship between neighborhood conditions and patient violence yielded no significant results, despite the finding that neighborhood disadvantage was negatively related to available social support and positively related to patient violence. Finally, analyses of the conditioning effects of neighborhood disadvantage and mobility on the relationship between specific diagnoses (i.e, diagnosed drug disorders and diagnosed paranoid disorders) and patient violence yielded no evidence of interaction effects.

Table 7.1. Examining Contextual Effects on Individual-level Risk Factors Using Three Statistical Procedures (exponentiated coefficients)

LOGISTIC REGRESSION	Model 1A Risk Factor = **Age (in years)**				Model 2A Risk Factor = **Anger (contin)**				Model 3A Risk Factor = **Black**			
Risk Factor	.97	.97	.95	.96	1.07**	1.07*	1.05*	1.05	2.70**	2.55*	1.27	1.17
Neighborhood Mobility	--	.74	--	.75	--	0.77	--	0.78	--	0.77	--	0.75
Neighborhood Disadvantage	--	--	1.71***	1.68***	--	--	1.58**	1.56**	--	--	1.56*	1.57*
Model Imp. (χ^2) (degrees of freedom)	0.8 (df=1)	2.4 (df=1)	12.7*** (df=1)	14.5*** (df=2)	7.3** (df=1)	1.6 (df=1)	8.7** (df=1)	9.9** (df=2)	6.9** (df=1)	1.7 (df=1)	4.9* (df=1)	6.6* (df=2)
COX REGRESSION	**Model 1B**				**Model 2B**				**Model 3B**			
Risk Factor	0.98	0.98	0.97	0.97	1.06**	1.06*	1.05*	1.04	2.54**	2.42*	1.37	1.27
Neighborhood Mobility	--	0.76	--	0.75	–	0.79	--	0.79	--	0.78	--	0.76
Neighborhood Disadvantage	--	--	1.59***	1.57	--	--	1.48**	1.47**	--	--	1.44*	1.45*
Model Imp. (χ^2) (degrees of freedom)	0.6 (df=1)	2.5 (df=1)	11.6*** (df=1)	13.5** (df=2)	6.9** (df=1)	1.6 (df=1)	7.7** (df=1)	9.1* (df=2)	7.1** (df=1)	1.7 (df=1)	4.0* (df=1)	5.8 (df=2)

* $p<.05$ ** $p<.01$ *** $p<.001$

Table 7.1 - Continued

NEGATIVE BINOMIAL	Model 1C Risk Factor = **Age (in years)**				Model 2C Risk Factor = **Anger (contin)**				Model 3C Risk Factor = **Black**			
Risk Factor	0.96	0.97	0.93	0.94	1.12**	1.11**	1.10**	1.09**	3.62***	3.35**	1.41	1.41
Neighborhood Mobility	--	0.63	--	0.74	--	0.72	--	0.78	--	0.67	--	0.71
Neighborhood Disadvantage	--	--	1.96***	1.89**	--	--	1.72**	1.69**	--	--	1.65	1.59
Model Imp. (χ^2) (degrees of freedom)	1.0 (df=1)	2.9 (df=1)	12.8*** (df=1)	14.4** (df=2)	10.0** (df=1)	1.6 (df=1)	9.0** (df=1)	10.1** (df=2)	13.2*** (df=1)	2.6 (df=1)	3.8 (df=1)	5.7 (df=2)

* p<.05 ** p<.01 *** p<.001

Table 7.1 - Continued

LOGISTIC REGRESSION	Model 4A Risk Factor = **Drug Disorder (0/1)**				Model 5A Risk Factor: **Impulsiveness (contin.)**				Model 6A Risk Factor = **Male (0/1)**			
Risk Factor	3.30**	3.21**	2.43 *	2.37*	1.06*	1.06*	1.07*	1.07*	2.85*	2.97*	2.78*	2.82*
Neighborhood Mobility	--	0.76	--	0.76	--	0.70	--	0.72	--	0.72	--	0.74
Neighborhood Disadvantage	--	--	1.50*	1.48*	--	--	1.71***	1.68***	--	--	1.64***	1.61**
Model Imp. (χ^2) (degrees of freedom)	10.0** (df=1)	1.9 (df=1)	6.5* (df=1)	8.0* (df=2)	5.6* (df=1)	3.3 (df=1)	12.1*** (df=1)	14.4*** (df=2)	6.8* (df=1)	3.0 (df=1)	11.0*** (df=1)	13.0** (df=2)
COX REGRESSION	Model 4B				Model 5B				Model 6B			
Risk Factor	3.01**	2.98**	2.30*	2.26*	1.06*	1.06**	1.06*	1.06**	2.79*	2.83*	2.68*	2.67*
Neighborhood Mobility	--	0.76	--	0.77	--	0.73	--	0.74	--	0.75	--	0.76
Neighborhood Disadvantage	--	--	1.41*	1.40*	--	--	1.59***	1.56**	--	--	1.53**	1.51**
Model Imp. (χ^2) (degrees of freedom)	9.9** (df=1)	2.2 (df=1)	5.8* (df=1)	7.6* (df=2)	6.5* (df=1)	3.2 (df=1)	10.6 (df=1)	12.9** (df=2)	7.3 (df=1)	2.7 (df=1)	10.0** (df=1)	12.0** (df=2)

* p<.05   ** p<.01   *** p<.001

Table 7.1 - Continued

NEGATIVE BINOMIAL	Model 4C Risk Factor = **Drug Disorder (0/1)**				Model 5C Risk Factor: **Impulsiveness (contin.)**				Model 6C Risk Factor = **Male (0/1)** *MALE X DISADVANTAGE (0.38, p<.05)*			
Risk Factor	4.01**	3.86**	2.23	2.28	1.05	1.07*	1.05	1.06	1.83	2.25	3.71*	4.0**
Neighborhood Mobility	--	0.64	--	0.70	--	0.55*	--	.63	--	.56*	--	0.65
Neighborhood Disadvantage	--	--	1.53*	1.47	--	--	1.81**	1.75**	--	--	2.11***	2.03***
Model Imp. (χ^2) (degrees of freedom)	8.6** (df=1)	3.1 (df=1)	4.5* (df=1)	6.6* (df=2)	3.2 (df=1)	4.9* (df=1)	11.2** (df=2)	15.0** (df=2)	1.5 (df=1)	4.5* (df=1)	16.0*** (df=1)	19.0*** (df=2)

* p<.05   ** p<.01   *** p<.001

Table 7.1 - Continued

LOGISTIC REGRESSION	Model 7A Risk Factor = **Paranoid Disorder (0/1)**				Model 8A Risk Factor = **Violent Arrests (0/1)**				Model 9A Risk Factor= **Psychopathy (continuous)**			
Risk Factor	4.55***	4.79***	3.71**	3.87**	3.28**	3.14**	2.41*	2.32*	5.74***	5.44***	4.34***	4.13***
Neighborhood Mobility	--	0.70	--	0.72	--	0.77	--	0.77	--	0.82	--	0.81
Neighborhood Disadvantage	--	--	1.54**	1.51**	--	--	1.52**	1.51**	--	--	1.43*	1.43*
Model Imp. (χ^2) (degrees of freedom)	13.4*** (df=1)	3.1 (df=1)	7.7** (df=1)	9.9** (df=2)	9.0** (df=1)	1.7 (df=1)	7.1** (df=1)	8.5* (df=2)	19.2*** (df=1)	1.0 (df=1)	4.7* (df=1)	5.7 (df=2)
COX REGRESSION	Model 7B				Model 8B				Model 9B			
Risk Factor	3.73***	3.89***	3.04**	3.15**	3.0**	2.88**	2.29*	2.20*	5.0***	4.76***	3.91***	3.74***
Neighborhood Mobility	--	0.73	--	0.74	--	0.78	--	0.78	--	0.84	--	0.82
Neighborhood Disadvantage	--	--	1.45**	1.42*	--	--	1.43**	1.42*	--	--	1.36*	1.36*
Model Imp. (χ^2) (degrees of freedom)	12.3*** (df=1)	3.1 (df=1)	7.0** (df=1)	9.4** (df=2)	9.1** (df=1)	1.8 (df=1)	6.4* (df=1)	7.9* (df=2)	19.6*** (df=1)	1.0 (df=1)	4.0* (df=1)	5.1 (df=2)

* $p<.05$ ** $p<.01$ *** $p<.001$

Table 7.1 - Continued

NEGATIVE BINOMIAL	Model 7 Risk Factor = **Paranoid Disorder (0/1)**				Model 8C Risk Factor = **Violent Arrests (0/1)**				Model 9C Risk Factor= **Psychopathy (continuous)**			
Risk Factor	7.91***	7.81***	5.71***	5.93***	3.94**	3.51*	2.1	1.89	8.6***	7.85***	6.01***	5.64***
Neighborhood Mobility	--	0.64	--	0.67	--	0.70	--	0.73	--	0.75	--	0.79
Neighborhood Disadvantage	--	--	1.54*	1.49*	--	--	1.57*	1.55*	--	--	1.38	1.36
Model Imp. (χ^2) (degrees of freedom)	18.1*** (df=1)	3.7 (df=1)	5.8* (df=1)	8.8* (df=2)	7.7** (df=1)	2.0 (df=1)	4.7* (df=1)	6.4* (df=2)	20.9*** (df=1)	1.4 (df=1)	3.3 (df=1)	4.3 (df=2)

* p<.05 ** p<.01 *** p<.001

Table 7.1 - Continued

LOGISTIC REGRESSION	Model 10A Risk Factor = **Employed (0/1)**				Model 11A Risk Factor = **Individual SES (5-cat)**				Model 12A Risk Factor=**Length of Residence (mos)**			
Risk Factor	0.78	0.74	1.04	0.98	0.85	0.86	0.91	0.92	0.99	1.00	1.00	1.00
Neighborhood Mobility	--	0.73	--	0.74	--	0.74	--	0.75	--	0.69	--	0.71
Neighborhood Disadvantage	--	--	1.67***	1.64**	--	--	1.66***	1.63**	--	--	1.66***	1.63**
Model Imp. (χ^2) (degrees of freedom)	0.4 (df=1)	2.7 (df=1)	11.2*** (df=1)	13.1** (df=2)	0.6 (df=1)	2.4 (df=1)	11.2*** (df=1)	13.0** (df=2)	0.9 (df=1)	3.4 (df=1)	11.4*** (df=1)	13.9*** (df=2)
COX REGRESSION	Model 10B				Model 11B				Model 12B			
Risk Factor	0.81	0.76	1.00	0.93	0.88	0.88	0.95	0.95	1.00	1.00	1.00	1.00
Neighborhood Mobility	--	0.74	--	0.75	--	0.76	--	0.75	--	0.71	--	0.71
Neighborhood Disadvantage	--	--	1.56***	1.53**	--	--	1.56**	1.54	--	--	1.55**	1.52**
Model Imp. (χ^2) (degrees of freedom)	0.4 (df=1)	2.7 (df=1)	10.2** (df=1)	12.3** (df=2)	0.4 (df=1)	2.4 (df=1)	10.2** (df=1)	12.2** (df=2)	1.1 (df=1)	3.4 (df=1)	10.2** (df=1)	12.9** (df=2)

* $p<.05$ ** $p<.01$ *** $p<.001$

Table 7.1 - Continued

NEGATIVE BINOMIAL	Model 10C Risk Factor = **Employed (0/1)**				Model 11C Risk Factor = **Individual SES (5-cat)**				Model 12C Risk Factor=**Length of Residence (mos)**			
Risk Factor	0.56	0.55	1.22	1.12	0.83	0.81	0.97	0.94	1.00	1.00	1.00	1.00
Neighborhood Mobility	--	0.61	--	0.71	--	0.61	--	0.71	--	0.58*	--	0.67
Neighborhood Disadvantage	--	--	1.88**	1.79**	--	--	1.81**	1.74**	--	--	1.84**	1.77**
Model Imp. (χ^2) (degrees of freedom)	1.4 (df=1)	3.6 (df=1)	9.6** (df=1)	11.5** (df=2)	0.5 (df=1)	3.4 (df=1)	10.3** (df=1)	12.3** (df=2)	0.6 (df=1)	4.6* (df=1)	12.0** (df=1)	14.6** (df=2)

* p<.05   ** p<.01   *** p<.001

Table 7.1 - Continued

LOGISTIC REGRESSION	Model 13A Risk Factor = **Spouse/Partner (0/1)**				Model 14A Risk Factor:**Social Support (# indiv)**			
Risk Factor	2.48*	2.27*	2.56*	2.37*	0.86	0.85	0.90	0.89
Neighborhood Mobility	--	0.80	--	0.82	--	0.72	--	0.74
Neighborhood Disadvantage	--	--	1.68***	1.66***	--	--	1.62**	1.59**
Model Imp. (χ^2) (degrees of freedom)	5.8* (df=1)	1.2 (df=1)	11.6*** (df=1)	12.4** (df=2)	2.8 (df=1)	2.8 (df=1)	9.8** (df=1)	11.9** (df=1)
COX REGRESSION	Model 13B				Model 14B			
Risk Factor	2.22*	2.05*	2.24*	2.08*	0.87	0.86	0.91	0.90
Neighborhood Mobility	--	0.81	--	0.82	--	0.73	--	0.74
Neighborhood Disadvantage	--	--	1.57***	1.55**	--	--	1.52**	1.49**
Model Imp. (χ^2) (degrees of freedom)	5.2* (df=1)	1.3 (df=1)	10.7** (df=1)	11.6** (df=2)	2.8 (df=1)	3.1 (df=1)	9.0** (df=1)	11.3** (df=2)

* p<.05   ** p<.01   *** p<.001

Table 7.1 - Continued

NEGATIVE BINOMIAL	Model 13C Risk Factor = **Spouse/Partner (0/1)**				Model 14C Risk Factor:**Social Support (# indiv)**			
Risk Factor	1.57	1.16	1.96	1.64	0.81*	0.84	0.86	0.86
Neighborhood Mobility	--	0.63	--	0.79	--	.67	--	0.72
Neighborhood Disadvantage	--	--	1.85***	1.80**	--	--	1.71**	1.67**
Model Imp. (χ^2) (degrees of freedom)	0.8 (df=1)	2.6 (df=1)	12.1*** (df=1)	12.9** (df=2)	4.5* (df=1)	2.3 (df=1)	8.5** (df=1)	10.3** (df=2)

* p<.05   ** p<.01   *** p<.001

Table 7.2. Logistic Regression Results (odds ratios)

Variables	Model 1	Model 2	Model 3	Model 4
Age (in years)	0.96	0.95	0.94	0.94
Anger	1.04	1.04	1.03	1.02
Black (0/1)	0.94	0.90	0.40	0.38
Drug Disorder (0/1)	1.94	1.87	1.92	1.87
Impulsiveness	1.02	1.02	1.03	1.03
Male (0/1)	2.87*	2.95*	2.92*	3.03*
Paranoid Disorder (0/1)	2.33 †	2.51 †	2.33 †	2.52 †
Prior Violent Arrests (0/1)	0.90	0.90	0.87	0.84
Psychopathy	3.23*	3.03*	3.15*	2.96*
Employed (0/1)	1.02	0.96	1.17	1.09
Length of Residence	1.00	1.00	1.00	1.00
SES (5 categories)	1.06	1.08	1.10	1.11
Spouse/Partner (0/1)	2.46*	2.22 †	2.66*	2.40 †
Time at Risk	1.00	1.00	1.00	1.00
Neighborhood Mobility	--	0.79	--	0.78
Neighborhood Disadvantage	--	--	1.71*	1.72*
Nagelkerke R^2 [a]	.28	.28	.31	.31
Model Improvement (χ^2) (degrees of freedom)	42.1*** (df=14)	1.1 (df=1)	5.0* (df=1	6.1* (df=2)

† p<.10 * p<.05 ** p<.01 *** p<.001

a The Nagelkerke R^2 quantifies the proportion of explained variation in a logistic regression equation (range: 0.0 to 1.0) (Nagelkerke 1991).

Table 7.3. Cox Regression Results (hazard ratios).

Variables	Model 1	Model 2	Model 3	Model 4
Age (in years)	0.97	0.97	0.96	0.96
Anger	1.03	1.02	1.02	1.01
Black (0/1)	0.96	0.91	0.50	0.46
Drug Disorder (0/1)	1.74	1.70	1.70	1.69
Impulsiveness	1.00	1.00	1.01	1.02
Male (0/1)	2.76*	2.77*	2.72*	2.79*
Paranoid Disorder (0/1)	2.09 †	2.25 †	2.10 †	2.25*
Prior Violent Arrests (0/1)	0.74	0.72	0.77	0.72
Psychopathy	3.10*	2.93*	2.81*	2.71*
Employed (0/1)	1.16	1.09	1.26	1.18
Length of Residence	1.00	1.00	1.00	1.00
SES (5 categories)	1.01	1.02	1.06	1.06
Spouse/Partner (0/1)	1.94 †	1.78	2.08 †	1.89 †
Time at Risk	1.00	1.00	1.00	1.00
Neighborhood Mobility	--	0.80	--	0.78
Neighborhood Disadvantage	--		1.52*	1.53*
Model Imp. (χ^2) (degrees of freedom)	40.0*** (df=14)	1.3 (df=1)	4.5* (df=1)	6.0* (df=2)

† p<.10 * p<.05 ** p<.01 *** p<.001

Table 7.4. Negative Binomial Regression Results (exponentiated coefficients).

Variables	Model 1	Model 2	Model 3	Model 4
Age (in years)	0.93*	0.92 †	0.91*	0.92 †
Anger	1.07	1.06	1.06	1.05
Black (0/1)	0.82	0.80	0.29 †	0.29 †
Drug Disorder (0/1)	2.54	2.44	2.60	2.54
Impulsiveness	1.04	1.04	1.04	1.04
Male (0/1)	2.80*	3.13*	3.56*	3.85*
Paranoid Disorder (0/1)	2.97*	3.14*	3.25*	3.37*
Prior Violent Arrests (0/1)	1.12	1.00	0.71	0.65
Psychopathy	4.5**	4.21**	4.82**	4.50**
Employed (0/1)	0.52	0.49	0.78	0.72
Length of Residence	1.00	1.00	1.00	1.00
SES (5 categories)	1.35	1.34	1.21	1.22
Spouse/Partner (0/1)	2.16	1.63	1.95	1.54
Time at Risk	1.00	1.00	1.00	1.00
Neighborhood Mobility	--	0.73	--	0.76
Neighborhood Disadvantage	--	--	1.91*	1.88*
Model Imp. (χ^2) (degrees of freedom)	53.3*** (df=14)	1.3 (df=1)	6.0* (df=1)	7.1* (df=2)

† p<.10 * p<.05 ** p<.01 *** p<.001

Table 7.5. Summary of Main Effects Results Across Three Models (exponentiated coefficients).

Variables	Logistic	Cox	Negative Binomial
Age (in years)	0.94	0.96	0.92 †
Anger	1.02	1.01	1.05
Black (0/1)	0.38	0.46	0.29 †
Drug Disorder (0/1)	1.87	1.69	2.54
Impulsiveness	1.03	1.02	1.04
Male (0/1)	3.03*	2.79*	3.85*
Paranoid Disorder (0/1)	2.52 †	2.25*	3.37*
Prior Violent Arrests (0/1)	0.84	0.72	0.65
Psychopathy	2.96*	2.71*	4.50**
Employed (0/1)	1.09	1.18	0.72
Length of Residence	1.00	1.00	1.00
SES (5 categories)	1.11	1.06	1.22
Spouse/Partner (0/1)	2.40 †	1.89 †	1.54
Time at Risk	1.00	1.00	1.00
Neighborhood Mobility	0.78	0.78	0.76
Neighborhood Disadvantage	1.72*	1.53*	1.88*

† p<.10 * p<.05 ** p<.01 *** p<.001

Table 7.6. Predicted Probabilities of Violence From Logistic Regression Equation at Varying Levels of Neighborhood Disadvantage.

Neighborhood Disadvantage	Predicted Probability of Violence †
-2 s.d. Below Mean	.03
-1 s.d. Below Mean	.04
Mean	.07
1 s.d Above Mean	.13
2 s.d. Above Mean	.21

† All other predictor variables fixed at their respective mean values.

Table 7.7. Analysis of Concentration Effects in Terms of Functional Form (exponentiated coefficients).

Variables	Logistic	Cox	Negative Binomial
Disadvantage Squared †	0.82	0.87	0.92
Model Improvement with squared term added (χ^2)	1.7 (df=1)	1.2 (df=1)	0.4 (df=1)
Mobility Squared †	1.04	0.99	1.03
Model Improvement with squared term added (χ^2)	0.1 (df=1)	0.1 (df=1)	0.2 (df=1)

* p<.05 ** p<.01 *** p<.001
† Holding constant individual-level variables and Factor Score.

Table 7.8. Social Support as Mediator of the Relationship Between Neighborhood Conditions and Patient Violence (Exponentiated coefficients).

Variables	Logistic Regression		Cox Regression		Negative Binomial	
Age (in years)	0.94	0.94	0.96	0.95	0.92	0.92
Anger	1.02	1.02	1.01	1.00	1.05	1.05
Black (0/1)	0.38	0.39	0.46	0.49	0.29	0.30
Drug Disorder (0/1)	1.87	1.84	1.69	1.65	2.54	2.64
Impulsiveness	1.03	1.03	1.02	1.02	1.04	1.04
Male (0/1)	3.03*	2.94*	2.79*	2.74*	3.85*	4.06*
Paranoid Disorder (0/1)	2.52	2.51	2.25*	2.23	3.37*	3.05*
Prior Violent Arrests (0/1)	0.84	0.83	0.72	0.72	0.65	0.56
Psychopathy	2.96*	3.03*	2.71*	2.76*	4.50**	4.76**
Employed (0/1)	1.09	1.14	1.18	1.21	0.72	0.75
Length of Residence	1.00	1.00	1.00	1.00	1.00	1.00
SES (5 categories)	1.11	1.09	1.06	1.05	1.22	1.15
Spouse/Partner (0/1)	2.40	2.40	1.89	1.91	1.54	1.60
Time at Risk	1.00	1.00	1.00	1.00	1.00	1.00
Neighborhood Mobility	0.78	0.78	0.78	0.78	0.76	0.77
Neighborhood Disadvantage	1.72*	1.69*	1.53*	1.50*	1.88*	1.85*
Social Support	--	0.93	--	0.95	--	0.91
Model Imp.(χ^2) (degrees of freedom)	48.2*** (df=16)	0.3 (df=1)	46.0*** (df=16)	0.3 (df=1)	64.7*** (df=16)	0.7 (df=1)

* p<.05 ** p<.01 *** p<.001

Table 7.9. Moderating Effects of Social Support on the Relationship Between Paranoid Disorder and Patient Violence: Multivariate Results (exponentiated coefficients). †

Variables	Logistic	Cox	Negative Binomial
Social Support X Paranoid Disorder	1.07	1.15	0.80
Model Improvement with squared term added (χ^2)	0.1 (df=1)	0.5 (df=1)	1.0 (df=1)

* p<.05 ** p<.01 *** p<.001

† Holding constant all other predictors.

Table 7.10. Post-Discharge Drug Use Among Previously Diagnosed Drug Abusers by Neighborhood Disadvantage and Mobility.

	Neighborhood Disadvantage	
Drug Use	Below Median (n=28)	Above Median (n=60)
No	39.3	42.4
Yes	60.7	57.6

	Neighborhood Mobility	
Drug Use	Below Median (n=48)	Above Median (n=40)
No	35.4	48.7
Yes	64.6	51.3

Fisher's Exact Test
* p<.05 ** p<.01 *** p<.001

Table 7.11. Moderating Effects of Neighborhood Social Disorganization on the Relationship Between Drug Disorder and Patient Violence: Multivariate Results (exponentiated coefficients)

Variables	Logistic	Cox	Negative Binomial
Disadvantage X Drug Disorder †	1.13	1.07	1.23
Model Improvement with interaction term added (χ^2)	0.1 (df=1)	0.1 (df=1)	0.3 (df=1)
Mobility X Drug Disorder †	1.72	1.60	1.53
Model Improvement with interaction term added (χ^2)	1.3 (df=1)	1.3 (df=1)	0.7 (df=1)

* p<.05 ** p<.01 *** p<.001

† Holding constant main effect terms

CHAPTER 8

Implications for Theory and Research in the Area of Violence and Mental Illness

Over the course of this century, a voluminous literature has accrued suggesting the importance of social disorganization as an explanatory mechanism underpinning differential rates of crime and violence between and within communities. Yet, to date the relevance of the social disorganization perspective for explaining the violent behavior of persons with mental illnesses has not been addressed. To explore this issue, this project applied social disorganization theory to the study of violence among a sample of individuals recently treated and discharged from a Pittsburgh psychiatric hospital. The purpose of the study was to assess the extent to which neighborhood social disorganization explained variation in the violent behavior of discharged psychiatric patients, over and above the effects of their individual characteristics, and to assess whether social disorganization conditioned the effects of these individual characteristics.

To accomplish this purpose, individual-level data from the Pittsburgh site of the MacArthur Foundation's

Violence Risk Assessment Study - the largest study of risk factors for violence among discharged psychiatric patients ever conducted - were linked with aggregate data on the characteristics of the neighborhoods in which patients resided after discharge - gathered from 1990 U.S. Census Summary Tape Files. This data linkage was accomplished by translating subjects' post-discharge addresses into census tract identifiers. To characterize the neighborhood environments into which the patients had been discharged, census tract measures were factor analyzed into two Factors: a Neighborhood Disadvantage Factor and a Neighborhood Mobility Factor. Following a long line of research, these factors were conceptualized as structural determinants of the social disorganization process.

Violence in this study consisted of serious acts of physical aggression toward others committed while subjects were living in the community. These acts included battery resulting in injury, sexual assaults, and assaults that involved the use of a weapon (or threats made with a weapon in hand). The study operationalized patient violence in three ways: (1) whether any violent act occurred during the followup; (2) as the time to a first violent act; and (3) as a count of violent incidents, each of which reflected a different aspect of what is generally referred to as violence risk (i.e., prevalence, imminence, and amount). The follow-up period included the first 20 weeks following discharge from the hospital.

As reported in the previous two chapters, the following results were obtained:

-- Neighborhood disadvantage was found to have a significant positive effect on patient violence over and above the effects of significant individual-level risk factors and control variables.

-- Neighborhood mobility was found not to be

statistically related to patient violence

-- The effects of neighborhood social disorganization accounted for less of the explained variation in patient violence than did the individual-level predictors (pseudo-R^2=3% vs. 22%). In addition, a good amount of the explained variation in patient violence (6% out of a total pseudo-R^2 of 31%) was shared by both individual- and neighborhood-level factors.

-- No evidence of concentration effects was found in the relationship between neighborhood social disorganization and patient violence.

-- Individual-level social support did not mediate the relationship between neighborhood conditions and patient violence.

-- The effects of substance abuse and paranoid disorders were found not to interact with levels of social support (or neighborhood social disorganization) in their relationship with patient violence.

In the remainder of this chapter, the implications of this study for social disorganization theory and for research in the area of violence and mental illness are discussed.

Discussion

Social Disorganization Theory. Faris and Dunham (1939) were the first American sociologists to apply a social disorganization perspective to the study of mentally ill people. Their pioneering work challenged the perception that the behaviors of persons with mental illnesses were determined solely by their individual characteristics. Specifically, Faris and Dunham argued that the "confused, frustrated, and chaotic" expressions of behavior often exhibited by mentally ill persons resulted, in part, from their location in socially disorganized neighborhoods. Although Faris and Dunham did not explicitly focus on the aggressive behavior of persons with mental illnesses, it was a straightforward extension of their theoretical framework to hypothesize that part of this complex of "confused, frustrated, and chaotic" behavior might include acts of aggression. Yet, since the publication of their work in 1939, and despite a long line of research linking neighborhood social disorganization to rates of crime and violence, no attempts have been reported by researchers to assess the relevance of neighborhood social disorganization for predicting violence among persons with mental illnesses.

Social disorganization theory posits that neighborhoods high in social disorganization are less able to exert informal social control over residents, exhibit normative structures which may facilitate interpersonal aggression, and, based on the arguments of Cullen (1994), provide less opportunity to obtain needed social supports. Accordingly, it was hypothesized that psychiatric patients discharged into socially disorganized neighborhoods would be more apt to engage in violence against others than those discharged into less disorganized neighborhoods. The results of this study provided substantial support for this hypothesis. Most importantly, patients discharged into disadvantaged neighborhoods were found to be significantly more likely to commit violent acts sooner after discharge and with greater frequency than those discharged into less disadvantage neighborhoods. This finding held after controlling for known individual-level risk factors.

The effect of neighborhood disadvantage on patient

violence can be attributed to the fact that place locates mentally ill people not only in geographical space but also in social contexts conducive to violence. Disadvantaged neighborhoods in which most residents are poor may be less able to maintain neighborhood surveillance and provide needed social supports. In addition, part of the effect of disadvantage may be to increase the average level of violence in the neighborhood, thereby increasing the likelihood that individuals with mental illnesses will act violently. Massey (1996) suggests that a logical adaptation to living in an environment in which violence is endemic is to become violent oneself (see also Anderson, 1990; Miles-Doan, 1998; Hiday, 1997). Although the findings reported here suggest that this process may extend to the violent behavior of persons with mental illnesses, a more precise assessment would require data on neighborhood violence rates - data which were not available in the current study.

In considering this core finding, it is important to note that this study of Pittsburgh neighborhoods found neighborhood disadvantage to consist not only of indicators of economic deprivation (i.e., poverty, income, and occupational structure), but also to include such measures as the percentage black in the neighborhood and the percentage of households that were female-headed. This factor structure differs from the theory of social disorganization originally formulated by Shaw and McKay (1942) and Faris and Dunham (1939) in which socioeconomic deprivation and population heterogeneity were treated as distinct dimensions affecting the social disorganization process. However, this factor structure is consistent with more recent presentations of social disorganization theory in which it has been suggested that the structural conditions underpinning the social disorganization process have changed since the theory was developed in the 1930's (Liska and Messner, 1999;

Sampson and Lauritsen, 1994; Warner and Pierce, 1993). Specifically, it has been observed that in today's disorganized communities, racial composition, family disruption, and socioeconomic disadvantage correlate so highly that they cannot be separated empirically (Miles-Doan, 1998; Sampson and Lauritsen, 1994; Wilson, 1987; Massey and Denton, 1993). Although these covariates are conceptually distinct, they are empirically highly correlated. This pattern of disadvantage appears to hold for this sample of Pittsburgh neighborhoods and, perhaps most importantly, it is in such disadvantaged neighborhoods that discharged psychiatric patients were found to be at greatest risk of engaging in violence.[32]

---

[32]The strong association between socioeconomic deprivation, racial composition, and family disruption in today's disorganized neighborhoods is substantively consistent with Massey and Denton's (1993) conceptualization of residential segregation and with Wilson's (1987) conceptualization of social isolation and concentration effects. Wilson argues that the social transformation of the inner-city has resulted in a disproportionate concentration of the most disadvantaged segments of the urban population - especially poor, black, female-headed families with children. According to Massey and Denton (1993), factors leading to the increased segregation of poor blacks include weak enforcement of Fair Housing laws, opposition from organized community groups to public housing projects in stable neighborhoods, and discrimination by individuals, financial institutions, and government. Urban minorities have also been especially vulnerable to structural economic changes related to the deindustrialization of central cities (e.g., the shift from goods-producing to service-producing industries). In particular, Wilson (1987) argues that the exodus of middle- and upper-income black families from inner-city neighborhoods has removed an important social buffer that might have deflected the full negative impact of prolonged joblessness and industrial transformation observed in these areas (see also Sampson and Lauritsen, 1994). The end-result of these processes is that socioeconomic deprivation, racial

Further, this study found no evidence that neighborhood residential mobility increased rates of violence among discharged patients thus providing additional evidence that structural changes have occurred in the underlying factors related to social disorganization.[33] As Liska and Messner (1999:84) suggest, "it may be that in some cities, especially those in the East and Midwest, we are witnessing a decline in the urban dynamics, expressed in social disorganization theory, wherein poor immigrants and migrants move into low-income housing in low-income neighborhoods; in time are replaced by newer immigrants and migrants in an ongoing cycle, leading to social instability and heterogeneity, which in turn produces low social control and high rates of deviance." Warner and Pierce (1993:507) suggest that today's socially disorganized neighborhoods appear to be "neighborhoods of last resort, neighborhoods where people remain, perhaps not because they choose to, but because they have no other choice." Thus, mobility appears to be less relevant a factor in explaining crime and violence within today's socially disorganized neighborhoods than perhaps it once was. This finding suggests that census variables commonly used to measure low levels of guardianship, such as residential mobility and percent foreign born, may not be universally applicable. To better understand the control mechanisms operating within today's disorganized

---

composition, and family disruption have become so highly correlated as to be empirically indistinguishable using factor analytic techniques.

[33]Although the effect of mobility on patient violence was observed to be negative (i.e., patients discharged into higher-mobility neighborhoods were found to exhibit lower levels of violence), this effect was not found to be statistically significant in any of the multivariate models.

communities, future research efforts must focus on obtaining a more extensive array of measures of control than those currently available from census data. In addition, future research must evaluate the extent to which these findings regarding a lack of association between neighborhood mobility and patient violence generalize beyond this Pittsburgh sample to other locations and time periods (i.e., particularly to those areas in which rates of mobility show greater variation than observed here).

The Role of Social Support. Sampson and Lauritsen's (1994) comprehensive review of the research literature on social disorganization highlights the centrality of *social control* and *cultural differentiation* as key mediating factors. In reviewing much of the same literature, Cullen (1994) emphasized the equally important role of *social support* in understanding the relationship between social disorganization and rates of illegal behavior, including interpersonal violence. For example Cullen points out that high rates of family disruption may operationalize not only surveillance over residents, but also the viability of social support networks and the opportunity to develop intimate relations. Further, in interpreting Sampson, Raudenbush, and Earls' (1997) recent results, Cullen, Wright, and Chamlin (1998:10) point out that the "construct of collective efficacy includes not only a measure of informal social control, but also a measure of cohesion and trust among residents - or what we would term the existence of helpful or supportive relationships in a community."

In light of these arguments, this study sought to assess social support as a partial mediating factor in the relationship between neighborhood conditions and patient violence.[34] Results indicated that neighborhood disadvantage was negatively related to the number of social supporters available to patients, thus providing some evidence in support of Cullen's notion that neighborhood social disorganization constrains the amounts of social support available to individual patients. However, the effect of neighborhood disadvantage on patient violence was not mediated by the amount of social support available to individual patients. The relationship between neighborhood disadvantage and patient violence remained unchanged when the social support was held constant. Although residents of disadvantaged neighborhoods tended to report fewer available social supporters, the number of social supporters appeared to have little effect in reducing patient violence.

One interpretation of this finding is that, contrary to Cullen's theoretical argument, social support is inconsequential as a mediating factor in the relationship between neighborhood conditions and patient violence. However, caution is advised in accepting this interpretation for two reasons. First, as mentioned above, this study was not able to measure the strength of *neighborhood-level* social support networks (as described by Cullen) but rather relied on a measure of individual supports as a proxy. Yet, it is conceivable - given current communication technology - that some proportion of the support reportedly provided to mentally ill individuals may come from persons located outside of the neighborhood boundaries. Unfortunately, the

---

[34]Partial (as opposed to complete) mediation was hypothesized due to the multiple pathways through which social disorganization is predicted to affect patient violence (i.e., through informal social control, cultural differentiation, and neighborhood-level social supports).

residential locations of these social supporters cannot be determined from these data. Thus, the measure of support used here may not have adequately tapped into the viability of social support networks *rooted in the ecology of the neighborhood*, a type of support which, according to Cullen, may be crucial for understanding the relationship between social disorganization and violent behavior. To address this issue, future research on the social ecology of violence and mental illness should attempt to measure the geographic span of the social support networks of the mentally ill to determine the extent to which they are rooted in the neighborhood environment (for a discussion of this issue, see Wellman, 1979; Logan and Spitze, 1994).

Second, it is conceivable that by assessing the number of individuals *self-reported* (i.e., perceived) by subjects as providing help during times of need, this study did not adequately measure the types of support that may be most influential in protecting against violence. For example, it may be that the types of assistance provided in neighborhoods with strong social support networks are subtle to the point of being invisible to the person with mental illness. For example, a neighbor may notice a mentally ill person acting in an odd or disruptive way, may then contact a family member, who subsequently shows up at the scene to talk to the person and take him or her home. Although this type of support may have indirectly prevented the mentally ill person's behavior from escalating to violence, it is at the same time a type of support (rooted in the ecology of the neighborhood) that may go unnoticed by the subject, and thus may not become included in self-reported counts of available social supporters.

This distinction between individual-level and aggregate-level measures of social support coincides with a network analytic approach to assessing social relationships

(Morrissey, Tausig, and Lindsey, 1985; Wellman, 1979). The network perspective is nicely summarized by Knoke and Kuklinski (1982:9-10):

> "...network analysis incorporates two significant assumptions about social behavior. It's first essential insight is that any actor typically participates in a social system involving many other actors, who are significant reference points in one another's decisions....Its second essential insight lies in the importance of elucidating the various levels of structure in a social system...The organization of social relations thus becomes a central concept in analyzing the structural properties of the networks within which individual actors are embedded, and for detecting *emergent social phenomena that have no existence and the level of the individual actor*" [emphasis added].

Therefore, before discounting the relevance of social support as a mediating factor in the relationship between social disorganization and patient violence, future studies must pay more attention to developing better measures of social support networks operating at (and/or beyond) the neighborhood-level. Only then may a complete understanding of the mediating role of social support be obtained.

Nonetheless, the lack of an effect of individual-level social support leaves open the possibility that other factors might mediate the effects of neighborhood disadvantage on patient violence. One such factor might be the accessibility of mental health services. To the extent that access to mental health services is related to the improved management of symptoms, then such access may also be related, indirectly, to reductions in violence risk. Furthermore, to the extent that mental health services are more difficult for residents of disadvantaged neighborhoods to access (perhaps because of a lack of resources to deliver such services or because their effective delivery requires higher levels of organizational participation than is typically found in such neighborhoods), then mental health service accessibility might be an important contextual factor related to violence. To assess this hypothesis, future studies will need to gather data on the accessibility and utilization of mental health services across neighborhoods - a measure which cannot be obtained with Census data.

Contextualizing Individual-Level Risk Factors. As mentioned throughout this text, the vast majority of studies of violence among the mentally ill have focused on individual-level characteristics, a focus which has reinforced the assumption that the symptoms and correlates of mental illnesses (e.g., including aggression) are determined primarily by factors rooted within the individual. However, as the current study demonstrates, limiting the selection of explanatory variables to individual-level measures imposes an artificial limit on the amount of variation in violent behavior that may be explained. The significant main effect of neighborhood disadvantage on patient violence reported here - holding constant known individual-level risk factors - emphasizes the importance of incorporating contextual measures into violence prediction models. Absent such measures, a unique amount of the variation in violence is left unexplained.

In addition, this study found that the effect sizes of specific individual-level predictors (e.g., black racial status, drug disorder, paranoid disorder, prior violent arrests, and psychopathy) were substantially reduced when neighborhood disadvantage was held constant. These results raise significant questions regarding the validity of the effect sizes reported in previous studies of these measures and, perhaps more importantly, suggest that part of the bivariate association between each of these risk factors and violence was due to the fact that scoring as high-risk on these measures was positively correlated with residence in a disadvantaged neighborhood. By omitting contextual measures from studies of violence among the mentally ill, researchers run the risk of overestimating the effects sizes of particular risk factors, thereby erroneously directing clinical attention toward points of intervention that might be more effectively addressed by taking into account the neighborhood context within which the patient resides.

Of great significance in this regard was the attenuation of the effect of black racial status on patient violence when neighborhood disadvantage was controlled. This finding suggests that the positive bivariate effect of black racial status on patient violence observed in this and other studies may simply reflect the fact that African American patients tend to reside in disadvantaged neighborhoods where *all* patients, regardless of racial status, are at greater risk of engaging in violence. Specifically, black patients were far more likely than white patients to return to disadvantaged neighborhoods after psychiatric treatment (Pearson $r=.66$, $p<.001$) and it was their neighborhood locations, and not their racial status per se, that maximally accounted for their increased rates of violent behavior. Had neighborhood disadvantage not been operationalized in these analyses, clinical attention may have been incorrectly directed toward the effects of black racial status as a risk factor for violence, rather than toward the effects of neighborhood social disorganization.

The importance of Individual-level Predictors. In suggesting that neighborhood conditions affect the violent behavior of persons with mental illnesses, this study does not take the position that mental illness is unimportant as a cause of violence; nor does the study necessarily contradict the biological foundations upon which many mental illnesses are believed to rest. Rather, this study follows Hiday (1997:412) in taking the position that "neurobiological factors may be the origin of severe mental illness; but social factors affects its course, manifestations, and connections to violence."

Indeed, support for the importance of individual-level characteristics in predicting patient violence was found throughout this study. First, although neighborhood conditions were found to account for a significant part of the explained variation in violent behavior, the overall amount of variation uniquely attributable to the neighborhood factors was small compared to that of the individual-level factors (unique pseudo-R^2=3% vs. 22%). Finally, the almost complete lack of cross-level interaction effects observed between neighborhood conditions and individual-level predictors suggested quite clearly that the effects of these individual-level predictors maintained across neighborhood contexts. Taken together, these findings lead to the conclusion that although neighborhood conditions are important factors to consider in predicting patient violence, the effects of individual-level predictors cannot be underestimated. The results of this study thus call for a comprehensive approach to the study of violence and mental illness that simultaneously examines the effects of individual- and community-level risk factors.

Policy Implications. Violence risk assessment remains a core feature of clinical practice in a wide variety of institutional and community settings. Beginning in the late 1960s, "dangerousness to others" became one of the primary criteria for the involuntary inpatient hospitalization of people with mental disorders throughout the United States. In the 1970's, tort liability was imposed on psychiatrists and psychologists who negligently failed to accurately predict their patients' violence. In the 1980s, the "dangerousness standard" expanded to statutes authorizing involuntary outpatient treatment (Appelbaum, 1994). In the 1990's, risk assessments of violence were formally invoked in the Americans with Disabilities Act, which protects the employment rights of people with mental disabilities, unless those disabilities result in a person being assessed as a "direct threat" of violence to other employees or to customers (Bonnie & Monahan, 1997).

Despite the pervasiveness of violence risk assessment, the research literature on clinical prediction remains disconcerting. The most sophisticated recent study found clinicians' unstructured violence risk assessments to be only modestly more accurate than chance (Lidz, Mulvey, & Gardner, 1993). The implications of the findings reported here for mental health policy lie in emphasizing the importance of assessing contextual conditions, as well as individual characteristics, when predicting and managing the risk for violence among discharged psychiatric patients. The documented effect of neighborhood disadvantage on patient violence suggests that the prediction and management of patient violence might be enhanced if mental health clinicians were to focus more attention on the neighborhood environments into which patients are discharged, in addition to assessing their psychiatric conditions at the time of discharge. In addition, these findings suggest that clinical interventions aimed at treating individual behaviors or characteristics in order to reduce violence may be more or less effective when applied in different neighborhood settings.

Conclusions

In summarizing the literature on social disorganization, Liska and Messner (1999) point out that the vast majority of studies informed by social disorganization theory have not operationalized the social disorganization process. Rather, these studies have sought to demonstrate an association between the hypothesized determinants of social disorganization and the hypothesized consequences of social disorganization. The current study is no exception, as census data were used to derive neighborhood measures. Unfortunately, census data do not contain information on social processes such as the social relationships and networks linking neighborhood residents to one another - processes which are central to the social disorganization theory. As a result, the current study - along with much prior research informed by social disorganization theory - sought indirect evidence in support of the theory. In particular, the current study sought merely to demonstrate that the determinants of social disorganization (in this case, neighborhood disadvantage and neighborhood mobility) were associated with the hypothesized consequences of social disorganization (in this case, violence among discharged psychiatric patients).

Thus, a significant difficulty in this and other research informed by social disorganization theory is that the key mediating processes by which neighborhood effects may be transmitted have not been measured, and therefore interpretations and conclusions regarding such effects must remain speculative. Although social support was raised as a potentially important mediating factor, concerns about the measurement of this construct render the null findings reported here inconclusive. What we are left with, therefore, is a contextual effect whose mediating mechanisms have yet to be identified. Therefore, it remains for future research into the social ecology of violence and mental illness to seek out better measurements of the social disorganization process in order to better assess the mediating mechanisms by which the contextual effect on patient violence occurs. Only then will we understand *how* social disorganization operates to increase the occurrence of violence among persons with mental illnesses.

Further, as Sampson and Lauritsen (1994:80) note: "the lack of measurement of social interactions and mediating processes is also directly linked to the definition and conceptualization of communities themselves." This comment refers to the fact that most criminological research (including that reported here) relies on "statistical neighborhoods" (i.e., census tracts) that may or may not correspond to social patterns of interaction and cohesion. As Tienda (1986:6) has argued, "the social dimensions of the definition of neighborhoods are crucial because they derive from interaction patterns, which ultimately are the primary mechanisms through which neighborhood effects can be transmitted." Thus, future work in this area should seek to achieve better measurements of the neighborhood interaction patterns suggested by social disorganization theory as leading to increases in violent behavior among neighborhood residents.

Finally, in broadening the focus of research on violence and mental illness, greater attention must be paid to differentiating contextual effects from the effects of selection. Although the results of this study suggested that individual-SES was *not* a key factor in determining the neighborhood locations of discharged patients (i.e., the Pearson correlation between individual SES and residence in a disadvantaged neighborhood was a modest -.15, $p<.05$), the extent to which the relationship between neighborhood disadvantage and patient violence is determined by other potential selection factors is not known. Unfortunately, descriptive data capable of explaining precisely *why* discharged psychiatric patients were found to reside in one neighborhood location as opposed to another were not available in the current study. Such data, however, are of crucial importance to a research agenda aimed at further developing our understanding of the role of ecological factors in assessing risk for violence among the mentally ill.

Directions for Future Research

Although this project represents an important step toward applying contextual measures to the study of violence and mental illness, a number of important measurement issues remain. First, since neighborhood mobility - which is typically conceptualized as a factor influencing informal social control and surveillance - was found to be less relevant a factor in explaining patient violence, a better understanding of the role of informal social control will require a more extensive array of measures than those currently available from census data, as well as an examination of mobility effects in other geographic locations. Second, although social support was explored as a potentially important mediating factor, concerns about the measurement of this construct - particularly the fact that no measure of *neighborhood-level* social support was available - render the null findings reported here inconclusive. Future studies must therefore develop better measures of the social support networks operating at the neighborhood-level. For this purpose, network analysis seems a promising direction. Fourth, to further assess whether the effect of neighborhood disadvantage on patient violence is due, in part, to increased levels of violence in disadvantaged neighborhoods, measures of neighborhood violence rates are needed. Finally, to assess the possibility that access to mental health services varies by neighborhood context, future studies will need to gather data on the availability and use of mental health services across neighborhoods.

Unfortunately, readily available data, such as the Census, do not contain information on such social and structural characteristics. Such data must therefore be gathered independently using techniques capable of producing reliable measures of neighborhood-level processes, techniques which tend to be costly (see Sampson, Raudenbush, and Earls (1997) for a rare example of such an effort). Nonetheless, greater attention to these measurement issues will be required in order to further enhance our knowledge of the ecological correlates of violence among persons with mental illnesses for purpose of improving policy, practice, and decision making.

BIBLIOGRAPHY

Abrahamsen, D. (1952). *Who Are the Guilty?*. New York: Rinehart.

Abram, K. M. & Teplin, L. A.. (1991). Co-occurring disorders among mentally ill jail detainees: Implications for public policy. *American Psychologist*, 46, 1036-1045.

Allison, P. D. (1984). *Event History Analysis: Regression for Longitudinal Event Data*. Beverly Hills, CA: Sage Publications.

American Bar Association (1989). *ABA Criminal Justice Mental Health Standards*. Washington DC: American Bar Association.

American Psychiatric Association (1987). *Diagnostic and Statistical Manual of Mental Disorders*. 3rd ed. Washington, D.C.: American Psychiatric Association.

American Psychiatric Association (1983). Guidelines for legislation on the psychiatric hospitalization of adults. *American Journal of Psychiatry*, 140, 672-679.

Anderson, E. (1997). Violence and the Inner-City Street Code. In J. McCord (Ed.), *Violence and Childhood in the Inner City* (pp. 1-30). Cambridge, MA: Cambridge University Press.

Anderson, E. (1990). *Streetwise: Race, Class, and Change in an Urban Community*. The University of Chicago Press.

Anderson, E. (1978). *A Place on the Corner.* Chicago: University of Chicago Press.

Aneshensel, C. S. & Sucoff, C. A. (1996). The neighborhood context of adolescent mental health. *Journal of Health and Social Behavior*, 37, 293-310.

Appelbaum, P. S., Robbins, P. C., and Monahan, J. (2000). Violence and delusions: Data from the MacArthur Violence Risk Assessment Study. *American Journal of Psychiatry*, 157, 566-572.

Appelbaum, P. S. (1997). Almost a revolution: An international perspective on the law of involuntary commitment. *Journal of American Academy of Psychiatry Law*, 25(2),135-147.

Barratt, E. S. (1994). Impulsiveness and aggression. In J. Monahan and H. J. Steadman (Eds.), *Violence and Mental Disorder: Developments in Risk Assessment* (pp. 61-79). Chicago: University of Chicago Press.

Bellair, P. E. (1997). Social interaction and community crime: Examining the importance of neighbor networks. *Criminology*, 35, 677-703.

Billy, J. O. G. & Moore, D. E. (1992). A multilevel analysis of marital and nonmarital fertility in the United States. *Social Forces*, 70, 977-1011.

Bland, R., & Orn, H. (1986). Family violence and psychiatric disorder. Canadian *Journal of Psychiatry*, 31, 129-137.

Bonovitz, J. & Bonovitz, J. (1981). Diversion of the mentally ill into the criminal justice system: The police intervention perspective. *American Journal of Psychiatry*, 138, 973-976.

Bordua, D. (1958). Juvenile delinquency and "anomie": An attempt at replication. *Social Problems*, 6, 230-238.

Borum, R. (1996). Improving the clinical practice of violence risk assessment. *American Psychologist*, 51(9), 945-956.

Breiman, L., Freidman, J., Olshen, R., & Stone, C. (1984). *Classification and Regression Trees.* Pacific Grove, CA: Wadsworth and Brooks/Cole.

Brewster, K. L., J. O. G. Billy, & W. R. Grady (1993). Social context and adolescent behavior: The impact of community on the transition to sexual activity. *Social Forces*, 71,713-740.

Brooks-Gunn, Duncan, G. & Aber, J. (1997). *Neighborhood Poverty.* New York: Russell Sage Foundation.

Brooks-Gunn, J. Duncan, G. J., Klebanou, P. K., & Sealand, N. (1993). Do neighborhoods influence child and adolescent development?. *American Journal of Sociology*, 99, 353-395.

Bryk, A., Raudenbush, S. and Congdon, R. (1996). *Hierarchical Linear and Nonlinear Modeling with the HLM/2L and HLM/3L Programs*. Chicago, IL: Scientific Software Inc.

Bryk, A. & Raudenbush, S. (1992). *Hierarchical Linear Models: Applications and Data Analysis Methods*. Newbury Park: Sage.

Bursik, R. J. (1988). Social disorganization and theories of crime and delinquency: Problems and prospects. *Criminology*, 26, 519-551.

Bursik, R. J. & Grasmick, H. G. (1993). *Neighborhoods and Crime: The Dimensions of Effective Community Control*. New York: Lexington.

Bushman, B. J. & Cooper, H. M. (1990). Effects of alcohol on human aggression: An integrative research review. *Psychological Bulletin*, 107, 341-354.

Byrne, J. & Sampson, R. J. (1986). The ecological/nonecological debate reconsidered. In (Eds.) J. Byrne and R. J. Sampson, *The Social Ecology of Crime*. New York: Springer-Verlag.

Campbell, K. & Lee, B. (1990). Gender differences in urban neighboring. *Sociological Quarterly*, 31, 495-512.

Chilton, R. (1964). Continuity in delinquency area research: A comparison of studies for Baltimore, Detroit and Indianapolis. *American Sociological Review*, 29, 71-83.

Cohen, P. & Cohen, J. (1984). The clinician's illusion. *Archives of General Psychiatry*, 41, 1178-1182.

Cohen, L. E. & Felson, M. (1979). Social change and crime rate trends: A routine activity approach. *American Sociological Review*, 44, 588-608.

Craig, T. (1982). An epidemiologic study of problems associated with violence among psychiatric inpatients. *American Journal of Psychiatry*, 139, 1262-1266.

Cote, G. & Hodgins, S. (1990). Co-occurring mental disorders among criminal offenders. *Bulletin of the American Academy of Psychiatry and Law*, 18, 271-281.

Crane, J. (1991). The epidemic theory of ghettos and neighborhood effects on dropping out and teenage childbearing. *American Journal of Sociology*, 96, 1226-1259.

Cullen, F. T., Wright, J. P., & Chamlin, M. B. (1998). Social support and social reform: A progressive crime control agenda. Paper presented at the 1998 American Sociological Association's annual meeting, San Francisco.

Cullen, F. T. (1994). Social support as an organizing concept for criminology: Presidential address to the Academy of Criminal Justice Sciences. *Justice Quarterly,* 11, 527-559.

Diez-Roux, A. V. (1998). Bringing context back into epidemiology: Variables and fallacies in multilevel analysis. *American Journal of Public Health*, 88(2), 216-222.

Dohrenwend, B. P. (1990). Socioeconomic status (SES) and psychiatric disorders. *Social Psychiatry and Psychiatric Epidemiology*, 25, 41-47.

Dohrenwend, B. P. (1983). The epidemiology of mental disorders. In D. Mechanic (Ed.) *Handbook of Health, Health Care, and the Health Professions* (pp.157-194). New York: Free Press.

Dohrenwend, B. P., Dohrenwend, B. S., Gould, M. S., Link, B. Neugebauer, R., Wunsch-Hitzig, R. (1980). *Mental Illness in the United States: Epidemiological Estimates*. New York: Praeger.

Duncan. G. J. & Aber, J. L. (1997). Neighborhood models and measures. In J. Brooks-Gunn, G. Duncan, and J. Aber (Eds.), *Neighborhood Poverty* (pp.62-78). New York: Russell Sage Foundation.

Duncan. G. J., Connell, J. P., & Klebanov, P. K. (1997). Conceptual and methodological issues in estimating causal effects of neighborhoods and family conditions on individual development. In J. Brooks-Gunn, G. Duncan, and J. Aber (Eds.), *Neighborhood Poverty* (pp.219-250). New York: Russell Sage Foundation.

Durkheim, E. (1966) (1938). *The Rules of Sociological Method.* New York, NY: Free Press.

Ellen, Ingrid G. & Turner, M. A. (1997). Does neighborhood matter?: Assessing recent evidence. *Housing Policy Debate*, 8, 833-866.

Elliot, D. S., Wilson, W. J., Huizinga, D., Sampson, R. J., Elliot, A. & Rankin, B. (1996). The effects of neighborhood disadvantage on adolescent development. *Journal of Research in Crime and Delinquency*, 33(4), 389-426.

Estroff, S. E. & Zimmer, C. (1994). Social networks, social support, and violence among Persons with severe, persistent mental illness. In J. Monahan and H. J. Steadman (Eds.). *Violence and Mental Disorder* (pp.269-295). Chicago: University of Chicago Press.

Ewalt, J. R., & Ewalt, P. L. (1969). History of the community psychiatry movement. *American Journal of Psychiatry*, 126, 41-52.

Faris, R. E., & Dunham, H. W. (1939/1965). *Mental Disorders in Urban Areas: An Ecological Study of Schizophrenia and Other Psychoses.* Chicago: University of Chicago Press.

Farrington, D. (1992). Explaining the beginning, progress, and ending of antisocial behavior from birth to adulthood. In J. McCord (Ed.) *Facts, Frameworks, and Forecasts* (pp. 253-286). New Brunswick, NJ: Transaction.

Farrington, D., Sampson, R. J., & Wilkstrom, P. O. (1993). *Integrating Individual and Ecological Aspects of Crime.* Stockholm, Sweden: National Council on Crime Prevention.

Fischer, C. (1995). The subcultural theory of urbanism - A 20th year assessment. *American Journal of Sociology*, 101, 543-577.

Fernandez, R. M. & Kulik, J. C. (1981). A multilevel model of life satisfaction: Effects of individual characteristics and neighborhood composition. *American Sociological Review*, 46, 840-580.

Firebaugh, G. (1978). A rule for inferring individual-level relationships from aggregate data. *American Sociological Review*, 43, 557-572.

Forth, A. E., Hart, S. D., and Hare, R. D. (1990). Assessment of psychopathy in male young offenders. *Psychological Assessment: A Journal of Consulting and Clinical Psychology*, 2, 342-344.

Fox, J. (1984). *Linear Statistical Models and Related Methods.* New York: Wiley.

Garner, C. & Raudenbush, S. (1991). Neighborhood effects on educational attainment. *Sociology of Education*, 64, 251-262.

Gardner, W.C., Lidz, C.W., Mulvey, E.P., and Shaw, E.C. (1996). A comparison of actuarial methods for identifying repetitively violent patients with mental illnesses. *Law and Human Behavior* 20(1), 35-48.

Gardner, W., Mulvey, E. P., and Shaw, C. (1995). Regression analysis of counts and rates: Poisson, Overdispersed Poisson, and negative binomial models. *Psychological Bulletin*, 118, 392-404.

Gerbner, G., Gross, L., Morgan, M., & Signorielli, N. (1981). Health and medicine on television. *New England Journal of Medicine*, 305, 901-904.

Glueck, S. and Glueck, E. (1950). *Unraveling Juvenile Delinquency.* Cambridge, MA: Harvard University Press.

Goffman, E. (1961). *Asylum: Essays on the Social Situation of Mental Patients and Other Inmates*. New York: Doubleday.

Gordon. R. A. (1968). Issues in multiple regression. *American Journal of Sociology*, 73, 592-616.

Gottdiener, M. and Feagin, J. R. (1988). The paradigm shift in urban sociology. *Urban Affairs Quarterly*, 24, 163-87.

Gove, W. (1980). Labeling and mental illness: A critique. In W. Gove (Ed.), *The Labeling of Deviance: Evaluating a Perspective* (pp. 264-270). Beverly Hills: Sage.

Gramlitch, E.. Laren, D., & Sealand, N. (1992). Moving into and out of poor urban areas. *Journal of Policy Analysis and Management* 11, 273-287.

Greene, W. H. (1993). *Econometric Analysis*. New York: Macmillan Publishing Company.

Hafner, H. & Boker, W. (1982). *Crimes of Violence by Mentally Disordered Offenders*. Cambridge, England: Cambridge University Press.

Hare, R. D. (1991). *Manual for the Hare Psychopathy Checklist - Revised.* Toronto: Multi-Health Systems.

Hare, R. D. , & McPhearson, L. M. (1984). Violent and aggressive behavior in criminal psychopaths. *International Journal of Law and Psychiatry*, 7, 35-90.

Harris, G. T., Rice, M. E., and Cormier, C. A. (1991). Psychopathy and violent recidivism. *Law and Human Behavior*,15(6), 625-637.

Harris, G. T., Rice, M. E. & Quinsey, V. L. (1993). Violent recidivism of mentally disordered offenders: The development of a statistical prediction instrument. *Criminal Justice and Behavior*, 20, 315-335.

Harris, G. T., & Varney, G. W. (1986). A ten-year study of assaults and assaulters on a maximum security psychiatric unit. *Journal of Interpersonal Violence*, 1, 173-191.

Harry, B. & Steadman, H. J. (1988). Arrest rates of patients treated at a community mental health center. *Hospital and Community Psychiatry*, 39, 862-866.

Hart, S. D. & Dempster, R. J. (1997). Impulsivity and psychopathy. In C. D. Webster & M. A. Jackson (Eds.), *Impulsivity: Theory, Assessment, and Treatment*. New York: Guilford.

Hart, S. D., Cox, D.N., & Hare R. D. (1995). *The Hare Psychopathy Checklist: Screening Version (PCL:SV)*. Multi-Health Systems Inc., New York.

Hart, S. D., Hare, R. D., & Forth, A. E. (1994). Psychopathy as a risk marker for violence: Development and validation of a screening version of the Revised Psychopathy Checklist. In J. Monahan and H. J. Steadman (Eds.). *Violence and Mental Disorder* (pp.81-98). Chicago: University of Chicago Press.

Hiday, V. A. (1997). Understanding the connection between mental illness and violence. *International Journal of Law and Psychiatry*, 20(4), 399-417.

Hiday, V. A. (1995). The social context of mental illness and violence. *Journal of Health and Social Behavior* 36, 122-1237.

Hill, M. (1992). *The Panel Study of Income Dynamics: A User's Guide*. Newbury Park CA: Sage.

Hollingshead, A. & Redlich, F. (1958). *Social Class and Mental Illness*. New York: John Wiley and Sons.

Holzer, C. E., Shea, B. M., Swanson, J. W., Leaf, P. J., Myers, J. K., George, L., Weissman, M. M., Bednarski, P. (1986). The increased risk for specific psychiatric disorders among persons of low socioeconomic status: Evidence from the epidemiological catchment area surveys. *American Journal of Social Psychiatry*, 4, 59-271.

Isaac, R. J. & Armat, V. C. (1990). *Madness in the Streets: How Psychiatry and the Law Abandoned the Mentally Ill*. New York: Free Press.

Jacobson, A. (1989). Physical and sexual histories among psychiatric outpatients. *American Journal of Psychiatry*, 146, 755-758.

Janca A, Helzer J. (1990. DSM-III-R Criteria Checklist. *DIS Newsletter*, 7,17.

Jarvis, E. (1971). *Insanity and Idiocy in Massachusetts: Report of the Commission of Lunacy, 1855*. Cambridge, MA: Harvard University Press.

Jencks, C & Mayer, S. E. (1990). *The social consequences of growing up in a poor neighborhood*. In L. E. Lynn & M. G. McGeary (Eds.) Inner-City Poverty in the United States. Washington, DC: National Academy Press.

Johnson, A. B. (1990). *Out of Bedlam: The Truth About Deinstitutionalization*. Basic Books, Inc., A Division of Harper Collins Publishers.

Kasarda, J & Janowitz, M (1974). Community attachment in mass society. *American Sociological Review*, 39, 328-339.

Kennedy, L. & Forde, D. (1990). Routine activities and crime: An analysis of victimization in Canada. *Criminology*, 28, 137-152.

Kim, J. & Mueller, C. W. (1978). *Introduction to Factor Analysis: What It Is and How to Do It.* Beverly Hills: Sage.

Klassen, D. & O'Conner, W. A. (1994). Demographic and case history variables in risk assessment. In J. Monahan and H. J. Steadman (Eds.) *Violence and Mental Disorder: Developments in Risk Assessment* (pp. 229-258). Chicago: University of Chicago Press.

Klassen D., & O'Conner, W. A. (1989). Assessing the risk of violence in released mental patients: A cross-validation study. Psychological Assessment: *A Journal of Consulting and Clinical Psychology*, 1, 75-81.

Klassen D., & O'Conner, W. A. (1988). A prospective study of predictors of violence in adult male mental health admissions. *Law and Human Behavior*, 12, 143-158.

Knoke, D. & Kuklinski, J. H. (1982). *Network Analysis*. Beverly Hills, CA: Sage.

Kornhauser, R. (1978). *Social Sources of Delinquency.* Chicago: University of Chicago Press.

Krakowski, M., Volavka, J., & Brizer, D. (1986). Psychopathology and violence: A review of the literature. *Comprehensive Psychiatry*, 27, 131-148.

LaFree, G. (1999). "A Summary and Review of Cross-National Studies of Homicide." In (eds) M. Dwayne Smith and Margaret A. Zahn (pp.125-145), *Homicide: A Sourcebook of Social Research*. Thousand Oaks, CA: Sage.

Laing, R. D. (1967). *The Politics of Experience*. New York: Ballantine Books.

Land, K. C., McCall, P. L., & Cohen, L. E. (1990). Structural covariates of homicide rates: Are there any invariances across time and social space. *American Journal of Sociology*, 95, 922-963.

Lander, B. (1954). *Toward an Understanding of Juvenile Delinquency.* New York: Columbia University Press.

Lee, B. A., Oropesa, R. S. & Kanan, J. W. (1994). Neighborhood context and residential mobility. *Demography,* 31, 249-270.

Lee, B. A., & Campbell, K. E. (1997). Common ground?: Urban neighborhoods as survey respondents see them. *Social Science Quarterly*, 78, 923-936.

Leighton, D. C., Harding, J. S., Macklin, D. B., MacMillan, A. M., Leighton, A. H. (1963). *The Character of Danger: The Sterling County Study of Psychiatric Disorder and Sociocultural Environment*, Vol 3. New York: Basic Books.

Lemert, E. M. (1951). Social Pathology. New York: McGraw-Hill.

Levy, L. & Rowitz, L. (1973). *The Ecology of Mental Disorder*. New York: Behavioral Publications.

Lewis, D. O., Pincus, T. H., Shanok, S. S., & Glaser, G. H. (1982). Psychomotor epilepsy and violence in a group of incarcerated adolescent boys. *American Journal of Psychiatry*, 139, 882-887.

Lidz, C. W., Mulvey, E. P., & Gardner, W. (1993). The accuracy of predictions of violence to others. *Journal of the American Medical Association*, 24, 1007-1011.

Lin, N. (1986). Conceptualizing social support. In N. Lin, A. Dean and W. Edsel (Eds.), *Social Support, Life Events, and Depression* (pp.17-30). Orlando: Academic Press.

Link, B. G., Monahan, J., Stueve, A., & Cullen, F. T. (1999). Real in their consequences: A sociological approach to understanding the association between psychotic symptoms and violence. *American Sociological Review*, 64, 316-332.

Link, B. G. & Stueve, A. (1995). Evidence bearing on mental illness as a possible cause of violent behavior. *Epidemiologic Reviews*, 17(1), 1-10.

Link, B. G. & Stueve, A. (1994). Psychotic symptoms and the violent/illegal behavior of mental patients compared to community controls. In J. Monahan and H. J. Steadman (Eds.). *Violence and Mental Disorder* (pp.137-159). Chicago: University of Chicago Press.

Link, B. G., Andrews, H. & Cullen, F. T. (1992). The violent and illegal behavior of mental patients reconsidered. *American Sociological Review*, 57, 275-292.

Link, B. G. & Cullen, F. T. (1990). The labeling theory of mental disorder: A review of the evidence. In J. Greenley (Eds.). *Research in Community and Mental Health* (pp.203-233). Greenwich: JAI Press.

Link, B. G., Cullen, F. T., Frank, J., Wozniak, J. F. (1987). The social rejection of former mental patients: Understanding why labels matter. *American Journal of Sociology*, 92, 1461-1500.

Liska, A. E. & Warner, B. D. (1991). Functions of crime: A paradoxical process. *American Journal of Sociology*, 96, 1441-1463.

Liska, A. E, and Messner, S.. (1999). *Perspectives on Crime and Deviance*. Third Edition. New Jersey: Prentice Hall.

Loeber R. & Stouthamer-Loeber, M. (1986). Family factors as correlates and predictors of juvenile conduct problems and delinquency. In M. Tonry and N. Morris (Eds.), *Crime and Justice: An Annual Review of Research*, Vol 7, (pp.29-149). Chicago: University of Chicago Press.

Logan, J. & Molotch, H. L. (1987). *Urban Fortunes: The Political Economy of Place*. Berkeley: University of California Press.

Lowenstein, M., Binder, R. L., and McNiel, D. E. (1990). The relationship between admission symptoms and hospital assaults. *Hospital and Community Psychiatry*, 41, 311-313.

Maddala, G. S. (1983). *Limited Dependent and Qualitative Variables in Econometrics*. New York: Cambridge University Press.

Massey, D. S. (1996). The age of extremes: Concentrated affluence and poverty in the twenty-first century. *Demography*, 33, 395-412.

Massey, D. S., Gross, A. B. & Shibuya, K. (1994). Migration, segregation and the geographic concentration of poverty. *American Sociological Review*, 59, 425-445.

Massey, D. S. & Denton, N. A. (1993). *American Apartheid: Segregation and the Making of the Underclass*. Cambridge: Harvard University Press.

McCord, W. & McCord, J. (1964). *The Psychopath: An Essay on the Criminal Mind*. Princeton, NJ: Van Nostrand.

McNiel, D. E. (1994). Hallucinations and Violence. In J. Monahan and H. J. Steadman (Eds.), *Violence and Mental Disorder: Developments in Risk Assessment* (pp. 183-202). Chicago: University of Chicago Press.

Menzies, R. J., Webster, C. D., McMain, S., Staley, S. & Scaglione, R. (1994). The dimensions of dangerousness revisited. *Law and Human Behavior*, 18(1), 1-28.

Menzies, R., Webster, C., & Sepejak, D. (1985). The dimensions of dangerousness: Evaluating the accuracy of psychometric predictions of violence among forensic patients. *Law and Human Behavior*, 9, 49-70.

Merton, R. K. (1938). *Social structure and anomie.* American Sociological Review, 3, 672-682.

Messner, S. F., & Rosenfeld, R. (1994). *Crime and the American Dream.* Belmont Calif.: Wadsworth Publishing Company.

Miczek, K. A., DeBold, J. F., Haney, M., Tidey, J., Vivian, J., & Weertz, E. M. (1993). Alcohol, drugs of abuse, aggression, and violence. In A. J. Reiss & J. A. Roth (Eds.), *Understanding and Preventing Violence* (pp. 37-62). Washington, DC: National Academy Press.

Miethe, T. D. & McDowall, D. (1993). Contextual effects in models of criminal victimization. *Social Forces*, 71(3), 741-759.

Miles-Doan, R. (1998). Violence between spouses and intimates: Does neighborhood context matter? *Social Forces*, 77, 623-645.

Monahan, J. (1997a). Clinical and actuarial predictions of violence. In D. Faigman, D. Kaye, M. Saks, & J. Sanders, (Eds.), *Modern Scientific Evidence: The Law and Science of Expert Testimony*, Vol. 1. St. Paul, MN: West Publishing Company.

Monahan, J. (1997b). Actuarial support for the clinical assessment of violence risk. *International Review of Psychiatry*, 9, 167-169.

Monahan, J. (1993). Limiting therapist exposure to Tarasoff liability." *American Psychologist*, 48(3), 242-50.

Monahan, J. (1992a). "A terror to their neighbors": Beliefs about mental disorder and violence in historical and cultural perspective. *Bulletin of the American Academy of Psychiatry and the Law*, 20(2), 191-195.

Monahan, J. (1992b). Mental disorder and violent behavior: Perceptions and evidence. *American Psychologist*, 47, 511-21.

Monahan, J. (1988). Risk assessment of violence among the mentally disordered: Generating useful knowledge. *International Journal of Law and Psychiatry,* 11, 249-257.

Monahan, J. (1973). The psychiatrization of criminal behavior: A reply. *Hospital and Community Psychiatry*, 24, 105-7.

Monahan, J., Steadman, H. J., Appelbaum, P. S., Robbins, P. C., Mulvey, E. P., Silver, E., Roth, L. H., and Grisso, T. (2000). Developing a clinically useful actuarial tool for assessing violence risk. *British Journal of Psychiatry*, 176, 213-319.

Monahan, J. & Steadman, H. J. (1994). *Violence and Mental Disorder: Developments in Risk Assessment.* Chicago: University of Chicago Press.

Morrissey, J. P., Tausig, M., & Lindsey, M. L. (1985). *Network Analysis Methods for Mental Health Service System Research: A Comparison of Two Community Support Systems.* U.S. Department of Health and Human Services, 1985.

Mulvey, E. P. (1994). Assessing the evidence for a link between mental illness and violence. *Hospital and Community Psychiatry,*45(7), 663-668.

Mulvey, E. P. & Lidz, C. W. (1995). Conditional prediction: A Model for research on dangerousness to others in a new era. *International Journal of Law and Psychiatry*, 18(2), 129-142.

Mulvey, E. P., Blumstein, A., and Cohen, J, (1986). Reframing the research question of mental patient criminality. *International Journal of Law and Psychiatry*, 9, 57-65.

National Center for State Courts (1986). Guidelines for involuntary commitment. *Mental and Physical Disability Law Reporter*, 10, 409-514.

Novaco, R. W. (1994). Anger as a risk factor for violence among the mentally disordered. In J. Monahan and H. J. Steadman (Eds.). *Violence and Mental Disorder* (pp.269-95). Chicago: University of Chicago Press.

Odegaard, O. (1956). The incidence of psychosis on various occupations. *International Journal of Social Psychiatry*, 2, 85-104.

Park, R. E., Burgess, E., & McKenzie, R. (1925). The City. Chicago: University of Chicago Press.

Pescosolido, B. A., Monahan, J. Link, B. G., Stueve, A., & Kikusawa, S. (1999). The public's view of the competence, dangerousness and need for legal coercion among persons with mental illness. *American Journal of Public Health* 89, 1339-1345.

Pfohl, B., Blum, N., Zimmerman, M., & Stangl, D. (1989). *Structured Interview for DSM-III-R Personality.* University of Iowa, Department of Psychiatry.

Phil, R. O., & Peterson, J. B. (1993). Alcohol/drug use and aggressive behavior. In S. Hodgins (Eds.), *Mental Disorder and Crime* (pp.104-15). Newbury Park, CA: Sage.

Pokorny, A., Miller, B., & Kaplan, H. (1972). The Brief MAST: A shortened version of the Michigan Alcohol Screening Test. *American Journal of Psychiatry*, 129, 342-345.

Przeworski, A. (1974). Contextual models of political behavior. *Political Methodology*, 1, 27-61.

Quinsey, V. & Maguire, A. (1986). Maximum security psychiatric patients: Actuarial and clinical predictions of dangerousness. *Journal of Interpersonal Violence*, 1(2), 143-171.

Quinsey, V. L., Rice, M. E., & Harris, G. T. (1995). Actuarial prediction of sexual recidivism. *Journal of Interpersonal Violence*, 10, 85-105.

Rabkin, J. (1979). Criminal behavior of discharged mental patients. *Psychological Bulletin*, 86, 1-27.

Reiss, A. J. & Tonry, M. (1986). *Communities and Crime*. Chicago: University of Chicago Press.

Rice, M.. & Harris, G. T. (1997). Cross-validation and extension of the violence risk appraisal guide for child molesters and rapists. *Law and Human Behavior,* 21(2), 231-241.

Rice, M., & Harris, G. T. (1995). Psychopathy, schizophrenia, alcohol abuse and violent recidivism. *International Journal of Law and Psychiatry*, 18, 333-342.

Rice, M., & Harris, G. T. (1992). A comparison of criminal recidivism among schizophrenic and nonschizophrenic offenders. *International Journal of Law and Psychiatry*, 15, 397-408.

Ricketts, E. R. & Sawhill, I. V. (1988). Defining and measuring the underclass. *Journal of Policy Analysis and Management*, 7, 316-325.

Riley, M. W. (1963). Special problems of sociological analysis (700-725). In *Sociological Research I: A Case Approach*. New York: Harcourt, Brace, and World, Inc..

Robert, S. A., (1998). Community-level socioeconomic status effects on adult health. *Journal of Health and Social Behavior*, 39, 18-37.

Robins, L. & Regier, D. A.. (1991). *Psychiatric Disorders in America: The Epidemiological Catchment Area Study.* New York: Free Press.

Robins, L., Tipp, J., & Przybeck, T. (1991). Antisocial personality. In L. N. Robins & D. Regier (Eds.), *Psychiatric Disorders in America* (258-290). New York: Free Press.

Robinson, W. S. (1950). Ecological correlations and the behavior of individuals. *American Sociological review*, 15, 351-357.

Robson, B. T. (1969). Urban Analysis*: A Study of City Structure with Special Reference to Sutherland.* Cambridge, England: University Press.

Rosenbaum, J. (1991). Black pioneers: Do their moves to the suburbs increase economic opportunity for mothers and children? *Housing Policy Debate*, 2, 1179-1213.

Rossi, A. M., Jacobs, M., Monteleone, M., Olser, R., Surber, W., Winkler, E. L., & Womak, A. (1985). Characteristics of psychiatric patients who engage in assaultive or other fear-inducing behavior. *Journal of Nervous and Mental Disorder,* 174, 154-160.

Rountree, P. W., Land, K. & Miethe, T. (1994) Macro-micro integration in the study of victimization: A hierarchical logistic model analysis across Seattle neighborhoods. *Criminology*, 32, 387-414.

Salekin, R. T., Rogers, R., & Sewell, K. W. (1996). A review and meta-analysis of the psychopathy checklist and psychopathy checklist-revised: Predictive validity of dangerousness. *Clinical Psychology: Science and Practice*, 3, 203-215.

Sampson, R. J. (1997). The embeddedness of child and adolescent development: A community-level perspective on urban violence. In J. McCord (Ed.), *Violence and Childhood in the Inner City* (pp. 31-77). Cambridge, MA: Cambridge University Press.

Sampson, R. J. (1993). Family and community-Level influences on crime: A contextual theory and strategies for research testing." In D. P. Farrington, R. J. Sampson, and P. H. Wikstrom (Eds.) *Integrating Individual and Ecological Aspects of Crime*, (pp.153-168). Stockholm, Sweden: National Council for Crime Prevention.

Sampson, R. J. (1988). Local friendship ties and community attachment. *American Sociological Review*, 53, 766-779

Sampson, R. J. (1985). Neighborhood and crime: The structural determinants of personal victimization. *Journal of Research in Crime and Delinquency*, 22, 7-40.

Sampson, R. J., Raudenbush, S. W. & Earls, F. (1997). Neighborhoods and violent crime: A multilevel study of collective efficacy. *Science*, 277, 918-924.

Sampson, R. J.& Morenoff, J. D. (1997). Ecological perspectives on the neighborhood context of urban poverty: Past and present. In J. Brooks-Gunn, G. Duncan, and J. Aber (Eds.), *Neighborhood Poverty* (pp.1-22). New York: Russell Sage Foundation.

Sampson, R. J., & Lauritsen, J. L. (1994). Violent victimization and offending: Individual-, situational-, and community-level risk factors. In A. J. Reiss & J. A. Roth (Eds.), *Understanding and Preventing Violence* (Vol 3. pp. 1-114). Washington, DC: National Academy Press.

Sampson, R. J. & Wilson, W. J. (1994). Race, crime and urban inequality. In J. Hagan & R. Peterson (Eds.), *Crime and Inequality*. Stanford, CA: Stanford University Press.

Sampson, R. J. & Groves, W. B. (1989). Community structures and crime: Testing social disorganization theory. *American Journal of Sociology*, 94, 774-802.

Sampson, R. J. & Woolredge, J. (1987). Linking the micro- and macro-level dimensions of lifestyle-routine activity and opportunity models of predatory victimization. *Journal of Quantitative Criminology*, 3, 371-393.

Sanchez-Jankowski, M. S. (1991). *Islands in the Street: Gangs and American Urban Society*. University of California Press.

Scheff, T. J. (1984). Being Mentally Ill: *A Sociological Theory*. Chicago: Aldine.

Segal, S. P., Watson, M. A., Goldfinger, S. M., & Averbuck, D. S. (1988). Civil commitment in the psychiatric emergency room. *Archives of General Psychiatry*, 45, 753-788.

Shain, R. & Phillips, J. (1991). The stigma of mental illness: Labeling and stereotyping in the news. In L. Wilkins & P. Patterson (Eds.), *Risky Business: Communicating Issues of Science, Risk, and Public Policy* (pp. 61-74). Westport, CN: Greenwood Press.

Shaw, C. R. & McKay, H. D. (1942). *Juvenile Delinquency and Urban Areas*. Chicago, IL: University of Chicago Press.

Silver, E. (2000a). Extending social disorganization theory: A multilevel approach to the study of violence among persons with mental illnesses. *Criminology*, 38, 301-331..

Silver, E. (2000b). Race, neighborhood disadvantage, and violence among discharged psychiatric patients: The Importance of contextual measurement. *Law and Human Behavior*, 24, 449-456.

Silver, E. (1995). Punishment or treatment?: Comparing the lengths of confinement of successful and unsuccessful insanity defendants. *Law and Human Behavior*, 19, 375-388.

Silver, E., Mulvey, E. P., & Monahan, J. (1999). Assessing violence risk among discharged psychiatric patients: Toward an ecological approach. *Law and Human Behavior*, 23(2), 235-253.

Silver, E., Cirincione, C. & Steadman, H. J. (1994). Demythologizing inaccurate perceptions of the insanity defense. *Law and Human Behavior*, 18(1), 63-70.

Simcha-Fagan, O. & Schwartz, J. E. (1986). Neighborhood and delinquency: An assessment of contextual effects. *Criminology*, 24, 667-699.

Skinner, H. (1982). The Drug Abuse Screening Test. *Addictive Behavior*, 7, 363-371

Skogan, W. G. (1990). *Disorder and Decline: Crime and Spiral of Decay in American Neighborhoods.* Berkeley: University of California Press.

Skogan, W. (1986). Assessing the behavioral context of criminal victimization. *Journal of Criminal Law and Criminology*, 72, 727-742.

Smith D. R. & Jarjoura, G. R. (1988). Social structure and criminal victimization. *Journal of Research in Crime and Delinquency*, 25, 27-53.

South, S. J. & Crowder, K. D. (1999). Neighborhood effects on family formation: Concentrated poverty and beyond. *American Sociological Review*, 63, 113-132.

South, S. J. & Crowder, K. D. (1997). Escaping distressed neighborhoods: Individual, community, and metropolitan influences. American *Journal of Sociology*, 4, 1040-1084.

Srole, L., Langner, T. S., Michael, S. T., Opler, M. K., Rennie, T. A. C. (1962). *Mental Health in the Metropolis: The Midtown Study*, Vol 1. New York: McGraw-Hill.

Steadman, H. J. (1981). Critically reassessing the accuracy of public perceptions of the dangerousness of the mentally ill. *Journal of Health and Social Behavior*, 22, 310-316.

Steadman, H. J., Silver, E., Monahan, J., Appelbaum, P. S., Robbins, P., Mulvey, E. P., Grisso, T., Roth, L., & Banks, S. (2000). Enhancing the clinical usefulness of actuarial violence risk assessment tools: A classification tree approach. *Law and Human Behavior*, 23, 237-255.

Steadman, H., Mulvey, E., Monahan, J., Robbins, P., Appelbaum, P., Grisso, T., Roth, L., & Silver, E. (1998). Violence by people discharged from acute psychiatric inpatient facilities and by others in the same neighborhoods. *Archives of General Psychiatry*, 55, 393-401.

Steadman, H. J., Monahan, J., Appelbaum, P. S., Grisso, T., Mulvey, E. P., Roth, L. H., Robbins, P.C., and Klassen, D. (1994). *Designing a new generation of risk assessment research.* In J. Monahan and H. J. Steadman (Eds.), *Violence and Mental Disorder: Developments in Risk Assessment* (pp. 297-318). Chicago: University of Chicago Press.

Steadman, H. J. & Felson, R. B. (1983). Situational factors in disputes leading to criminal violence. *Criminology*, 21(1), 59-74.

Steadman, H. J. & Morrissey, J. P. (1982). Predicting violent behavior: A not on a cross-validation study. *Social Forces*, 61, 475-483.

Steadman, H. J., & Ribner, S. A. (1982). Life stress and violence among ex-mental patients. *Social Science and Medicine*, 16, 1641-1647.

Steadman, H. J., Cocozza, J. J, & Melick, M. E. (1978). Explaining the increased arrest rate among mental patients: The changing clientele of state hospitals. *American Journal of Psychiatry*, 135, 816-20.

Steadman, H. J. & and Cocozza, J. J. (1978). Public perceptions of the criminally insane. *Hospital and Community Psychiatry*, 29(7), 457-459.

Steadman, H. J. & Cocozza, J. J. (1974). *Careers of the Criminally Insane: Excessive Social Control of Deviance.* Lexington, MA: Lexington Books.

Suttles, G. (1968). *The Social Order of the Slum.* Chicago: University of Chicago Press.

Swanson, J. W. (1994). Mental disorder, substance abuse, and community violence: An epidemiological approach. In J. Monahan and H. J. Steadman (Eds.). *Violence and Mental Disorder* (pp.101-136). Chicago: University of Chicago Press.

Swanson, J. W. (1993). Alcohol abuse, mental disorder, and assaultive behavior: An epidemiological inquiry. *Alcohol Health and Research World*, 17, 123-132.

Swanson, J. W., Holzer, C. E., Ganju, V. K., & Jono, R. T. (1990). Violence and psychiatric disorders in the community: Evidence from the Epidemiologic Catchment Area Surveys. *Hospital and Community Psychiatry*, 41, 761-770.

Swanson, J.W., Borum, R., Swartz, M.S., and Monahan, J. (1996). Psychotic symptoms and disorders and the risk of violent behavior in the community. *Criminal Behavior and Mental Health*, 6, 309-329.

Swartz, M. S., Swanson, J. W., Hiday, V. A., Borum, R., Wagner, R., & Burns, B. J. (1998). Violence and severe mental illness: The effects of substance abuse and nonadherence to medication. *American Journal of Psychiatry*, 155(2), 226-231.

Szaz, T. S. (1974). *The Myth of Mental Illness: Foundations of a Theory of Personal Conduct.* New York: Harper & Row Publishers.

Tarasoff v. Regents of the University of California. 131 Cal. Rptr. 14, 551 P 2d 334.

Tardiff, K., Marzuk, P. M., Leon, A. C., & Portera, L. (1997). A prospective study of violence by psychiatric patients after hospital discharge. *Psychiatric Services*, 48, 678-681.

Tardiff, K. & Sweillman, A. (1980). Assault, suicide, and mental illness. *American Journal of Psychiatry*, 37, 164-169.

Taylor, P. J., Garety, P., Buchanan, A., Reed, A., Wessely, S., Ray, K., Dunn, G., & Grubin, D. (1994). Hallucinations and Violence. In J. Monahan and H. J. Steadman (Eds.), *Violence and Mental Disorder: Developments in Risk Assessment* (pp. 161-182). Chicago: University of Chicago Press.

Taylor, P. & Gunn, J. (1984). Violence and Psychosis. I. Risk of violence Among psychotic men. *British Medical Journal of Clinical Research*, 288, 1945-1949.

Teplin, L. (1983). The criminalization of the mentally ill: Speculations in search of data. *Psychological Bulletin*, 94, 54-67.

Teplin, L. (1984). Criminalizing mental disorder: The comparative arrest rates of the mentally ill. *American Psychologist*, 39, 794-803.

Thornberry, T. P., & Jacoby, J. E. (1979). *The Criminally Insane: A Community Follow-up of Mentally Ill Offenders.* Chicago: University of Chicago Press.

Tienda, M.. (1991). Poor people and poor places: Deciphering neighborhood effects on poverty outcomes. In J. Huber (Eds.) *Macro-Micro Linkages in Sociology* . Newbury Park CA: Sage.

Valkonen, T. (1967). Individual and structural effects in ecological research. In M. Dogan and S. Rokkam (Eds.), *Social Ecology* (pp. 53-68). Boston, MA: MIT Press.

Warner, B. D. & Pierce, G. L. (1993). Reexamining social disorganization theory using calls to the police as a measure of crime. *Criminology*, 31, 493-517.

Webster, C. D., Douglas, K. S., Eaves, D. & Hart, S. D. (1997). HCR-20: Assessing Risk for Violence. Mental Health, Law, and Policy Institute, Simon Frazer University.

Webster, C. D., Harris, G. T., Rice, M. E., Cormier, C., & Quinsey, V. L. (1994). *The Violence Prediction Scheme: Assessing Dangerousness in High Risk Men.* Toronto: Center of Criminology, University of Toronto.

Webster, C. D., & Menzies, R. J. (1993). Supervision in the deinstitutionalized community. In S. Hodgins (Ed.), *Mental Disorder and Crime* (pp. 221-240). Newbury Park: Sage.

Wellman, B. (1979). The community question: The intimate networks of East Yorkers. *American Journal of Sociology*, 84, 1201-1231.

Wessely, S. (1993). Violence and psychosis. In C. Thompson and P. Cowen (Eds.), *Violence: Basic and Clinical Science* (pp.119-134). Oxford, England: Butterworth-Heinemann.

Widiger, T. A., & Trull, T. J. (1994). Personality Disorder and Violence. In J. Monahan and H. J. Steadman (Eds.), *Violence and Mental Disorder: Developments in Risk Assessment* (pp. 203-226). Chicago: University of Chicago Press.

Wilson, W. J. (1987). *The Truly Disadvantaged: The Inner-City, the Underclass, and Public Policy.* Chicago: Chicago University Press.

Wilson, J. Q. & Herrnstein, R. J. (1985). *Crime and Human Nature.* New York, NY: Simon and Schuster.

Wing, J. (1961). Institutionalism in mental hospitals. *British Journal of Clinical Psychology,* 1, 38-51.

Wirth, L. (1938). Urbanism as a way of life. *American Journal of Sociology*, 44, 2-24.

Wolfgang, M. & Ferracuti, F. (1967). *The Subculture of Violence.* London: Tavistock.

Wong, G. Y., & Mason, W. M. (1985). The hierarchical logistic regression model for multilevel analysis. *Journal of the American Statistical Association*, 80, 513-524.

Yamaguchi, K. (1991). *Event History Analysis.* Newbury Park: Sage Publications.

Yesavage, J. A., Werner, P. D., Becker, M. T., Holman, C., & Mills, M. (1981). Inpatient evaluation of aggression in psychiatric patients. *Journal of Nervous and Mental Disease,* 169, 299-302.

APPENDIX A
Violent Incident Coding Rules

INTRODUCTION

This document describes the coding rules used by the MacArthur Foundation Violence Risk Assessment Study to construct reconciled reports of violent incidents from a variety of sources, including subject self-reports, collateral informant reports, official arrest records, hospital admitting incident chart information, and rehospitalization records.

For all sources, the date of the incident was recorded along with the type of violent act engaged in by the subject (for arrest reports, arrest charges were recorded). Self-reports from subjects and collaterals also included detailed descriptions of each violent incident (i.e., in terms of incident location, victim relationships, seriousness and type of injury to victim, and whether a weapon was used). For serious incidents involving weapons or injury, a detailed narrative report was also obtained.

Subject and collateral sources were rated by project interviewers in terms of their honesty in reporting - on a five-point Likert scale ranging from 1=Honest to 5=Untruthful. These sources were also rated in terms of whether they were perceived as over or under-reporting violence, or accurately reporting violence.

All violent incidents were systematically reviewed, independently coded, and discussed by two trained coders whose tasks were: (1) to determine whether incident reports met the inclusion criteria for the reconciled variable; (2) to identify matching incident reports across multiple sources; and (3) for matching incident reports, to select the version of events that would be accepted in the reconciled variable.

The specific rules for accomplishing these tasks are described below.

I. INCLUSION CRITERIA

If the subject reported a violent incident(s) that did not match with a collateral report (and the subject was deemed 'accurate' by project interviewers), his or version of events was accepted.

The collateral's version of violent events was accepted if the collateral was (1) present during the incident; or (2) the victim of the incident; or (3) heard about the incident from either the subject or victim, regardless of whether the collateral's version matched with a subject version.

If either the subject or collateral was deemed unreliable by the interviewer, we did not include

their version of violent events. By unreliable, we refer to cases for which the interviewer rated the reporting of violence as extremely untruthful in the direction of over-reporting violence

We always incorporated official reports of violence into the reconciled variable (e.g., rap sheet, rehospitalization data, and admitting incident chart information) whether or not they matched with other sources.

II. IDENTIFY MATCHING INCIDENT REPORTS

Incidents reported by different sources were considering to **match** if they were recorded as occurring within **two weeks** of each other and seemed to depict the same violent event (e.g., based on the reported location, victim, and injury level). When no descriptive data were available, we relied solely on the incident date.

III. SELECT APPROPRIATE VERSION FROM INCIDENT MATCHES

If both the subject and collateral were judged by the interviewer as credible, we accepted the collateral's version of events (over the subject's) if the collateral was (1) present during the incident; or (2) the victim of the incident; or (3) heard about the incident from either the subject or victim.

This implies that we accepted the subject's version of

a matching incident (rather than the collateral's) only if the collateral had heard about the incident third-hand (i.e., from some other person not involved in the incident). There were no special rules for collaterals who were mental health professionals.

If the subject reported violence (regardless of the interviewer's assessment of truthfulness) and the collateral was judged as accurately reporting that no violence occurred, we accepted the subject's report because we assumed that the collateral could not have full knowledge of the subject's behavior.

We thus interpreted a collateral's report of no violence to mean that, regardless of frequency of contact, the collateral could not remain completely aware of all of the subject's violent behavior.

If the collateral was judged by the interviewer as over-reporting violence and the subject was judged as accurately reporting that no violence occurred, we accepted the subject's version.

Index